ALL THAT WE

ALL THAT WE SAY IS OURS

Guujaaw *and the* Reawakening
of the Haida Nation

SAY IS OURS

IAN GILL

Douglas & McIntyre
D&M PUBLISHERS INC.
Vancouver/Toronto/Berkeley

09 10 11 12 13   5 4 3 2 1

Douglas & McIntyre
An imprint of D&M Publishers Inc.
2323 Quebec Street, Suite 201
Vancouver BC Canada V5T 4S7
www.douglas-mcintyre.com

Library and Archives Canada Cataloguing in Publication
Gill, Ian, 1955–
All that we say is ours: Guujaaw and the reawakening of the Haida Nation / Ian Gill.

Includes bibliographical references and index.
ISBN 978-1-55365-186-4

1. Haida Indians. 2. Guujaaw, 1953–. 3. Haida Indians—Claims.
4. Haida Indians—Government relations. 5. Haida Indians—Biography. I. Title.

E99.H2G89 2009   971.1'120049728   C2008-908107-2

Editing by Barbara Pulling
Jacket design by Naomi MacDougall
Text design by Ingrid Paulson
Cover photograph copyright © Farah Nosh, 2009. The photograph, taken in
Skidegate, Haida Gwaii, in August 2008, is from a performance of *Sin Xiigangu*
(Sounding Gambling Sticks), the first play to be written in the threatened Haida language.
The play was performed by younger-generation Haida with the guidance of their elders.
Printed and bound in Canada by Friesens
Printed on acid-free paper that is forest friendly (100% post-consumer
recycled paper) and has been processed chlorine free.
Distributed in the U.S. by Publishers Group West

We gratefully acknowledge the financial support of the Canada Council for the Arts,
the British Columbia Arts Council, the Province of British Columbia through the Book
Publishing Tax Credit and the Government of Canada through the Book Publishing
Industry Development Program (BPIDP) for our publishing activities.

*This book is dedicated to my mother, Jane Fergusson,
for her love of language, and to my late father, Desmond Gill,
for his love of the well-made object.*

They became what they beheld.

—William Blake

They more than what we are,
Serenity and joy
We lost or never found,
The form of heart's desire,
We gave them what we could not keep,
We made them what we cannot be.

—from "Statues," by Kathleen Raine

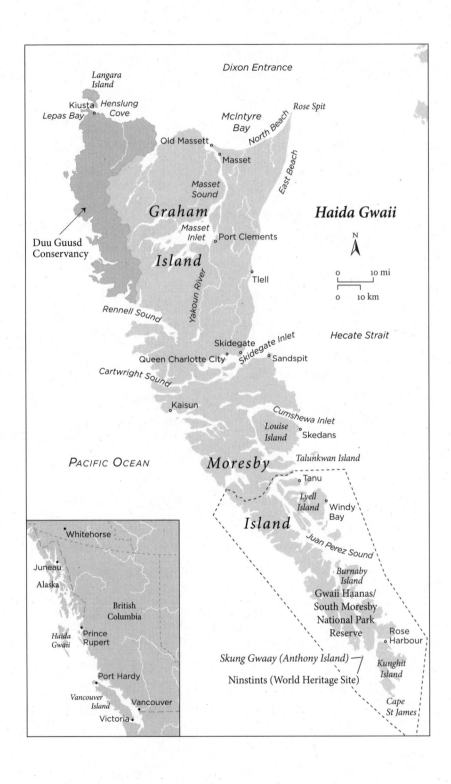

Dixon Entrance

Langara
Island

Kiusta   Henslung
Lepas Bay   Cove

McIntyre   Rose Spit
Bay

Old Massett

Masset

North Beach

East Beach

Masset
Sound

Graham

Masset
Inlet   Port Clements

Duu Guusd
Conservancy

Island

Tlell

Yakoun River

Rennell Sound

Haida Gwaii

N

0   10 mi

0   10 km

Hecate Strait

Skidegate

Queen Charlotte City   Sandspit

Skidegate Inlet

Cartwright Sound

Kaisun

Cumshewa Inlet

Louise
Island   Skedans

PACIFIC OCEAN   Moresby   Talunkwan Island

Tanu

Lyell
Island   Windy
Bay

Island

Juan Perez Sound

Whitehorse

Juneau

Alaska

British
Columbia

Haida   Prince
Gwaii   Rupert

Port Hardy

Vancouver
Island   Vancouver

Victoria

Burnaby
Island

Gwaii Haanas/
South Moresby
National Park
Reserve   Rose
Harbour

Skung Gwaay (Anthony Island)   Kunghit
Island

Ninstints (World Heritage Site)

Cape
St James

CONTENTS

ONE

THEN AND NOW

BACK THEN, PEOPLE rounded the point at G̲aw, or maybe came from out by Yan, and when they entered Masset Inlet there was a long line of totem poles and canoes and house fronts along the inlet's eastern shore. On the flood, now as then, the tidal rip adds eight knots or so to your hull speed, so the village goes by pretty fast. The old black-and-white photos show as many as forty totem poles along the shore, more in behind, but there are not so many poles now, no canoes on the beach, hardly any big houses, although the first house you see coming into Old Massett by boat these days is Jimmy Hart's Three Rainbow House, and it is a very big house.

It is fitting that Jim Hart has a big house. He is an important chief in these parts, Chief ʔIdansuu of the Staast'as Eagle clan, directly descended from Albert Edward Edenshaw, the name "Edenshaw" being as close as the white men came to getting their tongues around the word ʔIdansuu, back then.

Like Albert Edenshaw before him, Jim Hart is a powerful hereditary chief and a prominent Haida artist. This is readily apparent when you come into Old Massett by boat and see not just Jim Hart's house but, to the right of it, a totem pole that Hart carved and erected in 1999. Thirty years before, the famed artist Robert Davidson had erected a pole in the village, the first pole raised in Old Massett since the Haida emerged from the silent years and began to find their voice again. A profusion of totem poles has gone up in the village in the decades since. By day's end, on this Saturday in August, there will be another pole erected in Old Massett near another big house—Christian White's place, the Canoe People's House.

These days most people get to Jim Hart's house by road, not by boat. You leave the town of Masset and drive to the village of Old Massett, past Christian White's house and on down Raven Avenue till you can't go any farther, and that's Jimmy's house on the left, before the cemetery.

Inside, there are people working methodically but quickly towards a deadline, because Chief ?Idansuu is having a potlatch tomorrow, Sunday, and there is much still to do. Several young Haida apprentices hunch over a long, wide red cedar plank, painting bold ovoid shapes and strong lines in black and red, the traditional base colours of Northwest native art. The fresh lines will need to match up exactly with the board that came before and the one that will come after, twenty-four planks in all. Hart himself is off to one side, carving a cedar helmet, a raven. Two of his children, Carl and his twin, Mary, sit on a couch folding and rolling small hand towels and securing them with decorative ties, then tossing them into a plastic tote. A couple of folks are dragging and stacking endless other totes full of gifts shipped up from Vancouver, while someone else is unloading salmon, lots of salmon.

Over near the windows at the front of the house, Hart's oldest daughter, Lia, is bent over an impossibly wide sheet of brown paper, updating a massive genealogical chart that starts, as modern Haida history does, with ?Idansuu, Albert Edward Edenshaw, b. ca. 1812, d. 1894. The genealogy is a wonderfully complex thing to behold, charting as it does not just descendencies and gender, but splitting even further into moeties and clan lines, represented by circles and triangles, the geometric shapes and shadings linked by lines in a kaleidoscopic pattern that could be mistaken for a massive board for playing Chinese checkers.

The Hart house in Old Massett has been abuzz for weeks, but the Hart family has been working towards this weekend for more than a year. Hundreds of hours, thousands of acts small and large, will culminate in Sunday's house-front raising and feast. The invitations—sumptuously calligraphed cards that announce not one but two feasts this weekend—state that Jimmy Hart's deadline is one o'clock Sunday afternoon. Today, Saturday morning, it seems assured that he will miss his deadline by a goodly margin. There is so much left to do. For one thing, he and his apprentices have to down tools and head off back down the road to witness Christian White's pole raising, at the other end of the village. Later on, Hart will have to go to White's potlatch, too.

The joint invitation says that White's pole will be raised today at one o'clock, but he, too, is running a bit behind. A crowd that has swelled to about 300 souls doesn't seem to mind, milling about on a gorgeously bright blue sky day as White and his helpers use a backhoe to dig a hole. The Shark Mother totem pole—more than ten metres long, carved with the crests of White's Yahgu 'laanas Raven clan, and further adorned with eight copper-coloured shields—is missing its crowning piece, a large carved white raven that just now is being painted inside the Canoe People's House. The paint is still wet when the raven is brought out to be affixed to the top of the pole. The tenon is discovered to be a bit too fat for the mortise, prompting another short delay as White resorts first to a chisel, then to a chainsaw, to get the piece to fit.

The delays start to test the patience of Mary Swanson, clan matriarch, who grumbles that the pole raising is taking so long it's cutting into her preparation time for the feast. She complains, too, that all this feasting has produced a last-minute surge in demand for Haida names to be conferred over the next two nights. "Anyone would think I'm the only Haida on the islands," Swanson harrumphs, although it's clear she enjoys the attention that comes with being a venerated elder.

Finally, the raven's mortise is snug on the pole's tenon, and the paint is dry to the touch. White, in a dark tunic and a bright crested headdress, announces that the pole is being raised in honour of his grandfather. He says that sometimes, back then, slaves who had worked on a pole were killed and buried beneath it, a statement that makes even the kids in the crowd pay attention. His five assistants come forward, each with a power tool—orbital sanders, Skilsaws, jigsaws—and White dispatches each tool with a hard crack from a wooden club, consigning these modern-day "slaves" to the bottom of the earthen pit. Then, the artist and his apprentices circle the supine pole in a line, each making a chopping motion with an adze, mimicking the work that went into carving the pole, chanting as they ceremonially complete it. Their actions are also intended to expunge evil spirits and summon good ones.

By now, about 200 people are distributed along three ropes that fan out like tentacles from the totem pole, everyone bracing their backs for a mass tug-of-war. Another crowd stands behind the pole, holding two slack ropes and shouldering two wooden braces that will prevent the pole from overbalancing and taking out power lines and, maybe, some of the folks out front. There is a surge on the count of three, but the pressure on the front ropes seems to lodge the pole stubbornly in its hole, rather than to lever it up. Strong men scramble under the pole, and the next surge succeeds in getting the pole up high enough and on enough of an angle for a couple of braces to be cinched in behind it. Another concerted tug, and the pole is swinging outlandishly from side to side, the crowd recoiling in either direction, till the raven seems to shrug off gravity and, with a burst of effort from the crowd, soars in a clear arc up to its pride of place overlooking Masset Inlet, its beak turned slightly askew from the eagle atop the greying pole just a few metres away. All at once, the shoreline in Old Massett boasts another totem pole. Every new pole seems to confer a *gravitas* on the village and a deepening authority on the people who call Old Massett home—the Haida.

As the raven swoops into place, there is an appreciative roar from the crowd, lots of jostling and backslapping and, to add to the festive air, a quick clearing of the road while a wedding party goes by in a convoy of cars, all adorned with blue plastic flowers, amid a cacophony of horns. Jim Hart and his family don't linger long. They head back to their house to squeeze in a few more hours' work before joining White's feast at the Old Massett Community Hall. It's a magnificent gathering that lasts into the wee hours of Sunday morning.

There is a lull, a catching of the community's collective breath, and then it's late on Sunday morning and a crowd is building at Jim Hart's house, some people content to sit out on the grass by the inlet and picnic in the sun, others pitching in, helping the artists bring the planks down to the front of the house and to lay out, upside down, the numbered pieces of Hart's outsized cedar puzzle. No one, not even Hart, has seen all the completed boards together, but if anyone is nervous that there might be a panel missing or out of place, they do a good job of disguising it. When the planks are laid out on the grass, each piece toed into a concrete lip running along the foundation of the house and snugged tight against those on either side, it looks for all like a huge stage flat that has tipped over and landed face down.

Chief ʔIdansuu by this time has doffed his trademark beret and is wearing his chief's woven spruce root hat, his shoulders draped with a blanket and an apron around his waist. He stands on the balcony of the house and confidently declares that what the crowd is about to see hasn't happened on Haida Gwaii for well over a hundred years. Then, without any prompting, he remembers that "Robert did one in 1979, so this is the second one, actually," which draws a laugh.

The "Robert" he is referring to is Robert Davidson, not present at today's proceedings, although his brother Reg Davidson is, and so too another artist, Michael Nicoll Yahgulanaas, both of whom sing to a beat set by Davidson's drum. As with the previous day's pole raising, the amount of preparation preceding the house-front raising seems wildly disproportionate to the time it takes to actually raise the piece. With a dozen or so men standing on Hart's balcony, two or three to a rope, and another dozen on the ground to give the planks their initial lift, the front folds up like the side of a cardboard box, and to another round of cheers, hoots, hollers, claps and drumbeats, the house front is suddenly, magnificently, in place. Hart's house has been converted, in seconds, from a modernized big house—with a balcony, double-paned glass windows and doors—to what resembles more closely a traditional longhouse, though this one now lacks an opening at the front. But what a marvellous front! A huge red-and-black painting on a red cedar palette, not a brushstroke out of place over the entire expanse of wood, an emphatic new billboard that advertises the past and heralds the future.

As the planks are jostled more tightly into position, Hart stands in front of his work, explaining its features. He points first to the central depiction of a totem pole that he plans to put up in another three years, which bears some of the crests—bullhead, frog, beaver and eagle—of the Skedans people who have adopted his wife, Rosemary, and their four children. To the right of the pole, covering almost half the house front, is a resplendent eagle; to the left, a larger-than-life-sized two-fin killer whale. What Hart doesn't say is that painted house fronts were rare on Haida Gwaii, which seems strange given the artistry that attends almost everything the Haida ever touched. After introducing his four young assistants, two men, two women, Hart gives a quiet but forceful speech about how channelling their efforts into such a project is a powerful reminder that the Haida have a future. There is unbridled joy on the apprentices' faces, the joy of pride and achievement, and of confidence gained. Joy, too, on the face of ʔIdansuu—joy, and perhaps a little relief.

People drift away, to take advantage of a short lull in the proceedings. At five o'clock that afternoon, they start converging on the community hall. Some have come because they received the formal, hand-painted invitation, but most are here because it is known hereabouts, all over the islands, on the mainland, even in Alaska, that Jim Hart is putting up a "doings," a potlatch, and that it is an event not to be missed. So they come, couples, families, young and old, native, non-native, from near and far, mingling with easy familiarity, to an event that was banned from these shores between 1884 and 1951 by Canadian governments who feared the potlatch and its rituals, along with the people who practised them.

Tonight's program is spelled out on the invitation:

Welcoming ceremony
Relate Haida history as we know it
Feast
Acknowledgements
Clan namings
Clan adoptions
Relate our clan's history, traditional territories
and our living history
Performances throughout the evening

Many people are dressed in their Sunday best, and for some at least that's a holdover from the morning's visit to their church. Two dozen or so tables long enough to sit thirty people are arranged in rows either side of a large central cleared space, at one end of which stands a replica house front. At the other end are two speaking daises in front of a head table that is quickly populated by elders, important guests and Hart's close family. What is by day a basketball court is, this night, a feast house and a dance hall, adorned with cedar boughs and, over on one wall, Lia Hart's geneaological chart, taped in place between a fire alarm and a basketball hoop and drawing a lot of attention.

Ushers attired in decorated black tunics steer people to their seats. A man known by the single and singular name of Guujaaw enters without fanfare. Having been offered a place at the head table with his family, he instead makes way for the elders and takes a seat at a table with other Haida who, like him, have responded to the invitation's designation of "traditional dress" by donning some combination of vests, cedar hats, headbands, necklaces, bracelets, aprons, skirts, leggings and moccasins. Guujaaw wears his trademark waistcoat, fringed with abalone shells, and a fur-trimmed woven cedar headband over an otherwise ordinary long-sleeved shirt, brown pants and sensible shoes. Marcie, his wife, with their three young kids in tow, also makes room for the elders and ushers her children up to seats in the bleachers. As the hall fills to capacity, Michael Nicoll Yahgulanaas fairly bounces from table to table, dressed in a tunic and an adapted English top hat, to which he has added a crest on a thin board standing half a metre tall, giving him the appearance of a slightly manic town crier–cum–yeoman who just happens to have a killer whale fin poking out of his head.

When the tables are jam-packed and the bleachers are half full, ʔIdansuu is drummed into the hall through the main entrance, singers and dancers front and back, the chief resplendent in layers of clothing and jewellery, topped with his woven spruce root hat, his long ponytail tucked under his tunic. He holds aloft a gorgeously weathered copper shield, which he brandishes to loud cheers from the crowd.

It is great theatre, and after a prayer to the ancestors that signals the commencement of dinner, Oliver Bell, a small man, is hefted into the hall in a large pot, from which he springs and launches a lively skit while wearing a mask that's almost as big as he is. It seems there has been a bit of a miscue with the catering, and the first course, a seafood chowder, hasn't materialized. So when Bell leaps from the pot to perform a seafood chowder skit, it is Haida improv at its finest—and a gentle, good-humoured rebuke of the chief.

Chowder or nay, there is little risk anyone will go hungry. Each table already has plates filled with apples, oranges, cupcakes, bread rolls, and Rice Krispie squares. There are countless flower arrangements. On each plastic dinner plate rests a small jewellery pouch that contains a gift of a polished stone, or pretty shells, or both. Guests collect their gifts and pass their dinner plates up towards the head of each table, to see them return laden with roast beef, sliced smoked meat and salami, potato and pasta salad, and of course smoked and barbecued salmon. An extra flourish—an additional sign of wealth—is that each plate also has a cooked oolichan on it. These are consumed with obvious relish by most of the Haida, less enthusiastically by their non-native guests, and not at all by some too squeamish to tackle the legendary candlefish, a prized trading item between the Haida, whose rivers don't have oolichan, and north coast mainland nations, whose rivers do.

Perhaps 800 people are gathered in the hall now. On a hot night, the air in the hall is starting to thicken, but the Harts have anticipated that, too, thoughtfully supplying small hand fans that flutter such that, for a while, the bleachers look like a butterfly farm. Arnie Bellis, one of the evening's emcees, calls out from time to time for a show of hands from those who haven't been fed, and in a surprisingly short time, the crowd is happily stuffed. As the plates are cleared and coffee is served, Bellis takes the microphone and says, "I never thought I'd ever say this in [Old] Massett, but can you please turn off your cell-phones." There is much laughter. There are many cellphones, even though cell coverage came to the islands barely a month earlier.

Bellis's request signals that the potlatch is about to move from a sprawling, cheerful, social event into its business phase. A percepti-ble cohesion of interest and purpose takes hold, and from this point onwards, for the next couple of hours, a spell seems to fall over the crowd, as if the hall is somehow hermetically sealed off from the rest of the world. Which in many ways, it is.

One of the most important transactions of the evening happens early on, heralded by a loud song at centre stage from the trio of Michael Nicoll Yahgulanaas, Guujaaw and Guujaaw's nephew Donnie Edenshaw. When the song is over, Jimmy Hart singles out Guujaaw, who comes forward and is honoured for having adopted Hart's wife and children into the Skedans clan. Rosemary is non-native, so she and their children previously had no Haida status. By conferring it upon them, Hart says, Guujaaw has given them "bearing on the land." In reply, Guujaaw tells the crowd that Hart's doings have pulled people together and reminded them "of our ties to each other and to this land." Nicoll Yahgulanaas, Edenshaw and Guujaaw close this solemn bit of business with a song.

Chief ʔIdansuu turns his attention to Rosemary Hart, draping her with a blanket adorned with the same crest painted on his house front, the two-fin killer whale of Skedans. She looks luminous. He then honours each of their children—Lia, Mary, Carl, Geoffrey—with headbands fringed with fur, and Hart carefully thanks the two young women he had commissioned to weave the headbands. "If you need something woven, call these two," says Hart, which for the young weavers is a massive endorsement. Then the chief provokes peals of laughter as he haltingly disrobes, all fingers and thumbs, removing his hat, peeling off pendants and necklaces and his blanket, a pouch, his tunic, before gifting his tunic and an array of ornaments to Aaron Hands, his once estranged eldest son from an earlier liaison. In the public manner of the potlatch, Jim Hart is telling not just his oldest boy but their community that the two are father and son, and that he is a proud father of all his children.

Chief ʔIdansuu turns next to an onlooker who sits in the thick of things at the front of the hall, two canes propped up against his knees, a broad smile on his storied face, his head dressed in white ermine skin adorned with a thin round copper frontlet above his forehead. This is Chief Niis Wes, Ernie Wilson, who, being from Skedans, is chief of Guujaaw's clan and now, by extension, Rosemary Hart and the kids' chief, too. "I would like to gift this to the chief from my uncle, Morris White," Hart says of the copper shield that he once again holds aloft. As a measure of respect to Chief Niis Wes, Chief ʔIdansuu offers him the shield, but he adds one condition: that he can buy it back at some time in the future. "My uncle made the copper, and it came to me when he passed away," Hart says. "It means a lot to me. Like I said, I'd like to approach him [Chief Niis Wes] in the future and buy it back."

Chief Niis Wes gives a kingly nod of assent, and the deal is done. Huge cheers rise up, the significance of this gesture lost on no one. "This is the highest honour a Haida can give another one," the old chief says in a quavering but clear voice, beaming with delight. "It's not the size of the gift, it's the feeling behind it that makes it precious." Guujaaw leaps forward to seal the contract with a raven song. A dancer dressed as a large raven circles the floor, his hinged wooden beak clacking out a sharp percussion, at once lighthearted and mildly menacing.

The evening takes on a solemn hue when Jim Hart offers Guujaaw a gift "for all the things he's done for my children." It is also Hart's way of bringing honour to Guujaaw's own connection to the Edenshaw family, despite the fact that Guujaaw—born Gary Edenshaw—has long since chosen not to use the Edenshaw name himself. Hart looks and sounds quite earnest as he reaches over to the dais, but when it becomes apparent that the gift is the carved cedar helmet that he was working on just hours earlier—recognizably a raven, but demonstrably incomplete—Guujaaw and Hart burst into laughter. Hart has now famously missed another deadline, and while he holds up the helmet and explains how close it is to being finished, Guujaaw steals the show—the raven steals the limelight. Before Hart can react, Guujaaw has slapped down a piece of paper torn from the corner of a brown paper bag on which are scrawled words to a song that Michael Nicoll Yahgulanaas joins him in singing, the two wearing huge grins and exuding an air of unbridled mischief. They belt out the song, and it might just be the shortest tune in the history of the Haida people. It lasts precisely seventeen seconds. Guujaaw had finished composing it in the parking lot outside the community centre, another piece of artistic spontaneity on a weekend full of them. "Well, I didn't really have that one ready till about five o'clock that night," he later recalls. "Like other things, you keep fiddling around and ignoring things until it's getting a little late in the game. Anyway, I was kinda teasing Jimmy a little bit, eh?"

Waiting for the chief
Like ravens on the beach
We're waiting for the chief.

"Kinda teasing ourselves as well, we're waiting, but in the end it comes through as something supernatural. He was happy, anyway." In the way of the potlatch, once Guujaaw's song is sung it is no longer his, but passes into the ownership of Jim Hart. "It's his, he can let other people sing it, but it's his. Did you like it?" At the conclusion of the song, Guujaaw and Chief ʔIdansuu embrace.

Nika Collison and Taxulang guud ʔad k'ajuu (Friends Playing Music Together) from Skidegate are drummed into the hall, a troupe of ten women and one man who perform a headdress dance from Skedans. Chief Niis Wes keeps time, old curled fingers tapping steadily on his newly acquired copper shield. Collison, granddaughter of Mabel Stevens and the legendary Haida artist Bill Reid, then leads the group in another song, one that belongs to ʔIdansuu and was first sung at a potlatch when Jim Hart took his chief's name. At that time, the long-forgotten song was reintroduced to the Staast'as Eagle clan by Terri-Lynn Williams-Davidson, general counsel for the Haida Nation and a persuasive legal advocate for Haida rights and title. Collison and her group gyrate in a gorgeous swirl of button blankets, drums held aloft, a slow beat setting time for two dancers brandishing canoe paddles on their imaginary journey. The hall reverberates so loudly to the singing and drumming that, for a while at least, it feels as if the gathering is inside one giant drum, the roof stretched tight over those in attendance, the pulse of the drummers and the dancers and the singers connecting everyone with an invisible percussive thread.

The Skidegate dancers then perform an eagle dance to honour the Staast'as. This has been carefully choreographed, not just the dance itself but the hierarchy of honour. "[Haida] song and dance is in its rebirth stage still," Collison says, and so in consultation with Jim Hart and with her elders, she has pieced together "little bits of knowledge." Enough to know, for instance, that while they have an eagle dance that is well practised, they do not have a beaver or a frog dance—"So we'll just figure it out, we'll choreograph something." That something starts with a beaver, who dances into view while the drummers feather their drums with a murmuring beat, but no song is sung because "there's no song we know of for that," says Collison. The eagle comes next, a lusty, full-throated song-and-dance affair, a performer in a brilliant costume tipped by actual eagle wings spanning out from either hand of the dancer. Then, again just to drumming, a frog emerges in a green waistcoat, bobbing up and down with a fantastically lugubrious look conveyed by its wooden mask. "Again, this is new, what we are doing," Collison explains. "We don't know how to do the beaver or frog dance, so it seemed fitting that they were short, not like the eagle dance, and because beavers and frogs are shy, they came, peeked out and went back in."

There are several more dances by Collison's group, but one in particular stands out, not so much a dance but a play. It is the bear mother's story, and Collison is almost giddy with enthusiasm as she introduces it. It is a new dance born of many old stories about the bear mother, she says, but what all the stories have in common is that as women are out in the woods picking berries, one is captured by a bear and spirited off and, later, gives birth to cubs. Here in the gymnasium, a dancer springs onto the floor in a full-length bear costume, head, paws, the whole thing, while women dancers mimic the picking of berries, plopping the imaginary fruit into their upturned cedar hats with not a care in the world—until the bear jumps on one of the women and drags her screaming out of sight. Collison says her group chose the story because it's about respect. "And Jim is, I think, like Guujaaw, he's an excellent leader, and he has wonderful qualities that younger people observe and look up to and strive to attain. And so we wanted to do a song that had to do with honour and respect, and to honour Jim."

Then once again, there is a shift in mood from the theatrical to the transactional. Hart adopts a nephew, Jordan, who takes his new name and dances his way into Haida history and onto the genealogical chart. At the same time, Hart's children and friends have fanned out across the hall and are handing out gifts to everyone in the crowd: an extraordinary profusion of tea towels, knitted pot warmers, scarves, bath towels, salad servers, bowls, cups, toy dolls, potpourri, teapots, socks, baby powder, tablecloths, toys. It's an extravagant cascade of gifts, many of them handmade, not just one per person but thousands of gifts intended to both display and share ʔIdansuu's wealth.

Now Christian White enters the building at the centre of a noisy procession. Minus his eyeglasses and the studiousness they ordinarily add to his face, replete with headdress and regalia and waving a long spike of wood in the air, White looks positively fierce. His potlatch from the previous evening has spilled over into Hart's doings, and for a while some unfinished business from the Yahgu 'laanas agenda takes over from the Staast'as. White's cousin, the artist April White, fits him with a blanket that Pendleton Woolen Mills of Oregon has just added to its Native American line, her depiction of White Raven's Moonlit Flight. White completes some adoptions of his own, and there is a marvellous dance to honour the matriarchs, the "ladies of high esteem," as they are known. Soon a large knot of women and girls is on the move, swirling and swaying to a beat set by barechested young men of the Yahgu 'laanas clan. As White and his clan are drummed out of the hall, brandishing clubs and blades, there is an air of celebration, even triumph.

And then, the proceedings begin to wane. Some of the air has leaked out of the big drum. Some people leave—it is after midnight by now—though others remember that potlatches of old lasted for days at a time and you stayed till all was said and done. In this case, Hart has more adoptions to do—two friends from off-islands, Lois Sherr Dubin and Lindsay Eberts, who are celebrated because they "do good things in the outside world." Their new names will stay with them until they pass on, Hart says, and then will be returned home to Haida Gwaii: "And that's the way it is." The two are given their names by an elder, Robert Davidson's aunt Emily Goertzen, who insists they repeat them into the microphone. Three times they say their names, as is the tradition when the Haida confer a name. Then, with their new blankets, they take a turn on the floor, like so many before them, and thus are inducted into the living history of the Haida, Guujaaw drumming and singing accompaniment until the potlatch shows signs of petering out altogether. And then, suddenly, it has.

Outside, a boat slips down Masset Inlet. A car drives by. A scattering of kids plays noisily in the corner of a field despite the late hour and the evening chill. Dogs feast on scraps from the dinner. A screen door slams. There is a satellite blinking overhead. All but a handful of Canada's 30 million citizens live east of this point, and most are no doubt fast asleep now, in the wee hours of Monday morning. But if the satellite could send them a picture of what just happened here, surely many would blink twice at what they saw. They would see that, in this country they call Canada, there is another country called Haida Gwaii. To the people who live here, the Haida, theirs is not just another country: it is another culture, another cosmology, another reality, another economy, another history—another world.

TWO

LAND

TROUBLES

ONE SUMMER FRIDAY afternoon, the president, political leader and first speaker of the Council of the Haida Nation, who by constitutional diktat must be a natural-born Haida citizen, is in his office, dressed in a manner that takes the notion of casual Friday to a new level. Guujaaw wears a golf shirt whose unmistakable Royal Bank insignia has been defaced. He says he's been trying, without success, to remove the words but retain the logo, which for some reason appeals to him. With the shirt he wears a pair of loose-fitting work pants. He looks less like the president of a nation than he does a fisherman dressed for a day doing repairs at the net loft. If that were a Harley-Davidson T-shirt and he were in a city, people would no doubt give him a wide berth.

It's actually uncommon to find the president of the Haida Nation in his office. As often as not he is working from his home, just up the hill on the Skidegate Reserve, or he is travelling—to the villages on Haida Gwaii, where the people are; to Vancouver, where the money and the courts and the politicians are; to Ottawa and Victoria, if he really has to, because there are more politicians and lawyers there; and otherwise across Canada and around the world on a crusade for not just his people's rights but the rights of all indigenous peoples. He can also be found out on the land or the waters of Haida Gwaii, though these days a lot less often than he would like, due to the weight of his duties as head man of Haida Gwaii. Guujaaw's quest—no matter how far-flung the stops along the path he has chosen—begins and ends on the land. "Our people come from every part of these islands," he says, "and there is no place we can give up." *No pasarán.*

Guujaaw could add to his list of titles and responsibilities that of defendant-in-chief of the Haida Nation, though it is neither an accident nor a contradiction that in Action No. L020662 filed in the Vancouver Registry of the Supreme Court of British Columbia in 2004 he is listed as a plaintiff. The action is

BETWEEN:

THE COUNCIL OF THE HAIDA NATION and Guujaaw, suing on his own behalf and on behalf of all members of the HAIDA NATION

PLAINTIFFS

AND:

HER MAJESTY THE QUEEN IN RIGHT OF THE PROVINCE OF BRITISH COLUMBIA AND THE ATTORNEY GENERAL OF CANADA

DEFENDANTS

It is in the ten-page Statement of Claim in Action No. L020662 that the Haida lay claim to their entire homeland, seek title to all the lands and the seabed and the waters of Haida Gwaii, and demand the rights that attend to that title. (Title and rights are two different things, though in law their meanings are still evolving. Aboriginal title is a unique interest in the land, as opposed to fee-simple interest, and it includes the right to exclusive use and occupancy of the land. Aboriginal title also means the land is held communally rather than by individual aboriginal persons. Aboriginal rights is a broader concept based on activities, such as hunting, fishing and food gathering, that are an element of practice, custom or tradition. It is possible for there to be a valid aboriginal right without actual title to the land associated with that right. The ideal, for aboriginal people, is to secure both.) For many Haida, having to claim title before a court, a central fixture of the political system that took their land away in the first place, is, at best, an irritating contradiction; for the more militant Haida, going to court is a costly aggravation, a concession that perpetuates colonialism and plays into the dominant society's hands. For leaders like Guujaaw, laying claim to Haida Gwaii is like breathing. To him, every single act by every Haida citizen breathes life into the Haida assertion of rights and title, and the court case is one route among many—life by a thousand cuts—towards his people's renunciation of Canada's version of manifest destiny. The court case is a step on the path towards a destiny that is instead manifestly of the Haida's own design. Just one step, but in the world of aboriginal law, a huge leap: the Haida case is arguably the most sweeping indigenous rights claim in the world, and one of the most important land claims in Canadian history.

"So the title and rights thing," as Guujaaw laconically describes it one day, "isn't just to prove, just to show that we can establish aboriginal title under Canadian law, but also to show that they [the federal and provincial governments] have no claim to it [title] themselves." It sounds like a thoroughly uncompromising viewpoint, legally, but Guujaaw is prepared to concede that a form of sovereignty association between his nation and Canada might one day arise from the Haida winning their case. "The compromise is that we accept that we will make accommodation with Canada rather than the USA, Russia, or Japan—which are still options," he once told an interviewer. "And there are other [options], like decolonization. In doing this [compromising], we negotiate the interface and coexistence within

Canadian society." In a coffee shop in the Haida village of Skidegate, he elaborates upon this point: "The aboriginal title thing is a compromise. Haida title within Canada is what aboriginal title [for the Haida] boils down to. We could say they had absolutely no business claiming this land in the first place. That's the extreme, eh? Everybody should be getting on a boat and getting outta here. That's not in the cards for us. Our position is we'll make it work within Canada, holding title." Within Canada, another nation—not Quebec, but Haida Gwaii.

When the first Haida emerged from a cockle shell at Rose Spit perhaps 10,000 years ago, they inherited from the supernatural beings a place of incomparable physical beauty and abundance— even by the standards of British Columbia, which prides itself on its natural assets. The province is bounded to the west by a coastline that stretches more than 27,000 kilometres, or almost 17,000 miles. British Columbia's eastern boundary is formed by the Rocky Mountains, and the far north of the province has been compared with the Serengeti for the sheer volume and diversity of its wildlife. There are deserts and grasslands, huge lakes and fast-flowing rivers, forests and soaring mountain peaks, a stunning diversity of natural systems that represent five of the fifteen ecozones found across Canada. Amid this bounty, Haida Gwaii is arguably the most beguiling place of all. To hike among its huge trees is to step into a forest much older than the oldest buildings of Europe. To paddle its waters on a late summer's evening, and be treated to a visit from a pod of sleek orcas or a flock of clumsy pigeon guillemots, is to understand the profound human need for experiences that transcend the superficial offerings of modern life. To jig for halibut or ling cod off the west coast of Haida Gwaii—next stop, Japan—is to feel the pull of ancient rituals and the sense that, had the world turned out to be flat, a really big fish could tug you off the edge to be lost forever. Treading softly among the senescent remains of a Haida village site, a visitor may hear echoes of stories that reach back to a time beyond imagining; as native people themselves sometimes say, from time out of mind. From north latitude 52 to 54 degrees, between west longitudes 131 and 133 degrees, Haida Gwaii measures about 300 kilometres from top to bottom, and about 85 kilometres at its widest point. Its 150 or so islands comprise a land base of about one million hectares (about two and a half million acres), or a shade more than 1 per cent of British Columbia's land mass. It is a place so particular, so unique that it has been compared to the Galapagos Islands. Some people have even called it that, the Galapagos of the north.

In their land-use plan, the Haida describe their homeland eloquently as "an isolated archipelago of forest, muskeg and ocean, shaped like a bear's canine tooth shrouded in swirling clouds. The land is formed by ancient upheavals, volcanoes, sediments, ice flows and runoff. The surrounding ocean climate is warmer than the neighbouring mainland, so during the ice ages some parts of the islands remained free of glaciers. Most of the modern Hecate Strait and parts of our outer coastal regions were once above sea level, covered by tundra, streams and lakes, and inhabited by our ancestors. Over just the past few thousand years, the sea level has fluctuated by almost 200 metres, while the fish, forest life and our people adapted to the changing times. The weather is shaped by the dynamics of the largest ocean on Earth: there are high winds and rain, large tides, mild winter temperatures and cool, cloudy summers. Warm ocean currents mix with cold water upwellings rich in nutrients. The sea is abundant in plankton, seaweeds, fish, shellfish and mammals. Through the lives of everyone—people, seabirds and salmon, bear, and many others— the food webs of the ocean and land are woven tightly together. Because of our isolation, unique forms of life have evolved—birds, mammals, fish, plants and insects—in plenty. The forests are renowned for growing trees of high quality, for large seabird nesting colonies, unique salmon populations, raptors, the world's largest black bears, and an abundance of diverse ocean life. This is the physical and biological world in which Haida culture has grown for thousands of years, ever since Raven coaxed the first people from a cockle shell."

Although Haida Gwaii, like the Galapagos Islands, is often described as an enchanted place, there is nothing fey about it, nothing benign. It is periodically lashed with violent Pacific storms, battered by the strongest winds in the country and pounded by waves up to thirty-five metres high. The west coast of Haida Gwaii, an abrupt tectonic scarp rising from 3,000 metres below sea level to the 1,000-metre peaks of the San Cristoval range, confronts one of the most dangerous stretches of water along the entire length of the Pacific Northwest. Hecate Strait, which separates the east coast of the islands from the B.C. mainland, is equally feared for sudden squalls and tumultuous seas that make dangerous chores of sailing and fishing. Yet on a summer's day when the wind stops and a column of light beams through the oyster sky, it is possible to think you are in a kind of paradise on Haida Gwaii. On shore, there are dozens of unique species or subspecies of plants and animals. Sometimes, out from under the four metres of rainfall that occur every year, you can even see some of them. That rainfall is why the trees that grow on the islands are some of the largest free-standing structures in the world.

Haida Gwaii, Islands of the People, has an older name, X̱aaydlaga Gwaayaay, or Islands at the Boundary of the World. It has a younger name, too: the Queen Charlotte Islands. English sea captain George Dixon, who sailed there in 1787 aboard the *Queen Charlotte,* named the islands after his ship and, by extension, the wife of the reigning English king, George III. Looking south, you can see Haida Gwaii from Alaska on a clear day. You cannot see it, no matter how clear the day, looking west from the mainland of Canada.

On the walls of the Skidegate office of the Council of the Haida Nation, Guujaaw's office, hang handsome "salmon forest" maps produced by the Gowgaia Institute, a local non-profit that has worked closely with the Haida for more than two decades to document desecration by clear-cut logging and the consequences of logging for salmon habitat. These maps don't just record what's already been taken. They project logging plans out to the year 2250. Judging by those projections, the maps chart the destruction of any unprotected forest landscape on Haida Gwaii. What is interesting about these maps, apart from their dire predictions, is that they depict *only* Haida Gwaii. There is no locator map in the corner that situates Haida Gwaii in relation to anywhere else. The maps tell a story of one place. One separate place.

The Gowgaia maps reflect a biophysical reality but also a cultural and a metaphysical one. Haida Gwaii is at least in part defined by its separateness from the rest of the world. The Haida people are, too. The islands are sparsely settled, a few small towns and villages amounting to a population of fewer than 6,000 people. About half that number are Haida. The Haida were once were among the most accomplished of seafaring people, ranging north to Alaska and south to California in the great canoes that the massive old-growth trees enabled. They were artists, though there was no word for art in the Haida language; it was just something people did. The Haida had the luxury of time to make beautiful things because their islands were so tremendously abundant. Fish, salmon in particular, could be had easily. They were traders, too, often making the treacherous crossing to the mainland. But not every crossing contemplated commerce. The Haida were much feared along the coast as raiders and warriors. "The Haida, and only the Haida, were immune from attack," writes Christie Harris in *Raven's Cry*, her fictionalized retelling of the effect of European contact on the Haida. "In consequence, the pride of the Haida shaded even that of their mighty neighbours [the Tsimshian and Tlingit]. They were lords of the coast, the aristocrats of their world." These coastal sovereigns commissioned great art from the most talented among them to demonstrate their wealth and to keep their stories alive: totem poles, masks, canoes, woven baskets and a profusion of ceremonial attire. Theirs is a tradition of impressive, at times consciously intimidating displays of great craftsmanship, especially in that most generous medium, cedar. The Haida have their own language, too, classified by linguists as a language isolate. Haida is thought to be among the three or four most difficult languages in the world to learn and is today listed as endangered. Precisely because their language, their status, their livelihood, their culture, their songs and their very identity have been under such sustained assault, the Haida have chosen to fight not just for a portion of their land or a vestige of their culture but for all of it.

The Haida are determined not to trade away their rights in a negotiated treaty, like some other First Nations have decided to do or are thinking about doing. Says Guujaaw: "There's a real interesting and important little twist to this, and the advantage that we have is that because of the history of the Haidas and the artwork that's out there— Bill Reid, Jimmy Hart, Robert Davidson and all these guys that are putting stuff out there—wherever you go in the world, people know what the Haidas are to begin with, so when we make a stand they know who it is that's standing up. People pay attention to that because the ancestry, the culture, is respected. It's known." What is less well-known, and what Guujaaw and his fellow activists are determined to show, is that in addition to their notable ancestry and enviable skills as artists, the Haida once had an economy and systems of government that were equal to anything the outside world ever created. As with their art, their economy and their governance systems are continually evolving and adapting, and those systems are likewise deserving of respect. Since no senior government seems willing to accede to this view, the Haida have set out to demonstrate it once and for all.

The scope of the Haida's ambition is breathtaking. Their title and rights case uses as its judicial springboard more than a generation of Supreme Court of Canada decisions in cases concerning aboriginal peoples—*Calder, Sparrow, Van der Peet, N.T.C. Smokehouse, Gladstone, Delgamuukw, Haida*—and vaults the Haida on a long, high, expensive trajectory that will land them back in Ottawa in front of the nine justices of the Supreme Court of Canada. Undergirding both this judicial arc and a generation of incremental gains by aboriginal peoples in the courts is a span of obdurate resistance by the Haida, a history of stubborn, uncompromising leadership that has resisted every offer to settle the Haida's argument with Canada quickly or cheaply. Even today, when governments both federal and provincial have aligned around the notion that the "aboriginal question" really *does* need to be answered, the Haida seem as implacable as ever. "A lot of people are depending upon us bringing this forward and winning it," Guujaaw says. "We will win, cut and dried."

If they do, the Haida will bring a desperately needed clarity to an issue that remains perhaps the most profound failing of Canada as a nation, a deep stain on our claim to value fairness for all people in everything from our daily lives to our constitution. The Haida case could force governments to go beyond mere consultation and accommodation with native people. It could precipitate a wholesale revision of the rights and roles of governments in relation to aboriginal people and the resources to which they—in the view of industry, at least—continue to obstruct access. Depending how things turn out, business could finally get more of the "certainty" that it covets, or indigenous Canadians confronting unwanted developments could mount more blockades and direct action than ever before. The Haida case will undoubtedly set a new benchmark for indigenous rights in Canada. Beyond our shores, *Guujaaw et al.* will reverberate in the other English-speaking settler societies—the United States, Australia and New Zealand—at a minimum. The case could also profoundly influence the livelihood prospects for indigenous peoples around the world—peoples who presently occupy 22 per cent of the Earth's land surface, are stewards of 80 per cent of remaining biodiversity, and account for 90 per cent of global cultural diversity. This is no small thing that the Haida are taking on, and its resolution is long overdue.

THE LAND QUESTION goes to the very origins of Canada as a Confederation, much as it is central to the origin myth of the United States. In the rapid colonization of the Americas and their resources, native people were brushed aside, bought off or exterminated. In his book *1491*, Charles C. Mann refutes the long-held mainstream assumption that the Americas were a vast wilderness populated by small, nomadic bands of native people. He describes "indigenous America as a crowded, jostling place—'a beehive of people,' as [Bartolemé de] las Casas put it in 1542. To las Casas, the Americas seemed so thick with people 'that it looked as if God has placed all of or the greater part of the entire human race in these countries.'" So much for the notion of *terra nullius* ("land belonging to no one," literally "empty land"), a doctrine used by colonialists to justify settlement of indigenous lands.

The brutality of the Spanish in South America, Central America and Mexico—millions upon millions of indigenous people slaughtered in the first five decades after Columbus—had no numerical equivalent in North America, but western diseases took an unbelievable toll. "Nobody knows how many died in the pandemics of the 1770s and 1780s, but even if one had a number it wouldn't begin to tally the impact," Mann writes. "Languages, prayers, dreams, habits, and hopes—all gone. And not just once, but over and over again. In our antibiotic era, how can we imagine what it means to have entire ways of life hiss away like steam?" Mann's work acknowledges that there are "high counters" and "low counters" among anthropologists who have attempted to put a figure on long-extinguished populations. On Haida Gwaii, a "low counter" would have it that the historical Haida population was in the order of 10,000 people. American naval Captain William Sturgis, in 1799, suggested a total population of about 12,000 Haida based on a "warrior count" that extrapolated a total population from an observed number of Haida warriors and the estimated number of their dependants. This figure was considered more reliable than a "canoe projection," based on the number and capacity of canoes that were spotted by outsiders, or a house and lodge count that guessed at the number of occupants in Haida buildings. A Hudson's Bay Company census in the mid-1830s pegged the Haida population at about 8,500. Two other estimates from the same time were higher: about 9,500 in one case, 10,500 in the other. The Council of the Haida Nation's website describes the pre-contact Haida population as being in the tens of thousands.

Although there is no way of knowing exactly what the Haida's population was at its peak, by 1913 there was an exact count of the Haida still living on Haida Gwaii. The population, reduced to 7 per cent of the low estimate, was just 597 souls. The Haida weren't brushed aside, and they weren't bought off. Instead, they were nearly exterminated by disease, primarily smallpox and tuberculosis. Guujaaw once told *Maclean's* magazine the Haida had been victims of germ warfare. The colonizers could only have succeeded, he said, if "they wiped us out in that kind of way. That's part of our case in court: that kind of warfare isn't legitimate." But it was effective. The word *decimated* means to kill one-tenth of a population. The Haida were decimated over and over, till not even one-tenth of their population was left standing. Most gave up their lives, and those who remained were ordered to surrender their lands.

From an aboriginal perspective, ownership of the land was never in question until someone arrived to contest it. Entwined as it has been with the devastation of whole societies, the "land question" is as much about social justice as it is about actual land. Yet it is often characterized by non-natives as a latter-day land grab by aboriginal people; many non-natives cannot fathom any justification for wanting land other than to exploit it. For the dominant culture, the land question has always been, plain and simple, an issue of access to resources. The "settlement" of countries like Canada and Australia was based on the assumption that Europeans were arriving in unpopulated, unproductive lands. Where there were aboriginal inhabitants, they were considered to be nomads, with no claim to any particular place. Author J. Edward Chamberlin, in his book *If This Is Your Land, Where Are Your Stories?*, turns that notion on its head. "[Australian] Aborigines, who know the names of every plant and the location of all the water holes, as perpetual nomads? Europeans in a place ten thousand miles from home, as settlers? It doesn't make sense. For millennia, farming people have roamed the world looking for new places and dreaming of the home they left behind, moving on after a generation or so to other new places. And we call these people...my people, Us—'settlers'? The other people, the indigenous people who have lived in the same place for tens of thousands of years...we call Them 'wanderers'?...The truth is that We are the nomads and They are the settlers." Chamberlin underlines his point with a quote from British explorer Sir George Grey, who around 1840 wrote about the Australian aborigines' impression of Europeans who were moving onto the land. "He reported that since the Aborigines had no thought of ever leaving their land, they also had no notion of other folk leaving theirs. 'When they see white people suddenly appear in their country, and settl[e] themselves down in particular spots, they imagine that they must have formed an attachment for this land in some other state of existence, and hence conclude the settlers were at one period black men, and their own relations.'"

In British Columbia, the first "settlers" spread out across the land in much the same way that Australian and American "pioneers" did. As Robert Bringhurst writes in his book *A Story as Sharp as a Knife,* "Not many of the immigrants arriving in North America, from the sixteenth century through the twentieth, have grasped the fact that they were coming to take refuge with indigenous societies of genuine antiquity and cultural complexity." But the new arrivals neither sought edification nor saw cultural complexity. They saw land, and then as now they required government assistance to get it. From the outset of British Columbia's colonization, there has been no real distinction between the goals of government and those of business. The supreme embodiment of the nexus between business and government, money and power, was that first captain of industry, Sir James Douglas. In the mid-1800s, Douglas was posted to Fort Victoria as chief factor of the Hudson's Bay Company. He wanted access to land and to marine resources, especially sea otter pelts. In 1849, the whole of Vancouver Island was conveyed to the Hudson's Bay Company, and that same year the Crown Colony of Vancouver Island was established. Richard Blanshard was appointed as governor of the colony, but within months, he had resigned in frustration at his inability to impose any authority; all real authority lay with Douglas. The Crown dispensed with further pretence, and in 1851 Chief Factor Douglas became Governor Douglas as well. "He wore two hats," as former B.C. Supreme Court justice Thomas Berger later put it. The province's premiers have, for the most part, been wearing two hats ever since.

Douglas was curiously sympathetic to the notion that the Crown should not run roughshod over native people. He obviously felt duty bound by the Royal Proclamation of King George III, which in 1763 set out a policy by which aboriginal title should be surrendered before any settlement proceeded. James Douglas was signatory to fourteen such land settlements on Vancouver Island, the so-called Douglas Treaties. Other than in the far northeast of British Columbia, where an agreement called Treaty 8 took in aboriginal communities in the Peace River country, no other treaties applied to any lands in British Columbia during the colonial era. According to Thomas Berger, "Douglas's transactions with the Indians may look one-sided, and they were: a few pounds sterling and some blankets in exchange for all the Indians' land, except the reserves. But Douglas, at least, understood the Indians to have rights that had to be recognized, and that there had to be compensation; the white people could not simply enter their land and take it. That, however, was not the view of the settlers." Douglas's policy of obtaining surrenders, providing compensation and guaranteeing native hunting and fishing rights was soon discontinued. When British Columbia entered Confederation in 1871, the provincial government took the position that there would be no treaties with the Indians. One year later, Lieutenant-Governor Joseph Trutch wrote to then prime minister John A. Macdonald: "We have in B.C. a population of Indians numbering from 40,000 to 50,000 by far the larger proportion of who are utter savages living along the coast—frequently committing murder and robbery among themselves—one tribe upon another—and on white people...The Canadian system [of treaties] as I understand it will hardly work here. We have never bought out any Indian claims to lands nor do they expect we should."

Treaties had been signed in the United States, but they were proving a serious impediment to unbridled progress. In 1878, the U.S. government passed the General Allotment Act to abolish tribal control over land tenure and open the country up to further expansion of private property rights. President Theodore Roosevelt later referred to this as "a mighty pulverizing engine to break up the tribal mass." The engine worked, dividing up 90 million acres of land formerly reserved for Native American tribes and leasing much of the rest, usually to white ranchers. In Canada, the ruling business and political elites of the time were so confident of their imperial titles and rights, and held native people in such contempt, that they didn't bother to do the paperwork that could so easily have extinguished, for a pittance in compensation, the rights of all First Nations in British Columbia for all time, the Haida included. From the outset, aboriginal people knew they were being shabbily treated and pressed for a settlement of the land question, but Canada and British Columbia acted as if no such resolution were required. The failure of the colonial powers to heed the advice of James Douglas—what was later referred to as a "gaping hole in the colonizers' paperwork"—has since that time cost business its much-sought-after certainty over the land base; it has cost governments billions of dollars in compensation, and it continues to cost Canada billions of dollars every year, because a whole class of people are still under the putative "care" of the federal government. From the time Douglas first signed a treaty on Vancouver Island in 1850 till the first modern-day treaty was signed in British Columbia with the Nisga'a in 2000, fully a century and a half would elapse.

Successive B.C. governments went out of their way to avoid settling the land question, or even acknowledging that there was a "question" at all. Native people were herded onto reserves, disenfranchised and essentially left to rot. Their reserves took up a negligible amount of land, and much-reduced aboriginal populations were socially stigmatized, culturally ostracized, economically marginalized and politically ignored. "A strong race [has] supplanted a weaker...Indians must accept the inevitable. Progress and development [cannot] be stopped," said Commissioner James A.J. McKenna in 1913, when his Royal Commission convened to resolve a festering dispute between native leaders dissatisfied with their postage-stamp reserve allocations and settlers who wanted even more land freed for development. The Royal Commission itself had taken root in a dispute between the province and Sir Wilfrid Laurier's federal Liberal government, which recognized the risk inherent in British Columbia not having followed Douglas's advice to settle with the Indians. In the lucrative frenzy of frontier development, however, the provincial leadership saw nothing to be gained by pausing to deal with a minority population fast disappearing on the anvil of progress.

"The Indian land question, however, did not disappear," writes legal historian Douglas C. Harris. "In fact, growing and increasingly organized Native protest, including the emergence of three associations—the Indian Rights Association, the Interior Tribes, and the Nisga'a Land Committee that led delegations to London in 1904 and 1906 and to Ottawa in 1908—had raised its profile and brought it to an international stage." In light of those developments, the federal government was prepared to launch a court case to settle aboriginal title. British Columbia was bitterly opposed, and before Canada could put the land question to the Supreme Court of Canada over British Columbia's objections, the Liberal government fell in the 1911 election. "The new Conservative government under Robert Borden had no interest in pressing the controversial issue on behalf of a constituency that had no vote [the natives] with the prospect of antagonizing one that did [the settlers]," Harris notes. Instead of pursuing the case prepared by Laurier's Liberal government, Borden struck a deal with

B.C. premier Richard McBride. Canada would drop its reference to native title if the province would allow the issue of reserves to be studied in what became known as the McKenna-McBride Commission. McBride agreed, and an Indian Affairs official, James McKenna, set off with several commissioners to travel the province.

What McKenna's commission heard, from all the aboriginal leaders who stood before it, was an impassioned plea for their land. Chief Bob Anderson of the Heiltsuk Nation had this to say when the commission visited Bella Bella in 1913: "We are the natives of this Country and we want all the land we can get. We feel that we own the whole of this Country, every bit of it, and ought to have something to say about it. The Government have not bought any land from us so far as we know and we are simply lending this land to the Government. We own it all. We will never change our minds in that respect, and after we are dead our children will still hold on to the same ideas. It does not matter how long the Government take [sic] to determine this question, we will remain the same in our ideas about this matter. The British Columbia Government [are] selling the land all around us, and we do not know but they might sell it all, even including these Reserves, in time. We consider that the Government is stealing that land from us, and we also understand that it is unlawful for the Government to take this land."

GIDEON MINESQUE SPOKE on behalf of the Nisga'a when the commission stopped in the Nass Valley in 1915: "We haven't got any ill feelings in our hearts, but we are just waiting for this thing to be settled...we have been living here from time immemorial—it has been handed down in legends from the old people and that is what hurts us very much because the White people have come along and taken this land away from us...We have heard that some White men...said that the [Nisga'a] must be dreaming when they say they own the land upon which they live. It is not a dream—we are certain that this land belongs to us. Right up to this day the government never made any treaty, not even to our grandfathers or our great-grandfathers."

The commission visited the "Queen Charlotte Agency" from September 9 to 15, 1913. Inspections of the reserves took place, "the Commission being very favourably impressed by the evidences of substantial and intelligently directed progress presented in the more recent history of the Haidahs," according to the Royal Commission's final report. "These Indians at the time of the Commission's appointment had, with a total population of 597, twenty-five Reserves in all allotted for them, of an aggregate acreage of 3484.5, or 5.83 acres per capita for the Agency. The principal occupation of the Haidah (Queen Charlotte Agency) people being fishing, for the canneries and for food supply, the majority of their established Reserves are fishing stations of small area, which, however, they have manifested a desire to cultivate insofar as the character of the soil and opportunities generally permit."

On September 13, at the schoolhouse in Skidegate, with Henry Green sworn in as an interpreter, Amos Russ gave a statement on behalf of the Skidegate Indian Council: "We are glad that you people from Ottawa and the other law makers are here, and we are here to put before you our troubles... As far back as we can remember, without any doubt at all, the Queen Charlotte Islands practically belong to the Indians. It came about after a little while that the islands were called the Queen Charlotte Islands. We don't know who gave them that name. As far as we can remember we can claim that the islands fairly belong to us and as far back as we can remember there was never any treaty with respect to this land, between the government and the Indians. We never have had a fight for the islands. No nation ever came and fought us for them and won them from us. If we had had a treaty with the government we would not claim the islands... We see day by day that the government is selling land far down this coast and also down the west coast of the island. We know for a fact the government is selling this land and yet we can say the Queen Charlotte Islands are ours. You can see right around the island there are villages and villages and you can see our totem poles, which are the same to us as the white man's pre-emption stakes are to them."

The commission had come to the Queen Charlotte Islands to talk about land—specifically, the Haida's tiny reserves—but expressly *not* to talk about land claims. That didn't stop the Haida from pressing their case, as in this statement by Skidegate councillor James Sterling read out to the commission by Henry Green: "Our land troubles are, we understand, the principal reason for your visit, and we have no solution to offer you. Most of our land, of former days, is gone forever from us. What can we say regarding it? Our fishing and hunting grounds, our graveyards and woodland, it is all taken up by others. We have little to call our own, and cannot dispose of the little, if we want to. We are Wards of the Government, a people governed by a people, with no voice in the deliberations...We were told that this and that piece of land was all we could look forward to, and we have not been contented ever since...All we ask is justice and we pray that your visit will bring us nearer a settlement."

The commission chairman's response, as recorded, drips with paternalism. "It gives us great pleasure to visit this village as well as to have had the opportunity of visiting the village of the members of your tribe residing on the northern part of the island [Old Massett]. It is with pleasure we notice the progress you have made...we are especially pleased with the appearance of your village. We have found wherever we went, a very much improved and advanced condition of things where there has been a resident missionary of the Christian faith among the Indians...Perhaps the very best means of bringing about true civilization has been the Christian religion. Christianity and Western Civilization have always gone hand in hand. Now the best way to follow that up is by individual effort, that is, by the effort of each man in the tribe. Another great aid to civilization is Commercial enterprise, and that again is never going to be got by lying down on your back and expecting plums to fall into your mouth." The fruits of all this colonialist piety and entrepreneurship were of course unevenly distributed to the Haida, who had been busily converted to Christianity and, in the bargain, rendered essentially landless and unable to engage in commerce of any significant kind. But the commissioner would brook no discussion of native title: "All we can say with respect to that is, it is not in our powers to deal with and we have therefore nothing whatever to do with it."

The Haida would not relent. In fact, Amos Russ told the commission that the Haida "laid our claims before [our] lawyer…and left the matter in his hands, and he will take it before the Privy Council in England." The chairman was clearly shocked, saying he was "very much surprised" to hear that the Haida were preparing a submission to the Privy Council and speculating that they were "misinformed in some way or other. That is none of my business, I am only telling you this for your information. Somebody is misleading you or you have misunderstood something." The chairman asked the Haida to restrict their statements to describing the situation on their reserves, to which James Sterling replied, "We have been somewhat cramped and crushed up and we cannot move around as we want to." Sterling pressed the commissioners to explain who owned the Queen Charlotte Islands.

The chairman: "The British Columbia government claims to own the whole of the lands on the Queen Charlotte Islands outside of the reserves, except those places which they granted to private individuals." The Dominion government, he said, claimed those lands set aside for Indian reserves.

Sterling: "Why and in which way did they both get the Islands? If you could give us evidence of who [sic] they got the Islands, before all these people we would be contented."

The chairman: "I won't give an opinion in that respect."

Lunch was taken. During the break, according to the commission transcripts, commissioners Shaw and Macdowall succeeded in convincing James Sterling that the members of the commission were not biased. But after lunch, Solomon Wilson waded right back in, demanding to know if their title claim would be compromised by anything they said to the commission.

Solomon Wilson: "I want to say, really in regard to what you are here for, will this interfere with any of our lawyer questions?"

The chairman: "I am not prepared to say. It may or it may not."

Solomon Wilson: "I want a true answer please."

The chairman: "I cannot give you any other answer."

Solomon Wilson: "If we were to ask you for anything will it interfere with our claims?"

The chairman: "I say it may. I cannot say whether it will or will not…"

Solomon Wilson: "Then you are leaving us to risk it?"

A note by the chairman in the commission transcripts underlines how insistent the Haida were to not prejudice "their rights as to the Indian Title…I stated that it may [prejudice title], and thereupon being again asked if any person will testify, no-one responded. I therefore hold that they do not wish to give testimony." In other words, the Haida refused to further engage the commission in its inquiry about reserve lands, and soon after, the meeting ended.

The Royal Commission's final report makes it clear that the commissioners were in no mood to be drawn into a discussion about title. "While the representations of the Queen Charlotte Agency Indians for more adequate land allotments were hampered by their identification with the movement for recognition of Aboriginal Title and their fear that additional reserves might prejudice action in that connection (for which reason the Skidegates declined to discuss their land requirements with the Commission), the Commission did not permit this fact to militate against fair consideration of what investigation elsewhere shewed to be necessary and reasonable requirements of the Tribes." Indeed, the commission was so "fair" to the Haida that in 1916 the Queen Charlotte Agency was awarded seven new reserves, totaling another 360.1 acres, which pushed the Haida land allotment up to 6.44 acres per capita. "This per capita acreage, it may be remarked, is very low, a circumstance attributable largely to the fact that these

Indians are primarily fishermen and local conditions do not lend themselves to extensive farming operations. In view of the displayed progressiveness of the Haidah people and the rapidity to be noted in their evolution toward the goal of complete citizenship the Commission is of the opinion that encouragement and assistance should where possible be given them in their practical efforts to develop their holdings and improve their conditions." When their reserve lands were totalled up, the Haida people's share of the land mass of Haida Gwaii was just 0.15 per cent. In the rest of British Columbia, the effect of the Royal Commission's work was to take 47,000 acres of good land out of reserves and put 87,000 acres of poor land back in. "The value of land taken away was three times that added to the reserves," writes historian Jean Barman. "Reserve policy became a vehicle for pushing the Indian peoples as far out of sight as possible. Indian people were left with 843,000 acres as reserves. This represented less than 0.4 per cent of the province. There the matter rested." At least, it did for a while.

For the Haida, as with all First Nations in Canada, there was never any question that they had been dealt with unfairly by Canada and other governments. But the McKenna-McBride Commission seemed to settle the land question in the minds of federal and provincial politicians, and talk about entitlements and injustice was reduced to a murmur as native communities battled against the terrible effects of colonization. Drastically reduced in numbers, aboriginal communities nonetheless persisted with their claim for redress, but the odds against them were overwhelming. The same year the Royal Commission visited Haida Gwaii, the Nisga'a filed their petition, their land claim, with the Privy Council. But that year also saw the appointment of a celebrated Canadian poet, Duncan Campbell Scott, as deputy superintendent of Indian Affairs. Scott was fully committed to assimilating native people: "I want to get rid of the Indian problem," he said at one point, and he gave it his utmost, getting Parliament to beef up the Indian Act's prohibition against the potlatch and preparing an amendment to the act that prohibited any person or group from raising or receiving money for prosecuting Indian land claims. From 1927 until 1951, when it was repealed, section 141 of the Indian Act "quite simply made it impossible for any organization to exist if pursuing the land claim was one of its objectives," writes Paul Tennant in *Aboriginal Peoples and Politics*. The Allied Indian Tribes of British Columbia, formed in 1916 specifically to press for land claims, thus faltered and then failed. A successor group, the Native Brotherhood of British Columbia, made no progress on a central, though unspoken, reason for its existence — the pursuit of land claims. Governments in Ottawa and Victoria saw little need to accommodate a diminished and demoralized native population. Native people couldn't vote. Children were shipped off to residential schools and stripped of their language and culture, in many instances physically and sexually abused. It was not a time when a robust campaign for title and rights was on many minds. Most aboriginal people were concerned merely with surviving.

SOME CANADIANS HAVE fond memories of former prime minister Pierre Elliott Trudeau as a champion of human rights. Indeed, as the chief architect of the repatriation of Canada's constitution in 1982, Trudeau argued for and won inclusion of the Charter of Rights and Freedoms. What many are less likely to remember is that in 1969 Trudeau dismissed aboriginal rights as "historical might-have-beens." His remark, of a piece with his government's white paper urging the abolition of Indian status and the assimilation of natives into mainstream Canada, did not go unnoticed by aboriginal people. Trudeau's actions prompted Cree lawyer and writer Harold Cardinal, in his book *The Unjust Society*, to excoriate the federal government for its "thinly disguised programme of extermination through assimilation. For the Indian to survive, says the government in effect, he must become a good little brown white man. The Americans to the south of us used to have a saying: 'The only good Indian is a dead Indian.' The [Canadian] doctrine would amend this but slightly to,

'The only good Indian is a non-Indian.'" Cardinal's book, a bestseller, galvanized aboriginal resistance and would come to have huge consequences for public policy in Canada. Still, it was only reluctantly, and under tremendous pressure from New Democratic Party (NDP) activist MPs Ian Waddell and Jim Fulton, who had the vocal support of venerated Supreme Court of British Columbia justice Thomas Berger, that Trudeau, in 1982, allowed then justice minister Jean Chretien to sell him on the inclusion in the Charter of Rights and Freedoms of section 35, which reads: "The existing Aboriginal and treaty rights of the Aboriginal peoples of Canada are hereby recognized and affirmed."

However, for aboriginal people on the ground, including for the Haida, what the prime minister said and how Harold Cardinal responded made no immediate impact. Life on reserves and off them was often grim. Guujaaw refers to the 1960s as "the lowest part of the material culture as far as carving and singing had gotten" on Haida Gwaii. Nika Collison calls them the "silent years" for the Haida. "But even at that point they had a strong relationship to the land," Guujaaw says. "The intent and the mode of operation of the governments was to sever those ties to get at the resources, because if you have people close to the land they're prepared to fight for it."

So it was with the Nisga'a, on the mainland. Trudeau had been in power for less than a year when the Nisga'a, the People of the Nass, opened their land claim case, *Calder v. Attorney-General of British Columbia*, in the old courthouse in Vancouver on March 31, 1969. Their lawyer was a young Thomas Berger. When the Nisga'a lost their claim in the Supreme Court of British Columbia, Berger filed an appeal. The Nisga'a lost in the British Columbia Court of Appeal, too, so they took their claim to the Supreme Court of Canada. In 1973, Canada's highest court ruled four to three against the Nisga'a, but as Berger has written, "Sometimes a loss is almost as good as a win." Three judges had found in favour of the Nisga'a claim to title, three found against and one judge didn't address the question of title at all.

"It was effectively a hung jury in the highest court in the land," Berger wrote. While evenly divided on the Nisga'a claim that their title had not been extinguished, all six judges who ruled on the question of title agreed that at the time white settlers arrived in British Columbia, English law recognized aboriginal title. Justice Judson wrote, "The fact is that when the settlers came, the Indians were there, organized in societies and occupying the land as their forefathers had done for centuries. This is what Indian title means." The outcome of the case was sufficiently close (as had been the results of the federal election in 1972, which returned the Liberals with only a minority government), that the federal government agreed to negotiate native land claims in every region in Canada where no treaties had thus far been made. From this flowed treaties in northern Quebec and the Yukon, the Nunavut Agreement and, eventually, a treaty with the Nisga'a themselves in the year 2000.

One reason the Nisga'a claim took a generation to negotiate was that when the federal government sat down to talk, it did so safe in the knowledge that the negotiations could go nowhere without the province at the table. Dave Barrett's NDP government would come and go (1972–75) with no thought of joining the Nisga'a table. The Social Credit regime under Bill Bennett seemed almost to harken back to pioneer days, determined to smash the labour movement, eager to capitulate to the many demands of forest companies and mining interests, and happy to ignore anything coming out of the native camp. It was decidedly barren ground for aboriginal rights and title, and the horizon for native people became only mildly brighter with the repatriation of the constitution and its reluctant recognition of limited aboriginal rights.

Still, many First Nations took solace from the *Calder* decision in 1973 and the federal commitment to settle claims. The Old Massett Haida, in 1974, wrote to Premier Barrett to "respectfully DEMAND that any legislation of the Parliament affecting our Islands specifically stipulate in absolute terms that Aboriginal Title, whether acknowledged by the government or not, is NOT extinguished by said legislation. The subject matter of Aboriginal title is the single top priority item of concern to the Haida at this stage in our History. Aboriginal Title exists in English Common Law, and has never lawfully been extinguished on the Queen Charlotte Islands. There are absolutely no conditions under which we will be party to the extinguishing of Aboriginal Title at this time."

In October 1974, Barrett made the first ever visit to the Queen Charlotte Islands by a sitting premier. In Masset, according to the *Queen Charlotte Islands Observer,* "an ebullient David Barrett had a sympathetic audience of close to two hundred eating out of his hand." The premier gave a lengthy account of his government's first two years in power and of some of the fully 250 pieces of legislation tabled during that time. The *Observer* does not record if he made any comment about aboriginal title. All the same, at the end of Barrett's speech, the question-and-answer period was "upstaged by a Haida resident who announced himself as, 'The oldest man on the islands,' and went on to direct this question to the Premier: 'Who owns the Queen Charlotte Islands?'" The questioner apparently had an answer of his own, and he interrupted Barrett's attempts to reply until "Premier Barrett gave up and indicated he would attempt a personal response at the end of the meeting." No record of that exchange survives, but clearly the Haida were stirring into action again around the land question.

Just a few weeks later, something happened at Haida (the old name for the village of Old Massett) that would forever alter the political landscape for the Haida people. The *Observer* was, at the time, produced on a typewriter, and it featured handsome hand-drawn advertisements. Page 13 of the November 28 edition in 1974 displayed an ad for an anniversary sale at the Fields store in Masset (ladies' nylon ski jackets marked down to $12.88, a blue vinyl three-piece luggage set for $16.88, a five-pound box of Surf detergent, regular $2.43, sale price $1.99). There was a notice to the public about fare changes at Centennial Cabs. An old-time banjo and fiddle concert and dance sponsored by the Islands Protection Committee was coming up in Skidegate. And there, in between the ads for the dance and the cab fares, was an advertisement headed "Haida Land Claims." Those wishing ground transportation to a founding convention at Haida on December 7 were given a contact number and a deadline, "so that suitable arrangements can be made."

Two weeks later, the *Observer* ran a front-page headline in 12-point caps: "THE HAIDA NATION EXECUTIVE ELECTED AT FOUNDING CONVENTION." The story read: "'The founding convention was very successful and well attended despite adverse [weather] conditions,' reports Mr. Godfrey M. Kelly, newly elected president of this new entity. Mr. Godfrey Kelly continued, 'Six resolutions were submitted, all relating to Land Claims and all were passed. All were of a confidential nature.'" Thus was launched what would become, eventually, the Council of the Haida Nation. Thus was put in motion, though no one at the time could have predicted how long it would take, or what form it would take, the Haida title and rights claim. It is hardly surprising that the first six resolutions submitted and passed at the convention concerned land claims. Reynold Russ was the elected chief councillor of Haida at the time, and it was his council that had passed the resolution demanding that Barrett's government do nothing to extinguish aboriginal title. On December 7, 1974, the Haida leadership coalesced around the issue as never before.

Coincidentally, the benefit concert and dance sponsored by the Islands Protection Committee had gone off pretty well, too, as a different kind of land claim was beginning to percolate on the Queen Charlotte Islands. In this case it was environmentalists who began to cohere around an agenda, that of protecting the Queen Charlotte Islands from industrial logging and claiming areas for parks before chainsaws consumed the old-growth forests forever. In time, these two agendas—Haida title and rights and environmental protection—would fuse. In time, these two agendas would also find perhaps their best expression in one person, Giindajin Haawasti Guujaaw.

THREE

THE SPIRIT RUSHES
IN THE BLOOD

THERE IS AN old picture of Gary Edenshaw, as Guujaaw was known when he was a boy, standing on what appears to be the deck of a fishboat. He wears a sou'wester atop, gumboots below, shorts and a woollen sweater embroidered with a puppy. His right hand grips a railing, while his left is raised to head height, clenched in a fist, an oddly triumphal gesture for a five-year-old.

Guujaaw was born in 1953, second-last into a family of nine children in Masset. He was born of the Ḵak'yaals Ḵiigawaay Clan, the Ravens of Skedans, like his mother, Janet. His father, Lee, was of the Chiits Git'anaay Clan, the Eagles of the Yakoun River. Lee Edenshaw was not a descendant of the venerated Albert Edenshaw, but an Edenshaw through adoption. Theirs was not a wealthy family, but in towns like Masset and Skidegate, families typically weren't, and still aren't—at least if wealth is measured by income. David Phillips, one of Masset's most endearing raconteurs, and long a friend and co-conspirator of Guujaaw's, operates the Copper Beech House bed and breakfast in Masset. Both Phillips and his house are essential fixtures through which much of Masset's narrative has flowed for the past thirty-five years. According to Phillips, the Edenshaws' existence might have looked humble, "but you can't say that in Haida Gwaii, because as much as they *didn't* have, they had so much more than every other kid. They had many uncles who were talented in the forest and talented in the sea. They had wonderful women who taught them great stories and ideas, and the concept of being a Haida and what it meant. And with that, they became something special, something entirely different. Lots of people say, 'Oh, the Indians up there,' and I would correct them and say, 'They're not Indians, they're Haidas,' because Haida is something that is so fundamental, and it's in the blood. The spirit rushes in the blood."

Back then, in the 1950s, Masset was a little town that numbered about 300 souls. "I liked it there," Guujaaw recalls. "Yeah, it was a different kind of world than it is now. On every block there were trees in the middle, forested. Lots of old wrecks to play in, take the .22 out to the beach." Masset, now as then, spreads over a few square kilometres of mostly flat land, bounded to the north by a buffer of forest between it and the Haida village of Old Massett, to the east by an impressive wetland that is now a wildlife sanctuary and to the west by Masset Inlet. Towards the south, it is bisected by a slough of water that ebbs and flows out of and into the bird sanctuary and provides moorage for a dwindling fishing fleet. The fleet's presence today is more of an economic emblem than an engine. But when Guujaaw played at the water's edge here half a century ago, fishing was the economic soul of Masset, and the harbour was its heart.

Today, the waterfront is rather quaint. Old boat sheds are being spruced up for people to live in, and property values are tied more to recreation than to a working waterfront. In the 1950s, those sheds were where native and non-native craftsmen built and stored boats. Among the tumbledown buildings along the waterfront was Charlie Aberg's boat shed, a big place where the kids ran in and out, stealing cookies and quaffing the root beer Charlie made for them. Charlie also had a still, so there were lots of parties. There was a sawmill along there, too, Anderson's, now long gone. Michael Nicoll Yahgulanaas

grew up just a few houses away from Guujaaw and was his contemporary, as was Jim Hart. "Jimmy was a few blocks up—kind of a big
distance at that time—the other part of town. So you might see Jimmy
once a week, some sort of interaction, but Guujaaw was pretty much
every day," says Nicoll Yahgulanaas. "Building things, good rafting
adventures, a lot of splashing around in the water, constructing things
that float, that little kids can float on and act brave on." Nicoll Yahgulanaas recalls the Anderson mill, big beams, saw blades that somehow
the kids didn't fall onto and lots of jumping into piles of sawdust. A
local pervert lurking around. Games of cowboys and Indians, though
"no one wanted to be an Indian," he says, not even the Indians. Games
of cops and robbers, too, recalls Arnie Bellis, who ran in a gang with
Guujaaw and the Baker boys on Delkatla Street for a while. "He was a
scallywag," Bellis says about young Guujaaw, but never a real badass.
Guuj also played with friends up in the village of Old Massett, among
them Ron Russ. Russ remembers that an elder had made himself a
casket, which caught the eye of several young boys. "I remember us
stealing his casket and going out in the water, rowing around in it. He
built it out of one chunk of wood, like a canoe, so we were out paddling around in his casket, Gary, Arnie Bellis, there was a few of us.
Boy, did we ever get a licking for that one. We paid for days for that
one." Guujaaw, for his part, recalls that he "made many rafts and
makeshift watercraft as a kid...in regard to paddling around on a
casket, however, I was not on that vessel."

Guujaaw didn't just get up to youthful hijinks around the village.
From an early age, he accompanied his uncles into the woods. In the
matrilineal system that governs Haida family life, the most important mentoring influence on a young Haida boy is often not his father
but his mother's brothers. Although Guujaaw learned to gather food
with his parents, hunting and fishing with his father and digging
cockles and picking seaweed with his mother, he also came into the
care of his mother's brother Percy Williams, a legendary Haida political leader and an accomplished hunter, trapper and food gatherer.

And there was Jim Hart's uncle, Wilfred Bennett, who was known to be self-sufficient. "Eating like a king all the time," as Jimmy Hart recalls, and showing Hart and Guujaaw how it was done.

Until 1958 there was no road linking the town of Masset or the village of Old Massett with the other prominent Haida village on the islands, Skidegate. But people got around a lot by boat, and Guujaaw spent time in Skidegate early on. It was there that he fell under the spell of his great-grandmother, Gidʔahl Gudsllaay, Susan Williams, and the import of his Haida ancestry began to take root. "She came in from Skedans on a canoe to Skidegate," Guujaaw remembers. "There weren't enough people to keep the village there anymore. Yeah, she was pretty old. When I came into this world she was already over a hundred. She had tattoos, she showed us her tattoos. She had long hair when I knew her. Near the end they cut off her hair. When I came here, to Skidegate, she'd be making medicines, and singing. She'd throw a towel over us and make us dance."

There was Guujaaw the Younger, draped in a bath towel in place of a button blanket, dancing to songs sung by a woman who herself would have been a young girl when the Colony of British Columbia was founded. She lived through the cataclysmic decline of her people, finally canoeing north to Skidegate to live out her days, her ancestral village abandoned. Emily Carr captured Skedans as she saw it in her 1930 painting *Vanquished*. "It was kinda getting to be the end," Guujaaw says today. The Haida had lost so many of the songs and dances that had powered the potlatches of old. In Skidegate and in Old Massett, "it was kinda getting down to old people, and a few little kids."

It is almost as if there was a crease in the page of the history of the Haida at that time, as if the narrative of an unbroken decline since contact was interrupted, in those few years when Guujaaw and other young Haida were entering their power and the old people feared they were losing theirs. Clinging onto those songs was like clinging onto life itself. Young Guujaaw was understandably in awe of the old lady with the long hair, the tattoos, the songs and the stories of her village. If Susan Williams was born in the 1850s, as Guujaaw believes was the case, then fully a century later, the lyric of Guujaaw's formative years was composed by someone whose whole life was lived under the corrosive shadow of the land question, but who would have known Haida Gwaii close to the way it had always been, back then.

When Guujaaw's great-grandmother was born, the contact decades earlier with white people and the resultant smallpox, influenza and other diseases had already taken their shocking toll. But in the 1850s, before the first gold rush, there were no white settlers on Haida Gwaii, and only a few on the mainland. "By 1852 fewer than five hundred Britons had emigrated to the [Vancouver] Island colony, and about 30 had made some move to acquire land," writes political scientist Paul Tennant. So other than traders and missionaries, there was no great swarm of settlers displacing native people at the time, especially in the relative isolation of Haida Gwaii. "Although the Whites brought devastating diseases and disruptive change," Tennant writes, "there was no armed conquest, no widespread displacing of villages, and relatively little forced admixing of different communities. The Aboriginal past was not cut off. Many Aboriginal communities remained resident on ancestral sites. They could thus more easily keep alive their ways, their memories, and their ideals."

It is hard to imagine a more marvellous ancestral site than Skedans. During a survey of sites for the British Columbia government published in 1884, Newton H. Chittenden went to Skedans, along with Cumshewa, Tanu and Skung Gwaay (Ninstints) villages, and referred to them all as being "beautifully situated, facing the south from cozy sheltered nooks, with splendid beaches, and abundant supplies of food conveniently near. Besides the halibut bank marked on the chart, there is one near all of the villages mentioned, and inexhaustible quantities of clams and mussels along the neighboring shores. This is certainly one of the most favored regions in the world for the abode of the Indian." The Haida name for Skedans is Xuʔaji 'Laanas, or Grizzly-Bear Town. The Haida also called the village Ḵ'uuna, or Koona. Its head chief was Gidantsa, whose name was corrupted by early fur traders, such that on a list of trading sites prepared in the 1830s by John Work, Gidantsa's village was referred to as "Skee-dans." At the time, twenty-seven longhouses were strung like pearls along the shore of a curvaceous bay, a place described by John Smyly and Carolyn Smyly in their book *Those Born at Koona* as "almost unnaturally perfect in shape, like a basket turned to the south to trap the sun." When Work visited in the 1830s he counted 471 inhabitants, though at the village's peak it is thought to have been home to more than 700 people. The village had fifty-six carved monuments at the height of its fortunes. Today, most of them have been consumed by Haida Gwaii's famously luscious temperate climate and the constant erosion of the elements.

AT THE TIME of first contact, Xuʔaji 'Laanas, or Skedans, was one of fourteen main villages on Haida Gwaii. John Swanton, a linguist who arrived on the islands in 1900 and gathered a substantive record of its settlements, listed 126 towns, though some of those in his record appear to be duplicates. In any event, whether permanent settlements or seasonal camps, there were numerous places that the Haida called home. Today, only Skidegate and Old Massett are populated by the Haida year-round. In its statement of defence to the Haida's title and rights claim, the B.C. government says that "at or before the time persons of European ancestry first made contact with Aboriginal people who spoke the Haida language, these Aboriginal people lived in small autonomous family groups which were widely dispersed and were not politically unified or organized. Further, any Aboriginal title in the Queen Charlotte's [*sic*], which is not admitted, did not extend to the whole of the territory as claimed, but was only limited to specific sites." In other words, the government says, places like Skedans were not really villages at all, just places where "small autonomous family groups" gathered, and the fact that there were maybe only fourteen such "specific sites" on Haida Gwaii means the Haida cannot claim the land and resources that lie in between these sites. This ignores the fact that, by definition, rural towns are small, and they are hardly politically unified or organized. If British Columbia's non-native population were deemed to have title only to the "specific sites" they live in—the villages and towns of rural British Columbia— then about 95 per cent of the province (minus the 0.4 per cent occupied by native people) would be, by the same logic, as yet unclaimed by non-natives.

QUITE APART FROM how many villages the Haida once occupied, the Canadian and B.C. governments both say that aboriginal "family groups" like those at Skedans—governments are at pains not to accord them the status of communities, let alone a nation—"abandoned the sites they occupied, failed to maintain any substantial connection they may have had to these sites...and either left the Queen Charlotte's [sic], or consolidated at two sites, Skidegate and Masset." The lack of any sense of culpability for what caused the Haida, Guujaaw's great-grandmother Susan Williams among them, to abandon their villages is astonishing. But in fact, it is of a piece with the provincial government's position that "British Columbia does not admit the existence of the 'Haida Nation'." The federal government, while it admits that "an organization *styled* [emphasis added] the Haida Nation currently exists," denies that Haida people ever held aboriginal title to Haida Gwaii, or that members of the Haida Nation do today. It might stun some Canadians to know that their governments deny the very existence of the Haida, but it comes as no surprise to Guujaaw. "That's what they are. It's not a surprise. We know what we've been dealing with all this time. I don't think it's shocking that they don't care about us. Governments and industry are just made out of money, and that's the only thing that moves them. It isn't about right and wrong or good and bad, it's just about what is going to make money, how do they keep the economy moving, that's all."

THE FEDERAL AND provincial governments also deny another key claim of the Haida: that they were a trading nation, and their trade constituted part of an economy of their own. The governments insist that no Haida economy existed until white people arrived and created trade and economic activity, based on an exchange of goods for furs. But George F. MacDonald, a noted scholar on the Haida, says that Chief Gidantsa, at Skedans, maintained a special relationship with Chief Tsebassa, town chief of the Tsimshian village of Kitkatla, located on the mainland of British Columbia, across Hecate Strait. The town chiefs are said to have had a common ancestor from the Nass River. Through their alliance, trade and potlatches took place, the Haida exchanging their dried halibut, dried seaweed, herring roe and legendary canoes for the Tsimshian's prized oolichan grease, dried berries, goat wool and horns. It might not have been entered into the national GDP, but this import-export activity is cited in the field notes of George M. Dawson's expedition to Haida Gwaii in 1878, and of Dawson's visit to Skedans, where he observed at first-hand evidence of trade between the Haida and the mainland. "About sundown two large Canoes with two masts Each, & the forward one with a large flag hoisted, hove in sight round the point. Turn out to be Kit-Katla Chimseyan Indians with loads of oolachen grease for Sale. They have slept only two nights on the way from Kit-katla. They come here on a regular trading expedition."

Some might call a regular trading expedition evidence of a trading economy. But Dawson also said that, in 1878, Skedans showed signs "of having passed its best days some time since...Of houses there are about sixteen, of totem poles about 44. These last seem to be put up not merely as hereditary family Crests, but in memory of the dead." And it was in memory of the dead that, almost a century

later, Guujaaw travelled as a young man to the villages of his ancestors all over Haida Gwaii. "I think I pretty well slept in most of the
villages, among the bones and the totem poles and stuff like that. I
ended up burying a lot of the bones because they were beginning to
be tourist attractions, and showing up in books." According to
Haida lawyer Terri-Lynn Williams-Davidson, more than seventeen
Haida clans were made extinct, "and with them their ties to certain
parts of their territories. Our ancestors' final resting places were
also excavated and their remains and associated burial objects were
removed to institutions in faraway lands. And our repository for
cultural knowledge and ceremonies, our art and our cultural treasures were also removed."

In the years before Guujaaw set out to visit the old villages, he had
some growing up to do. Initially, the narrowest of threads—dancing
at the feet of his ancient great-grandmother—connected him to the
Haida's extraordinary culture and its near extinction. In Old Massett
he picked up dances and songs from a group of elders determined to
keep their traditions alive. He learned stories from Percy Williams.
Early on, Guujaaw developed a talent for listening to his elders that
would have a dramatic influence on how he would be seen by others
when he later stepped forward into a leadership role.

Importantly, Guujaaw did not go to residential school. Because
he lived in the non-native community of Masset, the government
dragnet that caught so many young native children in its assimila-
tionist web missed him, as it also missed Michael Nicoll Yahgulanaas,
as it also missed Jimmy Hart and Arnie Bellis. Ron Russ, however,
lived in Old Massett, and he got sent to Alert Bay, which he calls a
mixed blessing. "I learned a lot down there," he says, but he quickly
learned to forget his Haida tongue as well. "When I started to speak
it to my brother in residential school, we got beat up. It wasn't nice."
When Russ came back to Old Massett after three years, "it was bad,
because nobody knew me. I had to earn my respect." But Guujaaw,
he remembers, welcomed him back into the fold. "He understood

what we went through. He never used that against us, unlike some people." Fortunately, rather than being shipped off to a distant school to have their culture beaten out of them—the equivalent of which, in Australia, came to be known as the Stolen Generation—Guujaaw, Nicoll Yahgulanaas, Hart and Bellis managed to have an upbringing that was part elementary school and part schooling in the elements.

And then there was high school, which none of them paid much attention to. Ron Russ says he, Guujaaw, Jimmy and Arnie spent time on the land instead. "We went all over the north and south, paddled around, camped around, we just basically lived off the land, trapping, fishing, whatever. We never even seen each other for a month at a time, I'd be with my grandfather, and Guujaaw, he'd be with his father, or his uncle. Traplines cross, so we'd meet, and my grandparents, they used to sit down and we'd sit and talk. Well, *they'd* sit and talk, and we'd listen. They'd tell us stories. That's how we got all our stories from our people, being out on the land, hunting, fishing."

Inevitably, Masset had a feature that was standard issue in every hinterland B.C. town: a café offering "Chinese and Canadian cuisine" in which the proprietor never quite seems to have mastered either. In this case, the café was run by Dick Mah. Then Jimmy Seto moved to town and floated the idea of a bowling alley. Everyone was for it, so he built a four-lane alley (later expanded to eight), added some pool tables and a jukebox, and put the word out that he was looking for workers—pin setters. As Jim Hart explains, "We lined up outside, all excited about this job, and he'd call us in one at a time and interview us, so it was pretty intimidating. He showed us around to look at the whole show. Guujaaw got a job, I got a job. But Guujaaw's parents were a little more relaxed than mine. They let him stay out till eleven; I had to be in at nine. So he got the late shift, made oodles of money, because you could do two lanes when you got good at it, just jump back and forth between them, and then make more money." The Dragon Bowling Alley was "a favourite 'hangout' for Indian and white males," writes author Mary Lee Stearns, and the bowling leagues brought together folks from all over the northern part of the islands. When payday came around, Jimmy Seto would cook up hamburgers and chips and give the boys a big meal, washed down with a Coke. "That was big time, eh?" Jim Hart recalls with a laugh. Later on, the boys got another job, this time cleaning up at night at the cannery.

When they were in school, Jim Hart remembers taking music classes where they sang old slave songs, Guujaaw doing so with a lot of emotion—something of a showman even then, Hart says. It was Hart's shyness that in part led him to the more solitary pursuit of carving, but Guujaaw also carved, signing up in 1968 for a student argillite carving program led by the legendary Rufus Moody. Reynold Russ, Ron Russ's father and then the chief councillor in Old Massett, remembers Guujaaw as a solitary type, a bit of a loner. "I was sort of a woodsman, too, I went trapping as a young person with my grandfather. You couldn't starve if you were in the woods, if you knew what you could eat, taking juice from a branch. That's what I learned, and Guujaaw spent a great deal of time in the woods, more so than I did." Reynold Russ also remembers that Guujaaw asked questions all the time, and it became evident to everyone that he wasn't always satisfied with the answers. Guujaaw had been given his first Haida name, Haawasti, by his clan chief. His second Haida name, Giindajin— literally, "Argumentative One"—was given to him by his Uncle Percy. "It describes how I was," Guujaaw recalls. "You know, the argumentative one. Questions all the answers."

Guujaaw's mother died when he was fifteen, and he lived with his Uncle Percy before going to Prince Rupert, on the mainland, to finish high school. "You know school wasn't the most important thing to us at the time, as a teenager," Guujaaw says now with a smile. But he did well enough to graduate. He went on to learn carpentry in Rupert and at trade school in Terrace and Burnaby, and he worked as a house builder before heading back to Haida Gwaii.

Masset has always had a reputation as a tough town. It still hasn't quite shed its raw-knuckled, primary-industry feel. Most paycheques are hard to come by—earned in harsh weather, in dangerous jobs like fishing and logging—and plenty of incomes are all too easily flushed away on booze and, more recently, hard drugs. The town was dramatically altered after the Second World War with the advent of a military base, CFS Masset, that squatted right in the geographic centre of the community and distorted the social, political and economic life of the town. Commercial activity in the region had once been centred on Old Massett, the native community, but the co-op there fell on hard times, and the coming of the base was "fairly consistent with the Canadian approach, which is to stick all the Indians in one place and provide all the commercial services right outside, so they are basically a market pool for the corner store," says Michael Nicoll Yahgulanaas. Masset has long been stained with talk of racism, but Guujaaw doesn't see it that way. "For one thing, the Haidas never really got to be a minority. People were judged more on merit than anything else." Others recall, though, that the coming of the base exacerbated racial tensions.

By the early 1970s, when Guujaaw returned to his hometown, Haida Gwaii had begun to attract some counterculture types—the odd draft dodger, some hippies, some back-to-the-landers. David Phillips was a stowaway on a ship bound for China when he aborted his journey in the port of Prince Rupert. He washed up in Masset and never left. Jenny Nelson was a flower child who had drifted across the country from Ontario. A polyglot group of characters assembled along the shore of the Delkatla Slough, one of them a man called Hibby. According to Nelson, "He was an old drunk who lived in Nightmare Alley. There used to be four or five houses along there, all on stilts. Hibby lived there. Guuj lived there. Hibby carved floats with faces on them. You can see them, there's a whole section of Hibby's stuff at the museum. And Hibby was an avocado pit guy, too [carving faces into avocado pits]. I think Guuj started carving floats with Hibby, and making little avocado pit faces." Guujaaw recalls, "The old house was owned by Hibby, who was a locally well-known old carver and poet wino who rented bunks for a buck a night. Lots of drifters, hippies, mushroom pickers, biologists, birders and the like stayed there. Hibby and I were close from the time he showed up when I was a kid. He gave me a handwritten book of his poems."

There were soft drugs around, recalls Jim Hart, and everyone partook, though he remembers that Giin, as a lot of folks had taken to calling Gary Edenshaw before he became Guujaaw, wasn't a big drinker like some. There was a lot of music, too. "Yeah, Guuj played guitar back then, we all played guitar in those days," says Jenny Nelson. And bongo drums, "lots of jamming, lots of music." Nelson remembers it was mostly rock music people were playing then, except in Guujaaw's case. "He started singing, learning [Haida] songs. There was a real dedication. I remember there was a totem pole being carved at the boat shed, it was there for years, and Guuj worked on it. And he connected with a guy from Bella Bella who had learned a lot of songs. He had a tape playing all the time. And then he got tapes from his old Nonni [great-grandmother], so he had all those tapes playing constantly." As Guujaaw himself says, "I used to live with that old lady. That was one of the first tapes I owned, of her singing. Then after that we started collecting them from old shoeboxes and under people's beds, and then put them onto an archive tape. Of a hundred that we taped and transcribed in English and Haida, I learned probably sixty. Whole bunch of love songs."

The songs obviously had an effect on Nelson. She and Guujaaw started going together, though it wasn't just his singing that wooed her. "His storytelling, which of course I'm hooked on immediately, right?" And according to David Phillips, he was a commanding presence even then. "He always stood out. I mean, he dressed differently than everyone, he was the first guy that, when you came onto the scene, he was the one with the long hair, and just that kind of swagger of his, you know, that kind of 'I'm in control.' And no matter what he did, he *was* in control, and it wasn't anything he wanted, it was just that things came to him. The control came to him because he had a sort of magic. Guujaaw, when he comes into a room he turns heads, he *becomes* the room and it's nothing but him, and all that enormous spiritual baggage that goes with him."

Guujaaw moved in with Jenny Nelson, who was living out near North Beach, a gorgeous stretch of sand on Haida Gwaii's uppermost fringe. You can see Alaska from there. Their ramshackle cabin in the woods, a few kilometres east of Masset, was known locally as Chicken-shit Harry's. "That was before they subdivided it all," remembers Guujaaw, "so there weren't any other people there, just some clam diggers." The parcels of land there were all pre-emption lands from the settler period, Guujaaw says, but it was a tough place to make a go of it, and "none of the settlers made it." Today, there's little left on the site of Chickenshit Harry's but the shell of an old stove, a tangle of rusting wire and bits of an old vehicle. Over the road now, beach-front lots are selling for hundreds of thousands of dollars, much to the bemusement of the locals. What did Guujaaw do out there in the early seventies? "Chopped the wood, hauled the water," he says with a gruff laugh.

Guujaaw and Jenny would have their first-born son, Gwaai, in 1977, while they were out at the beach. There, after a fashion, they also got married. There wasn't a proper ceremony with a licence and all that, but there was a blessed gathering on the beach. One photo-graph of the occasion shows the back of Nelson's head, her hair entwined with a garland of flowers, and a slim-looking Guujaaw, hair parted, sporting a moustache and a goatee, about to drink from a cup. In that cup, so the story goes, was a healthy slug of oolichan grease. A young Michael Nicoll Yahgulanaas looks on cheerily.

These days, Arnie Bellis works alongside Guujaaw at the Council of the Haida Nation, as vice-president. Bellis is a big man with enor-mous arms, testament to years spent in the woods logging, and to hundreds of hours logged on the basketball court. He recalls that when Guujaaw first came back from the mainland, the two of them weren't as close as they had been growing up. A lot of young men like

Bellis had opted for industry jobs, logging and fishing, while Guu-jaaw was "a bit of a beatnik" out on the beach. But while he might have had his summers of love in a place not exactly famous for its summers, Guujaaw didn't exactly drop out. He maintained his prac-tice of spending time with the elders, and he later became principal singer for the Kaa.aads nee Dancers, a group led by Robert David-son's father, Claude, and stepmother, Sarah. He continued to roam the land, too, putting his carpentry skills to work building cabins and, at one point, experimenting with the construction of a traditional fishing weir in Naden Harbour. And he rowed everywhere. Whether to gather food or to go from place to place, he rowed. "He had a row-boat he was real proud of, and so he would row," Jenny Nelson recalls. Someone had run a car into William Charles's house in Old Massett and knocked the place off its foundations. Underneath, they discov-ered an old double-ended dugout canoe. "So we bought it from him, and that's what Guuj rowed around in. They're beautiful boats."

Guujaaw's arms are no match for Arnie Bellis's today, but he has the slab-like upper body of a former rower. "Yeah, lots [of rowing] between Masset and Naden, and Kiusta quite a few times. I had that dugout with oarlocks on it that I went all the way around on, Masset around to Skidegate. That wasn't uncommon, either, to row out like that. People used to fish like that. Rowing around the west coast was a little more challenging." In fact, the west coast of Haida Gwaii is more than just challenging. It is known to fishermen as one of the most treacherous stretches of open water anywhere and as one of the most unforgiving coastlines in North America. By the time Guujaaw had his boat, it was exceedingly rare for people to row at all anymore; motors had taken over. His Masset-to-Skidegate journey north and west around Graham Island is the stuff of local legend still. Nelson remembers getting dropped off at Kiusta in a motorboat. Guujaaw and his nephew Wayne rowed out to Kiusta, then around to Lepas Bay. Guujaaw rowed out on his own from there. "I think he had a fish hook when he left; he forgot the food. He just took off, but then he tended to do that," Nelson says. "He took off, just gone. We didn't hear from him again until he was in Skidegate. I was still out there [in Kiusta] and someone radio-phoned us. That was pretty neat, and that was part of following the old ways."

Guujaaw doesn't make so much of the trip, but he does remember a tough day when he was off Rennell Sound, the largest inlet on the west coast of Graham Island. He misread the tide and had to buck it for hours. "When you're rowing all day, you can start to faint," he says, adding quickly, "Didn't happen to me." He did other long solo trips, including one from Queen Charlotte City to Burnaby Island in the south. And trips closer to home in the years that followed, with Jenny, Gwaai and their second-born son, Jaalen. "We did this one trip," she remembers, "three days down into the inlet, into the Kumdis area, rowed down there. It was beautiful. We'd go out to sea, too, go out for seaweed. One time we'd been way out there, it was a beautiful day, and we had all this seaweed. We'd dried a lot of it on these hot, flat rocks. And then Guuj woke me up in the middle of the night, still dark, and there's a huge storm coming up. We had two kids. So anyway, soon we're rowing and the storm's coming up really fast and one oar breaks. We're like way out there, one oar, babies, but I was totally confident, blindly confident, because he always pulled us out of everything, he's really good at that. And he got us to where Jimmy Hart's longhouse is now, we got there with packs of seaweed. It was spooky." Today, the boat is safely stored in the boathouse next to Hart's longhouse, perhaps waiting for another young Haida to take to the waters.

From today's vantage point, it seems that Guujaaw's every act was freighted with cultural and political importance. By rowing, he was reclaiming the waters of Haida Gwaii. By building cabins, he was reclaiming the land. By singing and drumming, he was bringing back old songs. By gathering and retelling stories, he was performing the role of Haida historian. By learning to hunt and gather, he was participating in the most ancient of economies. By questioning everything,

Giindajin was becoming a willing conscript in the long battle over the land question. And by resisting everything from traditional industries like logging to the militarization of their town, he and Michael Nicoll Yahgulanaas and David Phillips and other young activists on Haida Gwaii were expressing a values shift that might have been more visible in places like Haight-Ashbury, Woodstock, Kent State or Cuba but had a northern redoubt in far-flung Masset.

MICHAEL NICOLL YAHGULANAAS sees it as one of the earliest incidents of civil disobedience in British Columbia, the tearing down of a federal lighthouse that had been constructed near the boat harbour at the edge of the village of Old Massett. It was the mid-1970s, a time when the Haida still built wooden seine boats and moored them in their own harbour. The village of Old Massett was trying to raise money to expand the reserve by buying land, and the chief councillor at the time, Bruce Brown, found out about an agreement that had been signed decades earlier between the federal government and the Haida. In exchange for money and the construction of a drawbridge over the slough to provide access to their harbour, the Haida had agreed the government could build "range" lights on reserve land to facilitate navigation in Masset Inlet. The feds put up the lights, but they never paid up the money, and they built a causeway instead of a drawbridge. The slough silted up, rendering the harbour useless. That meant the Haida had to walk five kilometres to the harbour in the non-native town of Masset, since at the time few of them had cars.

"Anyway," Nicoll Yahgulanaas recalls, "Bruce figures, 'Okay, these guys actually owe us, let's calculate the interest. My goodness, there's enough money here, we can buy all this land that's coming up for sale!' He said, 'Look, guys, you owe us this money,' the deal, the money, and the feds said no. So Bruce and the council said, 'Well, we're going to take those range lights out.' So the cops flew over from Prince Rupert: 'Don't you Indians go messing with government property.' And the Haida said, 'You owe us money and this is how it is.' And the cops said, 'Don't do it or we could get after you.' Well, the Haidas just went and knocked the lighthouse down. The cops never showed up. It was just like a training ground for 1985, Lyell Island."

Neither Michael Nicoll Yahgulanaas nor Guujaaw took part in tearing down the lighthouse, but Nicoll Yahgulanaas took possession of the lighthouse beacon. Later, he and Guujaaw placed it atop a cedar pole they then raised as a "trophy pole." For Nicoll Yahgulanaas, it was a pivotal moment in the history of resistance by not just the Haida but First Nations throughout British Columbia. There was a pattern to those events that has played out again and again since, he believes, and one that would play out later in the 1970s in Masset—this time with Guujaaw in a central role.

It was obvious from the beginning that the presence of a military base in Masset was going to distort the town's development, for better or for worse. The base began in 1943 as a naval radio station but was decommissioned after the war. However, it had established its credentials as a listening post for pulling in signals from marine traffic, and it was repurposed in the 1960s as part of the Canadian Forces supplementary radio system. By 1970, a large antenna had been built a few kilometres east of Masset. It is an entirely incongruous feature on the low shoreline, looking a bit like the Colosseum, except built of wire. The antenna is still there today, though it is now operated remotely from a CFS base in Ontario. The expansion of the base in the centre of Masset in the sixties and seventies was heralded by Prime Minister Pierre Trudeau as a new model for integrating the military into community life. It didn't really work out as planned. "Essentially what you have is three communities: Old Massett, new Masset and CFS Masset," explains Michael Nicoll Yahgulanaas. "CFS Masset and Old Massett, in terms of cash flow, were essentially federal enclaves. They were both welfare communities. So Trudeau was saying, 'You've got to integrate,' but there was no bloody way they were integrating. And then the tension really grew, the tension between those young settler men in their military uniforms and those young Haida men. There was a fair bit of smacking going on." Much of that "smacking" took place in a pub next to the base. The pub's owners, intentionally or otherwise, had co-opted a high-status Haida name, Siigaay, by calling their bar the Seagate. "That big status name is applied to a pub, so it's kinda like, 'Let's take all the parts together and create a sort of *West Side Story* kinda thing, just to fuel it up, to pump it up.' There was always this tension. I felt the tension," Nicoll Yahgulanaas says.

"You know, some people came around who thought they could push people around," recalls Guujaaw. "Here we had a military, all of a sudden, plunked into the middle of the village, a big social experiment. And the thing is, you could walk, practically bump into, somebody and there'd be no 'hello,' no acknowledgement there was even another human being there. Like living in a city, but we're just people living in a small town." Guujaaw didn't spend any time cracking heads in the pub, but he does remember his blood boiling when he was living out on the beach and heard shots up in the Sangan River area. He walked up the river and found bears that had been shot and just left there, dead. Another time he discovered garbage bags filled with dead geese. And halibut thrown out, wasted. To many locals, including Guujaaw, this could only have been the work of people stationed at the base. "Then they decided to reward them with the freedom of the village."

Looking back on the events of June 3, 1978, David Phillips remembers it as "another moment of Haida monumental presence." The good burghers of Masset had their vision of what the day would look like. There would be bleachers for dignitaries, citizenry lining the streets with cheerful children in the foreground. There would be flags and bunting and the sharp clacking of boots on the macadam as, to the accompaniment of marching music belted out by the Cape Naden Band, 200 of CFS Masset's finest would round the corner and swell into view. They would halt, there would be an inspection and, as the military men stood at ease and the children fidgeted, there would be speeches about honour and recognition and mutual regard.

The day would be freighted with even more meaning because the village of Masset would be honouring one of their own, Peter Stewart-Burton, who had left town to join the military and was returning as a commanding officer. What could be more perfect? The keys to the village handed to a local hero, and with them the right for the military to carry guns, fix bayonets and otherwise assert an emphatic superiority over the citizens of Masset. But not over Citizen Guujaaw, who laughs about it now. Question: "So you went up against the commanding officer?" Answer: "No, against the whole works of them."

Most Canadians remember the Oka Crisis, a land dispute between the Mohawk nation and the town of Oka, Quebec, which began on July 11, 1990, and lasted until September 26 of that year. The confrontation's most memorable, searing public image is that of a young Canadian military sentry, Private Patrick Cloutier, standing nose to nose in a staring contest with Mohawk warrior Brad Larocque. Oka was a rude awakening for Canadians, as a long hot summer of protests spilled across the country and Canada's negligent treatment of aboriginal claims was laid bare. It would have come as no surprise to anyone in Masset, however. The issues at the heart of the standoff, and the images that dominated the nightly news, bore an uncanny resemblance to the showdown in Masset twelve years earlier.

"I remember the day it happened," says David Phillips. "Word kind of just filtered out through the village, 'You'd better get up there, there's something happening.' The Cape Naden Band is playing away, great march music, and all of a sudden Guujaaw starts marching around with a whole bunch of people following him—where they came out of the woodwork from I don't know—just followed him around and...brilliant!...there was a whole bunch of kids with signs saying, 'No Sir!'" Most of the community had turned out for the official proceedings, and Phillips remembers a ripple of unhappiness among the onlookers as Guujaaw played Pied Piper to the straggle of protesters. Befittingly, his instrument of choice was a drum, not a flute. "And then three battalions, or whatever they were, turned the corner up Main Street. Guujaaw veered off and the whole gang followed him right down in front of the RCMP. You have the post office on one side and the RCMP office on the other, which is kind of perfect. And Guujaaw walked up nose to nose, I mean nose to nose, with the commanding officer and told him he's not going anywhere. And the commanding officer is demanding that Guujaaw move out of the way, and meanwhile some guy from Queen Charlotte is putting daisies in the barrels of all the guns. It was classic! All the elders were scolding Guujaaw and giving him hell and telling him to stop and how embarrassing it was. He wouldn't move. So I think they stood for forty-five minutes, nose to nose, and then it broke up a bit." In the end, the military got the keys to the village, but only on the condition that their bayonets were sheathed and remained that way.

A front-page report on the events in the *Queen Charlotte Islands Observer* the following week, headlined "Freedoms Don't Come Easily," said, "the nature of the exchange between Major Stewart-Burton and Gary Edenshaw is not known, but sufficient that, with the exception of 'the fixing of bayonets' the ceremonies were resumed to the cheers of folk lining Masset's Main Street for this festive occasion." Guujaaw remembers this exchange with the commanding officer: "Stewart-Burton said, 'Okay, you made your point, can you stand aside and let us pass?' Answer: 'No, sir.'" Peter Stewart-Burton, today retired from the military, says he doesn't put a lot of stock in what Guujaaw did back then. "With respect to the confrontation issue with Gary Edenshaw, there really wasn't much to it. He was looking for headlines and rounded up enough of his friends to make a small crowd objecting to the military members carrying firearms in town. We talked the next day, and it was quite obvious he was happy. He had gotten his name in the paper, and that was what it was all about. I must confess at the time I was more than a little miffed at the RCMP for not clearing the crowd, as it was a mayor-initiated Freedom of the City parade at which the mayor presented me with the key to the city. I was extremely proud of the military members on parade who were subject to hassling and poking by the Haida children, and yet restrained themselves from any response of any kind. It could have gotten nasty if they had lost their cool."

Michael Nicoll Yahgulanaas was conflicted about the protest, since Stewart-Burton was his uncle. "I just made a choice not to be there," he recalls. But he remembers it as a significant event in Guujaaw's evolution as an activist. Who knows how much more "smacking" went on down at the Seagate as a result of the stand Guujaaw led against the military? Certainly, he had angered official Masset, antagonized the entire CFS base and even upset some of the Haida. Rev. Ian MacKenzie straddled all the communities as Anglican rector for Old Massett and for the non-native parish of Masset, which was a shared ministry with the military. "Things were very, very tense," he recalls. "When those soldiers were dismissed, three or four of them, they took off after those Haidas like you wouldn't believe, to kinda beat them up if they could catch them." There was dark talk down at the Legion about the upstart native, but in letters published by the *Queen Charlotte Islands Observer,* people ranged in their views from accusing Guujaaw of leading an "ill-mannered and unwarranted provocation" to thanking him for bringing to light the ongoing tensions caused by the presence of the base. Michael Nicoll Yahgulanaas weighed in himself, writing that the confrontation could have been avoided if "appointed leaders of our stratified communities" had engaged in prior public dialogue. Helen Scully, a respected local teacher, wrote a letter to the newspaper defending Guujaaw's stance, Nicoll Yahgulanaas recalls, "articulating in an adult way, and an informed way, and saying to her fellow members of the Legion, 'Just hold on, guys, this guy is doing what we are all doing when we are off doing our bit to save the world.' And it contextualized it quite nicely and really had a big impact on the village, in Masset: this isn't just some punk kid, this isn't frivolous, this isn't like graffiti, there's something pretty serious going on here." Frank Collison wrote from Old Massett to say, "If there are any 'freedoms' to be granted to anyone, it should be done by the people who own the island." Collison seemed to take a swipe at Guujaaw: "When the Haida people decide that the time has come for them to take their destiny into their own hands it shall be done with dignity and respect by the people who have earned their place of leadership within the community." That said, though, Collison thought the failure to consult the Haida in awarding the freedom of the village of Masset to the military was "by far [the] grossest insult that the Band Council has endured since it was established in 1912... GO HOME—INDEED."

Which, eventually, they did. Today, Canadian Forces Station Masset is closed. It has been "stood down," as the military say. An indoor swimming pool and some sports courts were a decent legacy, but in 2008 the rec centre closed down. All that was usefully left behind are some of the PMQS (private military quarters) that used to house the uniformed young settlers and now make respectable housing for young families and retirees. The actual military headquarters, a tribute to seventies' government-industrial architecture at its unimaginative worst, are shuttered and awaiting merciful extinction. No one seems to know who kept the keys to Masset. Maybe Guujaaw's got them.

FOUR

OUT OF

HAND

STRATHCONA. MOUNT ROBSON. Garibaldi. Tweedsmuir. Clayoquot Sound. The Stein Valley. The Stikine. The Tatshenshini. The Skagit. The Kitlope. The Carmanah Valley. Gwaii Haanas. The Khutzeymateen. Valhalla. The Great Bear Rainforest.

British Columbia's most famous protected areas are notable for their beauty, their species richness, their sheer number of hectares, the rareness of their ecosystems and, as has come to be more appreciated over the past few decades, their role as repositories of indigenous cultures. In Haisla territory on the mainland, what the government calls the Kitlope Heritage Conservancy Protected Area, the Haisla Nation calls Huchsduwachsdu Nuyem Jees. Non-natives see lines on a map marking off a "protected" area, usually a "park," whereas the Haisla think of their people being born and living and dying in this "land of milky blue waters" (Huchsduwachsdu). For them, what has been protected are their ancient stories and myths, their *nuyem*. Lines on maps are not unimportant—without them, there would be no definitive way to thwart industrial logging, strip mining or other ill-considered resource grabs—but they tell only a partial story. Consider that the list of "protected area accomplishments" in more than a quarter century of campaigning by the Western Canada Wilderness Committee takes up just one page. A roll call of the fallen—of valleys laid waste by more than a hundred years of industrial logging, mining or flooding for power; of places that will forever be without "status," other than to be "zoned" for development—now *that* would be a long list. And on that list, maybe at the top, though well out of alphabetical order, would be Talunkwan Island. It could even be argued that every protected place on the Wilderness Committee's list of accomplishments can trace its provenance to the fact that Talunkwan Island was so utterly, unforgivably *unprotected*.

In *Big Trees Not Big Stumps,* Wilderness Committee founder Paul George's account of British Columbia's long-running wars in the woods, Talunkwan Island is featured in the first ugly picture. The photo appears early, on page 5—Richard Krieger posing beside a washed-out road in a clear-cut. But it is the photograph of Talunkwan Island on the next page, taken by Krieger himself, that most starkly depicts why a generation of British Columbians have fought their provincial and federal governments, and each other, in an attempt to drastically curtail old-growth logging. The photograph is of a massive clear-cut, scarred with logging roads and left, in effect, for dead. Talunkwan Island sits just off the east coast of Moresby Island, which in the 1980s became the focus of an intense international wilderness protection campaign. (Haida Gwaii's 150 or so islands are clustered around two large islands, Graham to the north—where most of the modern-day settlements are—and Moresby to the south.) Another book, *Islands at the Edge,* published in 1984 at the height of the campaign to save South Moresby, also features a picture of Talunkwan Island. It too is a picture of unspeakable ruin. In fact, the "Talunkwanization" of South Moresby led to an insurrection that began on Haida Gwaii and has since spread to every corner of British Columbia and also around the world.

Industrial logging arrived on the Queen Charlotte Islands in the early 1900s. The Gowgaia Institute estimates that about 170,000 hectares were logged over the century that followed. Says Gowgaia: "That's enough wood to circle the Earth with a six-foot diameter log worth about 20 billion dollars." As elsewhere in the province, the timber barons savaged the forests with impunity and, it must be said, imperfect knowledge about the effects their practices would have. They fed provincial coffers to the tune of about $2 billion in "stumpage," or resource rents, from logging on Haida Gwaii alone. Thus did a succession of development-minded premiers have money to throw at new roads, new towns, new dams: the works. A mutual dependency grew between the government and the companies, and the companies and their towns. The Charlottes—famous for the extraordinary size of their cedar and spruce trees in particular—proved irresistible to the timber barons, and many of the big names found their way to the islands: MacMillan Bloedel, Alaska Pine & Cellulose, Rayonier, Western Forest Products, Weyerhaeuser and Brascan, plus countless bit players. Whole hillsides were laid bare as the increasing mechanization of forestry allowed loggers to travel farther and take more. As Haida villages were entering perhaps the bleakest phase in their history, Sandspit and Queen Charlotte City and Port Clements and Masset were bulking up on forestry revenues and their marine concomitant, fishing dollars. A lot of Haida worked in both industries, but they were seldom owners. Assets were held by a few local grandees, though most commonly by off-island owners. For a period lasting about an average non-native Canadian's life expectancy, that's just the way it was.

Then, in October 1974, ITT-Rayonier (B.C.) Ltd. revealed plans to move a contractor logging operation south from Talunkwan Island to Burnaby Island. It was a completely unremarkable thing to do. The mechanics of British Columbia's resource industrial complex were such that if a mine was spent, a fishery exhausted or a timber licence logged out, a resource company would either shut down or move operations to the next best site. Rayonier's contractor had gone full throttle on Talunkwan, leaving behind what John Broadhead, a contributor to *Islands at the Edge,* called "the worst environmental horror show in British Columbia...They could not have left behind a more ecologically devastated area...Ravaged by landslides with every rainy season, the spectre of Talunkwan is a constantly renewing indictment of forestry practices on the Charlottes." At the time, the Goliath of the B.C. logging industry had no David to stand up to it. Today, swarms of professional environmentalists descend on every infraction in sight. Environmentalism is now an industry in its own right. But back then, only a stirring of discontent was heard. There was little organization, no money, no real infrastructure or process for citizens, be they Haida or no, to have a say in what happened on the land.

Talunkwan Island would become something of a poster child for bad logging practices, but what had happened there was hardly an exception. Vancouver Island was being ravaged from stem to stern. Over on the mainland, the Nass Valley was utterly ransacked, and the clear-cuts around the Bowron Lakes were so huge they were visible from outer space. On the Queen Charlottes, there were plenty of Talunkwans in the making, in Yakoun River and Cumshewa Inlet and Skidegate Inlet and in Tasu Sound and Naden Harbour and along the shores of Ian Lake and at Dead Tree Point and Rennell Sound and Maude Island and Sachs Creek. It was enough to instill a sense of urgency in a small but growing minority of island residents who thought industry had had its way for too long. Soon, logging in the Queen Charlotte Islands would come under the close and persistent scrutiny of a ragtag group called the Islands Protection Committee. Their publications *About Time for an Island* and *All Alone Stone* sounded some of the first clarion calls of British Columbia's environmental movement. Greenpeace had been founded a couple of years earlier in Vancouver, and in October 1974, on the banks Haida Gwaii's Tlell River, a grassroots environmental group was formed "to act as a voice on behalf of all island residents." Unbeknownst to Rayonier and the provincial government, a wrench was about to be thrown into what had worked so well for so long. Goliath was about to get his David, though at the time, his name was still Gary.

It was on the porch of a small cabin in Tlell that Thom Henley first met Guujaaw. Henley had been kayaking in the Charlottes, a fresh-faced American who had quit the United States and pitched up on the islands looking for adventure. In the summer of 1972, he planned to paddle down to South Moresby. The night before he left, Henley ended up staying at Glenn Naylor's house on Hippie Hill, just up the way from Queen Charlotte City. The house was crowded, so Henley slept on the porch. There was an all-night party going on up the hill, and "the most incredible conga drumming I'd ever heard," he remembers. "I asked Glenn the next day, 'Who was that?' and he said, 'Oh, that's Gary Edenshaw.' So I heard the name long before I met him."

In the fall of 1974, Henley paddled into Masset looking for a place to spend the winter. He met someone who had a cabin in Tlell, a hamlet about midway down the east coast of Graham Island, between Masset and Skidegate. "This Haida guy was hitching, couldn't get a ride, got stuck there, so we offered him a place to stay. I remember it was quite late at night, about eight of us sleeping on the porch, nice autumn night, I'm down on one far end, this guy's at the other far end. Suddenly I hear this voice: 'Anybody awake?' It's like middle of the night. I said, 'Yeah, I'm awake.' 'Oh, yeah? Whatcha thinking?' 'Well, I was just thinking about that area I was paddling, the southern part of your islands'—I didn't even know his name at the time. He says, 'What's that like?' I told him about it. Next thing I knew we were up, everybody was still asleep, and we went in the dining area, lit an oil lamp, pulled out a map of South Moresby and drew the line. That was the first time I met Guujaaw. Everybody who woke up that morning at the cabin, we had them sign on as the founding members of the Islands Protection Committee."

The line drawn that night by Guujaaw and Thom Henley (who would come to be known as Huckleberry, Huck for short) is surely one of the most incredible acts of kitchen table cartography in modern Canadian history. The line wasn't arrived at through scientific consensus or conventions or protocols or negotiations. It was just a couple of guys in the middle of the night with the hare-brained notion that everything below that line should be spared the fate of Talunkwan Island, which was just above it. "The irony is it's the exact same line today," says Henley, in reference to the northern boundary of Gwaii Haanas, now a world-renowned protected area. "We followed a TFL [tree farm licence] line, just followed that TFL line out to the ocean and followed it around, and even the marine sanctuary boundary today is the line we drew in '74. It's too bizarre." A few weeks later, the Islands Protection Committee held its first fundraiser.

The benefit dance was held at the Skidegate Community Hall on the November full moon. Ed Young and Percy and Terry Williams from Skidegate played accordion, sax and bass. Gary and Marlene from Queen Charlotte played folk guitar. Dick and Evan Walker from Cape Ball sang and played guitar. Steve and Rich from Tlell were there with a fiddle and banjo combination, and Vic from Masset accompanied on guitar. From Queen Charlotte, Ron Suza played guitar, with Pete Thompson on flute, Martin on electric piano, Dale on stand-up bass and Gary Edenshaw on conga drum. The concert raised more than $300, which was to be spent on "publication of an environmental newspaper to publicize the South Moresby Wilderness Proposal." So it was that within a few short weeks, Guujaaw and Huck's late-night line drawing had spawned an audacious conservation vision and had slapped on it an official-sounding name that would become part of the public discourse in Canada for more than a decade. On the strength of that proposal, now $300 to the good, one of the most famous wilderness battles in the world was joined.

THOM HENLEY RECALLS the first meeting he had with the chief of the Skidegate Band, Percy Williams. It was in Skedans, in the summer of 1974. Henley had been kayaking in South Moresby and pulled into Windy Bay, on Lyell Island, to sit out the tide. He hiked along a small stream, he recalls, and into "the most beautiful forest I'd ever seen in my life. I was so moved by it." At the time, the forest on Lyell Island was unlogged, and it contained some of the monumental cedar and spruce trees for which Haida Gwaii is renowned—thousand-year-old giants, gorgeous cathedral trees as old as many of the actual cathedrals of medieval Europe. Huck wandered through the woods in awe, then made his way back to the beach, where he lit a fire. Looking around, he was startled to see a dead eagle just a few feet away on the gravel, its body still warm, its mate perched in a tree, calling in lament. Huck was from Michigan, where America's emblematic bald eagle was rarely seen. He thought there must be a use for this eagle, perhaps as a specimen for the museum being built in Skidegate, so he gutted it, stuffed it with spaghnum moss to preserve it, and tucked it behind the seat of his kayak. With the tide now in flood, he launched his kayak, hoisting a sheet as a sail to take advantage of a following wind. On the sheet, he had earlier sketched an eagle with a felt pen. With the image of an eagle billowing above him, and a dead eagle nestled at his back, he set a course for Skedans.

"Percy Williams, who was grand chief of the Haida Nation at the time and chief councillor in Skidegate, too, had come down deer hunting, and he anchored his boat on the north side of the peninsula. When he hiked across and looked down the beach for deer, he didn't see any, and then like all good Haida he looked out to sea. He saw something he'd never seen before—he saw these wings flashing in the late evening sunlight and this big white eagle head coming towards him. He'd never seen a kayak. I didn't actually spot him until I landed on the beach. I was pulling the kayak up the beach and I looked up to where I was going to tie it up, and I saw this old man with grey hair, wearing a grey sweater, sitting on grey logs. He just blended in, beautifully camouflaged. And I thought, 'I want to show this guy my eagle.'"

"Why do you bring me this eagle?" Williams asked him.

"Because there aren't many left," Henley said.

And then the two of them got to talking, and Henley told Percy Williams of his travels through South Moresby, of his visit a few hours earlier to Windy Bay, and said how it pained him that what had happened to Talunkwan Island was going to happen all down the chain of islands that made up South Moresby. Percy Williams told Henley that Skedans had been logged by his own band to help build a hall in Skidegate, and how that had pained him, too. From their meeting on the shore, Henley paddled north towards what would be his chance encounter with Percy Williams's nephew, Guujaaw.

Barely weeks after they'd met, Guujaaw and Huck got wind of a meeting between Rayonier and the Skidegate Band Council. The meeting was really no more than a courtesy call on the part of the company. Rayonier owned the rights to log South Moresby, by virtue of what was known as Tree Farm Licence 24. Tree farm licences were granted by the Crown to timber companies that promised to log an agreed-upon (at least by government and industry) Allowable Annual Cut (AAC). In British Columbia, there were about 50 TFLs that covered most of the province. At that time, as now, AACs were wildly unsustainable, but overcutting the forests meant more timber volumes for the companies and more resource rents for the government. And it meant lots of jobs, lots of multipliers in the economy, including for the Haida. Licences were based on the volume of wood that could be extracted, and those volumes were achieved by cutting "blocks" of trees. Rayonier's contractor on the islands, Frank Beban, had exhausted Block 2 of TFL 24 on Talunkwan Island, and he wanted to shift to Block 4 on Burnaby Island. Routine stuff that no one dared gainsay.

Guujaaw and Thom Henley—sinewy young Haida hunter gatherer-cum–beatnik and his fresh-faced draft-dodger sidekick—had no official standing in the community, and there was no reason they would be invited to the meeting. But Guujaaw had standing with Percy Williams. It was from his Uncle Percy that he had learned much of what he knew about the land. It was with his Uncle Percy that Guujaaw had made his many early forays into South Moresby. Henley recalls, "So Guujaaw said, 'My uncle's the chief councillor, so let me go and see if we can attend that meeting.' Then he came back and said, 'Yeah, it's okay, we can go, but we're not allowed to talk. Just observers, sit at the back.' And I said, 'Well, it's better than nothing—information. Let's go.'"

The representatives Rayonier had assembled to promote the company's plans to log Burnaby Island can be forgiven for thinking that theirs would be a sympathetic audience. The Haida counted many loggers among their members, including Chief Percy Williams. The "land question" was no more settled for the Haida in the 1970s than it was in the 1920s, but for logging companies there was no question as to who called the shots in British Columbia's forests. British Columbia sits over the Cascadia subduction zone, however, one of the most volatile geological fault lines in the world, and even the largest, seemingly most immovable features of the landscape are in a state of constant, mostly imperceptible movement. If there was an equivalent to the Richter scale for measuring the impact of meetings between mortals, as opposed to tectonic plates, then the meeting in Skidegate in late 1974 might well have measured 9.5.

"So we go down to this meeting," recalls Huck. "I didn't recognize Percy, but he recognized me, I guess, because he gets up and starts telling this story. 'Not too long ago, I was deer hunting in Skedans,' and he talks about looking out and seeing this eagle coming over the water and stuff, and he goes on and on, and he's quite far into the story before I realize he's talking about me. And then he says, 'Well, the eagle messenger is here in the room today, and I'd like to turn the meeting over to him.' So suddenly Guuj and I had the floor to talk about what our concern was." From the back of the hall, having been told to come as mere observers, Guujaaw and Huck were invited to the front and given a platform to question the officials from Rayonier. Talunkwan Island had been devastated by landslides after the clear-cutting, they said, its streams choked with silt and debris. What guarantees could the company provide that the same thing wouldn't happen on Burnaby Island? Question after critical question was fired at the increasingly rattled corporate functionaries, who were totally unprepared for any sort of confrontation. By the end of the meeting, the Skidegate Band Council had voted to oppose Rayonier's plans to log on Burnaby Island. It was an unheard-of setback for the company, a huge and unexpected victory for Guujaaw and Huck. It was particularly important that Guujaaw had won the support of his Uncle Percy, though Williams did have misgivings about his nephew's vision for saving all the lands south of the line he'd drawn. "You're asking for too much," Henley remembers Williams telling Guujaaw. "No, Uncle, we're not asking for enough," Guujaaw replied.

True enough, because while Rayonier backed away from its plans to log Burnaby Island, and the B.C. government agreed to a five-year moratorium on logging there, the company filed a new plan to log on Block 3—Lyell Island. The plans were approved in haste, and Rayonier's logging contractor Frank Beban moved his machines south to the next frontier. By the spring of 1975, Beban had cutting permits for Lyell Island, and he wasted no time in getting to work. Environmentalists learned an early lesson: a victory in one location is often pyrrhic, because the government and the companies always have another place from which to extract wood and money. This is known in some quarters as the "waterbed" effect—you displace water (or logging) in one corner and it ends up in another. It still goes on today.

While the meeting in Skidegate didn't seem like a seismic event at the time, it was an immensely important turning point for the Haida and their century-long search for an answer to the land question. They had publicly rebuffed and rebuked a logging company for its behaviour on the land. Just as importantly, a young Guujaaw was launched on his journey to become an enormous influence on the future of the Haida, and indeed the future of indigenous people around the world. For the first time, his actions were sanctioned by the Haida power elite, his vision tacitly approved by his powerful uncle, his stance supported by the Skidegate Band Council. Later on, he would upset some of the elders in Old Massett with his protest against the military, but on this night he came away from the meeting in Skidegate with the respect of his elders. They recognized someone who had taken the time to live out on the land, to bring food to the elders, to listen to their stories, to learn their songs. They saw and heard someone with a vision for the land that generations of Haida had watched being taken from them, and then abused. Guujaaw started out at that meeting in the fall of 1974 as a silent observer. There would be many more meetings, but after that night in Skidegate, Guujaaw would never again be billed as an observer. From that night on, he was at the epicentre.

THAT SAID, LIFE intervened. Up in Masset, Guujaaw and Jenny Nelson were living at Chickenshit Harry's—at least until the loggers came and clear-cut all around their squat and forced them back into town. Nelson remembers a formative trip when the two of them travelled to the mainland, to Terrace, for a conference on northwest development that brought together "a Kispiox farmer, an elderly miner, labour members, professionals, Nishga [sic] leaders, conservation officers and Anglican priests." At the conference, multinationals were identified as the common enemy of communities. This was all earnestly written up by Nelson and published in *All Alone Stone*, the hand-set periodical published by the fledgling Islands Protection Committee. "I wasn't that political," Nelson says. "I was writing nursery rhymes and gathering food and stuff like that. Anyway, so we went off to the conference in our gumboots and all our North Beach clothes. Holy mackerel, it was hot there. We were the only ones stomping around in gumboots. Guuj had brought dried halibut and seaweed. After the conference we had this incredible journey. We hitchhiked up to New Aiyansh, which is Nisga'a territory. New Aiyansh was the only Nisga'a town you could get to by car. Then we went from there to Canyon City—like, huge cliffs. Canyon City nestled on the other side of the [Nass] river with this long, long swing rope bridge— must've been suspension—no cars. They used to make their bread with oolichan grease. That's one thing I really remember. It's just a beautiful little place. And then late that day we caught a truck ride down to Greenville. It's on the other side of the river. And they phoned ahead—radio-phoned—and they must've said we had dried seaweed and stuff 'cause as we're coming across someone sent a boat over. There's this little promontory where the boat was going to land—there's a horse grazing, no cars, and two old women with their grandchildren and these wine jugs full of oolichan grease coming down to greet us. We stayed the night there, and then we came to Kincolith, which is way down, no roads, and we stayed there two or three nights—ate bear meat, oolichan. I think the only food we had at one point was these oolichans, which I'd never eaten before—sundried oolichans strung on a bit of cedar bark five feet long that we'd bought for five bucks. Then there was a boat going to Rupert, so we caught a boat to the mouth and down to Rupert. We were trading in the old way, 'cause that was traditional, to trade seaweed and halibut with the Nisga'a for grease. I never saw stuff like that before. So it was this incredible time, where everything just falls into place." And by this time, of course, Nelson had also fallen for Guujaaw, for his mastery as a storyteller, a musician and a food gatherer, and for the ease with which he travelled in native communities and his intuition about the land and its traditions.

Back in Masset, Nelson wrote up her account of the northwest conference: "Land claims were supported and 'the unity of native people, trade unions, environmentalists, progressive church groups, community associations and others' was re-affirmed." In the same issue of *All Alone Stone*, Guujaaw and Nelson co-authored a short piece called "Brother Taan," a paean to the black bear, based on a story told by an elder, Henry Geddes: "He talked of the kinship between bear and man. How a bear packs a dead deer through the bush as a man might, thrown over his shoulder, holding the neck in his mouth...He said a hurt bear makes 'a real human cry that brings out the goosepimples. *"Ananiiyaa"* (I am hurt), it calls out to the Haida.' And though old-time trappers and bear were not friends, shooting bear was not something to be done lightly or unnecessarily.

'You never get over it. It brings sweat, and a sickness that isn't fear. When you skin it, you think it is a human being. I never got used to it. I can't eat it. I've got a lot of respect for them.'"

There was another story, "Out of Hand," about cedar trees, signed by Ghigndiging, an early declaration of a world view that Guujaaw would come to express with increasing sophistication and authority. Back then, he wrote:

In the olden days, the cedar tree was carefully chosen for use. The man embraced the tree, honouring the life that was to be taken; for he knew each tree, each plant, each animal, is a living spirit, like ourselves.

Giant cedars were taken apart and reassembled to house and home the people of the islands. From beautifully carved cedar utensils, they ate their food. In the cedar, they portrayed their identity; while visions and stories sprang to life. On the cedar, they travelled and hunted and battled. With the chips they warmed their backs. Yes, all the wood was accounted for. Cedar was very much a part of life.

By and by, came a new type of man and a new type of life. The wooden homes now had windows and dugouts were replaced by plank boats (schooners). Silver and china replaced traditional eating utensils. Woodworking took on new sophistication. Small sawmills sprang up throughout the island. Hemlock and spruce were harvested. Fishing vessels were a splendid sight to many a fine craftsman on launching day. Aeroplanes were being made of the spruce. This was accepted and lived by.

And then it came to pass that the forests became the property of profiteers, of takers who never see the tree, of those who cannot hear the cries over the noise of their anxious machines. Saw-mills disappeared along with boat-houses. Tree corpses were hauled from their birthplace by the barge load, in most cases destined to become pulp. The craftsman, practically a thing of the past, must buy his lumber from outside, at high prices. Orphaned trees were left to try and make it on washed out slopes. Things had literally gotten out of hand.

Ghigndiging's writings varied a lot in tone and content. There was also this poem:

> You are what you eat
>> What are you?
> A clam
>> or a weiner
> A cheezy
>> or a root
> A vegetable
>> or a noodle
> A candy
>> or a berry
>>> —Gary Edenshaw

A clam or a weiner, a Cheezie or a root, a candy or a berry? It seems that for Guujaaw, everything that had been introduced to the islands had an equivalent, or better, freely available on the land or in the sea. "Traditional foods were very important in [Guujaaw and Jenny's] house," remembers Huck. "They were always bringing in clams and salmon and halibut. Anyone tried to bring in Cheez Whiz or something like that, Guujaaw'd be right on their case. 'What are you, a weenie or a salmon?' He was always into healthy eating, people eating from the land. And whenever he'd go clam digging or for any type of food, he'd always go take it to the elders. This was a really important thing to him, to feed the elders."

All the while, commercial clam diggers were scouring North Beach for razor clams, a delicacy locally but shipped to the United States for crab bait. Guujaaw saw the stripping of clams from Haida Gwaii as yet another bad deal for the Haida. It eroded the Haida's connection to the land, damaging their health, creating unnatural dependencies. When a plant in Masset was established to harvest kelp and convert it into fertilizer—what the local Member of Parliament at the time called an "ignored resource"—it was Guujaaw who pointed out that kelp was actually an essential part of the marine ecosystem. He wrote in *About Time for an Island:*

> A while back on rowing to Wiah Point, we passed through a kelp field. About ten seals were peering out of the water at us, following us and studying us, while small fish jumped damn near a foot out of the water. There were blackfish nearby and seabirds swimming amongst the kelp. There was lots of activity above the water and even more beneath. We moved as quietly as we could, but not unnoticed.
>
> On travelling north again, soon after the kelp plant starting operating, the area was stripped clean...and still.
>
> In the past all the kelp patches had names.

There is something wistful about Guujaaw's early writings, though Thom Henley remembers that every word was weighed carefully. "When we were doing *All Alone Stone* magazine, Guujaaw had given us this beautiful quote for the front page. I think it said we'll live together on this island, apart from the rest, and if we all do what we can, no matter how small, things can't help but get better. I can't remember if the word was 'small' or 'little,' but we were doing the layout and we didn't have the original draft and were just trying to do it from memory, and whether we had 'small' or 'little' it wasn't what he wanted, he wanted the opposite. But he wasn't there to proof it. So he shows up, confiscates all the copies, sits in a closet, crosses out 'small' and writes 'little' on every copy—like, 500 copies of this thing. But that's the kind of stubbornness he has, attention to detail."

At this time, with the South Moresby Wilderness Proposal out in the open, Gary Edenshaw's name began to appear regularly in the *Queen Charlotte Islands Observer*. But though the letters were signed "Gary Edenshaw," their content was all Ghigndiging, the argumentative one. "We live in a world where silence means political consent," he co-wrote in 1975. Nothing wistful about that. Guujaaw took public issue with the largest forest corporation in the province, MacMillan Bloedel, demanding that they be prosecuted for dumping logging debris into fish-bearing waters in Haans Creek. When that didn't happen, he complained to the provincial Attorney General about the government's failure to act: "We seek justice for the creek, the fish and all else that was hurt." He argued with professional foresters, whose credentials he largely disdained. He argued with local senti-ment that resource development on the islands was well planned and there was no need for a committee to protect the islands. "Nothing will be changed, improved or even thought of if everyone sits and allows events to float past," Guujaaw wrote. And the Islands Protec-tion Committee "will probably die a quick death when it shrinks from calling a spade a spade."

Guujaaw wasn't the only member of the Islands Protection Com-mittee who was prepared to take unpopular stands. Thom Henley was with him at every turn, through every turn of phrase. Jenny Nel-son was no shrinking violet either. There were dozens of contributors to *All Alone Stone*, other signatories on letters to the editor; there were organizers, campaigners and advocates. More than 500 people on the islands had immediately signed on to a petition in 1974, demanding that the government agree to an immediate moratorium on logging in the area delineated in the South Moresby Wilderness Proposal. But Guujaaw was a rarity in that there were very few Haida at this point who had taken a prominent role in the South Moresby campaign or the other environmental campaigns on the islands. "He was...one of very few Haida really active on the [committee]," remembers Paul George, who met Guujaaw in 1976 on his first trip to the Queen Char-lotte Islands. George was to find out, first-hand, that off-islanders with an agenda aren't always welcomed on Haida Gwaii.

"Contrary to rumours, Guujaaw did not refuse to shake my hand," George writes in his book *Big Trees Not Big Stumps,* "but he did ask me whether or not I was a police agent." Paul George is a kind of Rumpole of the Bailey of the Canadian environmental movement, big, burly, dishevelled, with a disarmingly distracted air that belies a sharp mind and a ferocious zeal for wilderness protection. Like Thom Henley, George had left the United States and headed north to dodge the Vietnam War. From his base in Victoria he heard of efforts to save South Moresby, so he pitched up in Masset with an idea for "a definitive coffee-table book that would help save it from being logged. I even had the book's name picked out: *South Moresby: The Galapagos of the North.*" His book idea got a frosty reception from the Islands Protection Committee, or IPC, but "Guujaaw and I hit it off right from the start. I respected his ideas and blunt style of discourse."

Paul George would go on in 1980 to found the Western Canada Wilderness Committee, quite possibly the most effective grassroots environmental group in North America, thanks in part to its production of wilderness calendars, posters and glossy coffee-table books that extol the beauty of British Columbia's wild places and warn about the industrial threats to them. But in the spring of 1977, on his second trip to the Charlottes, the IPC told George they wanted to do a book of their own, not the book he had proposed. George was discouraged, and it seemed he would leave the islands empty-handed. He heard about a symposium in Skidegate, though, and when he got there he found that about 150 others had turned out to hear about the South Moresby Wilderness Proposal. "Amongst the many who gave speeches that day was Guujaaw," George writes. "He got sort of tongue-tied, stumbled over words and didn't say much. I learned later that day that it was Guujaaw's first big public speech. One of the Haida elders told Guujaaw afterwards that it was a good one because, 'It gave everyone there a chance to think about what you might have said.'"

Although George didn't get to do a book about the Charlottes, the IPC lightened up enough to realize that someone of his huge energy and obvious commitment could be an important ally. So George and his financial sponsor, Richard Krieger, a photographer, were encouraged to go ahead when they proposed an expedition to chronicle the beauty of the islands. But on their first trip, George and Krieger didn't make it to South Moresby. They didn't cross Huck and Guujaaw's magic line. They ended up just north of it, on Talunkwan Island, "an impressive monument to the destructiveness of clearcut logging," George writes. "I felt from the first sight of it that images of its ugliness were as important to the campaign to convince people to save South Moresby as images of the magnificent wild forests that remained." They got a lot of photographs of a lot of ugly things. On subsequent expeditions, the two were accompanied by Thom Henley, in one instance, and on several occasions by Guujaaw. It was Guujaaw who led them on a circumnavigation of Moresby Island, not a trip for the faint of heart. "I saw for the first time the extensive evidence of Haida use and traditional occupancy of the land," George recalls. "I became completely convinced that the Haida would ultimately have to be the ones to 'save' South Moresby. They had the power to protect the area. They just needed the will to do it."

George and Henley and Krieger took up Frank Beban, the logging contractor, on an offer to tour Beban's operations on Lyell Island. Their side of the bargain was that they would do a South Moresby slide show, at Beban's logging camp. At two logging camps, they gave a hard-hitting slideshow focussed on Talunkwan Island, and at the end there were some very unhappy faces atop some very large frames. They gave another show in Skidegate, hoping the Haida would turn out in numbers. They didn't. Barely a dozen people showed, but Guujaaw pointed out that one of the people who came was Chief Percy Williams. Paul George recalls Guujaaw saying, "The word will get out. The next time there will be lots of people." Sure enough, the next slide show, held later that summer in the Skidegate Hall, was packed with Haida. "They had come to see the 'beautiful pictures of South Moresby,'" George remembers. "They were deeply shocked. Richard had two trays of slides. In the first he just threw in slide after slide of recent clear-cuts and landslides caused by logging on Haida Gwaii. Most were of Talunkwan Island…some were recent ones of Lyell

Island. Richard showed them without any comments. People were in tears by the time he was done."

On the surface of it, Paul George was wrong to assume the Haida had any special power to save South Moresby; at least, there was nothing in the white man's rules that conferred that power upon them. Richard Krieger's slide show was one spark that helped to galvanize the Haida and awaken in them an unshakable will to save South Moresby. Guujaaw says that will had long been there, since logging "was in the face of our people for fifty years by then." But it was in exercising their will that the Haida would come to discover their unique power all over again.

FIVE

DRUM

THE ARTIST ROBERT DAVIDSON once said that to begin to know Haida Gwaii, you have to visit not just the venerated islands of South Moresby but the northern reaches of the archipelago as well. He said too that the way to arrive there is by boat. Only by spending time on the unquiet waters north and west of Old Massett can you start to appreciate what the Haida have navigated for thousands of years on and off the waters of their homeland. From Old Massett, the first really tricky piece of water to negotiate is Wiah Point, also known as Seven-Mile Point. It can get awfully lumpy there when the sea is up and the wind is blowing hard in unison, which it seems to do a lot. Shag Rock is another place where a boat can make heavy going of a western reach, and then there's a long stretch of open water before reaching Pillar Rock, which the Haida call Hlgat'aajiwas, a stunning column of sandstone and conglomerate rock that looks like a hundred-foot cigar planted off the shore of Graham Island, tipped with bushes and stunted trees. Soon, Langara Island appears on the starboard side, and with open ocean seething in the distance, a boat can slip in behind the crook of Marchand Reef to offload in relative calm at the village of Kiusta. Back in 1774, hundreds of Haida lived at Kiusta, and it was the Kiusta people who first saw Juan Perez and the crew of the *Santiago*, who in turn were the first Europeans on record to lay eyes on Haida Gwaii. Two hundred years before Chief Percy Williams saw Thom Henley in a winged kayak down south in Skedans, the Haida saw their first sailboat off the coast of Langara Island. A Haida chief recounted that first contact to George M. Dawson:

It was near winter, [the chief] said, a very long time ago, when a ship under sail appeared in the vicinity of North Island. The Indians were all very much afraid. The chief shaked in the general fear, but feeling that it was necessary for the sake of his dignity to act a bold part, he dressed himself in all the finery worn in dancing, went out to sea in his canoe, and on approaching the ship performed a dance...It would appear that the idea was at first vaguely entertained that the ship was a great bird of some kind, but on approaching it, the men on board were seen, and likened, from their long dark clothing and the general sound and unintelligible character of their talk, to shags [cormorants],—which sometimes indeed sound and look almost human as they sit upon the rocks. It was observed that one man would speak whereupon all the others would immediately go aloft, till, something more being said, they would rapidly descend.

The Haida sufficiently overcame their fear of this ghost ship to approach it in numbers in their canoes, paddlers singing. After eagle down was scattered on the waters by a shaman in the lead canoe, trade ensued. The encounter happened offshore, and there is no record of Juan Perez or his men ever setting foot in the village of Kiusta. The first European to see Kiusta is thought to have been the English Captain George Dixon, aboard *Queen Charlotte*, in 1787. It is in association with Kiusta that the name Edenshaw first surfaced in written records, mentioned by fur traders as far back as the 1790s. It was to Kiusta that Albert Edward Edenshaw moved in 1834, and there he built a house whose design came to him in a dream. He called it the Story House, and when it was completed he gave a great potlatch.

(Albert's nephew Charles, the great artist, would later make a model of the Story House, which today can be found at the Museum of Nat-. ural History in New York.) So it is entirely fitting that it was to Kiusta Guujaaw went in the late 1970s to begin the long process of putting the Haida's house back in order. He began by building a house.

In an online biography, Guujaaw lists the design and construction of the Kiusta longhouse "in the Haida style" as his first "architectural commission." He had already begun to make his mark as an environmental and political activist, but he was maturing as an artist and a performer, too. He had started early, as a high school student, enrolling in a student carving program hosted by Rufus Moody to encourage young argillite carvers. Argillite is a soft rock that is transitional between slate and shale. The dark stone looks a bit like coal and, if kept damp, carves easily, like soapstone. Access to an argillite quarry (or slatechuck) near Skidegate is tightly controlled by the Haida. Rufus Moody was a legendary Haida carver. Along with Robert Davidson's father, Claude, he began teaching young Haida artists to carve in the 1950s. Today, an intricate thirty-eight-centimetre argillite totem pole by Moody, who died in 1998, will fetch $7,500 in a downtown Vancouver gallery. Moody was one of the most prolific argillite carvers ever, and it was in studying with Moody that Guujaaw first found his form in the dark, earthly sediments of Haida Gwaii. "This kicked off a lifetime of studies of Haida artifacts and culture," his online biography says. In 1972, when he was only nineteen, Guujaaw was commissioned to make several masks for the ceremonial use of the Kaa.aads nee and Skidegate dancers. The following year, his argillite sculpture titled *Woman Washing Hair* was purchased for its Legacy Collection by the Royal British Columbia Museum in Victoria. It is a compressed piece of work, just twenty centimetres long, eight high, ten wide, although the woman in question, naked and supine, is sumptuous and full-bodied. The sculpture conveys a lusty sexuality seldom seen in Haida art. However, it was in another classic Haida form that Guujaaw produced one of his seminal, most enduring and most publicly visible works: the making in 1976 of a skin drum, adorned with a painted Haida bear design. More than thirty years later, he still uses that drum—his talisman, his telegraph, his transponder, his trademark.

It was to Guujaaw the drummer, the artist and, not incidentally, the carpenter that a group of chiefs turned when they drew up plans in the late seventies for the Kiusta longhouse. Guujaaw the activist was entirely sympathetic to the chiefs' desire to "help bring the village back to life" by constructing a longhouse in the Haida traditional style. It was the first such house to be built in decades on Haida Gwaii, other than in the populated villages of Old Massett and Skidegate. Today, the longhouse, crafted by Guujaaw's sure hands as a carpenter and his initiate's eye for detail, is the only building that stands on a shore where more than a dozen houses were once aligned, facing north. In the summer months it is home to the Haida Watchmen, young guardians and elders who play a part in reasserting Haida rights to their land by populating treasured sites of historical importance. During a potlatch in 1981 to celebrate the completion of the longhouse, Giindajin Haawasti was given another name that would thenceforth distinguish him: Guujaaw. In Massett Haida dialect, the word *guujaaw* means, simply, "drum." In conferring a new name on him, Claude Davidson and the Massett chiefs were recognizing the work Guujaaw had done to enlist a new generation of Haida in learning and performing the ancient dances and songs, and his work to place the elders more firmly back on their lands by building them a house. At Kiusta, in the judgement of the elders, Guujaaw graduated from being Giindajin, full of questions, to someone who was authorized to articulate a Haida world view through his oratory. To provide answers. From that moment on, the vibration of Guujaaw's deerskin drum—beside a fire, at a potlatch, at a blockade, at the head of a protest march, on the courthouse steps, in a canoe or on a stage thousands of kilometres away—would become a percussive underlay for the reawakening of an entire nation.

THE PRIMARY MATERIAL used in the construction of the Kiusta longhouse was red cedar, *Thuja plicata*. It is a tree, writes Hilary Stewart in her book *Cedar,* that "so thoroughly...permeate[d] the cultures of the Northwest Coast peoples that it is hard to envision their life without it." Traditionally, the cedar tree's roots were used for making baskets, the bark for making baskets and clothes and the withes for making ropes. The wood from the cedar was used for shelter, for making canoes and boxes and for carving totem poles. Arguably Guujaaw's deepest expression of a land-as-culture-as-art-as-people continuum has emerged in his most beloved medium, cedar. It was perhaps inevitable, then, that he would apprentice in cedar with one of the most famous Haida artists of modern times, Bill Reid.

Bill Reid wasn't just a feted Haida artist. He is claimed as one of Canada's greatest artists ever. He was, and remains, a controversial figure for the Haida, in part because he was not raised on the islands. Reid was of mixed heritage—son of a German-Scots-American father who was an "itinerant entrepreneur," according to Reid himself, and of a schoolteacher and seamstress who denied her Haida heritage. Bill Reid was born in 1920 and raised in Victoria and on the British Columbia mainland, not knowing of his Haida heritage until he was in his twenties. He began to develop an interest in Northwest Coast art forms at that time, and he made the first of many trips to Haida Gwaii soon after learning of his ancestry. Reid's grandfather was a nephew of Charles Edenshaw, a legendary Haida artist. But it was to Ontario, not Haida Gwaii, that Reid travelled in 1948 to begin his studies in design. When he moved back to Vancouver in 1951, he used the European jewellery-making methods he had learned to expand the repertoire of Haida jewellery-making from shallow engravings to fuller three-dimensional designs. Reid made visits to

Haida Gwaii to salvage works of classical Haida sculpture, and he became a fixture on the Vancouver and Victoria museum scene, contributing major works to the nascent Museum of Anthropology at the University of British Columbia and becoming an increasingly valued artist among galleries and collectors. In the late sixties he won a fellowship to study in Europe for a year and, when he returned from Europe, Reid settled in Montreal. In the early 1970s, he gravitated back to the West Coast for good. His tutelage in two very different cultural traditions—"the rich seahunting villages of the northern Northwest Coast of North America... [and] the city-states of Europe"—led to comparisons between Reid and artists like Donatello, Yeats and Bartók. In the years until his death in 1998, Reid grew in stature from talented artist to national treasure.

In 1977, at a time when Bill Reid's reputation in the cities of North America still far exceeded his regard in Haida Gwaii, he was commissioned to carve a 17.4-metre Dogfish totem pole to be raised in Skidegate and that stands there still. The pole was to be sited at the rear of a new administration complex built for the Skidegate Band Council on Second Beach, overlooking the entrance to Skidegate Inlet. The fact that the building was designed by architects from off-island probably contributed to the community's disdain for the project. The totem pole itself was seen at the time as a "symbol of the past," according to Reid, and "there was no interest, nobody, it was a subject of curiosity, it wasn't a village activity." No doubt Reid's temperament didn't help. He was a maverick, unafraid to ruffle feathers on the islands and to speak his mind. He was irreverent, disgruntled and openly dismissive, at times, of "these goddamn Indians [who] won't come to work and if you say anything to them, they just bugger off." According to Diane Brown, a Skidegate elder, at the outset Reid gave her and other Skidegate villagers the impression they were "pitiful remnants of what our ancestors were."

Reid desperately needed assistants, especially given that he was weakened by Parkinson's disease. Joe David, a Nuu-chah-nulth carver from Vancouver Island, came to Reid's aid. Robert Davidson joined in. So did Guujaaw, providing the muscle the project required. At the time, Guujaaw and Jenny Nelson had just had their first son. Gwaai was given his name when he was about three months old, on a trip to Burnaby Narrows in South Moresby. "We had a little rowboat down there," Jenny recalls. "I remember just being in bliss, hanging my diapers up on the point at Burnaby Narrows."

Once Guujaaw joined the Skidegate pole project, Jenny and Gwaai were never far away. "Gwaai used to hang from his jolly jumper on that pole," Nelson remembers. The pole featured legendary beings Reid often depicted in his art: a grizzly bear and bear mother, with their cubs; a raven and a frog; Nanasimgit, who rescues his wife after she is kidnapped by killer whales; a dogfish (shark). Atop them all, three traditional watchmen, the spiritual protectors of the Haida people. It was a monumental carving, and it took a monumental effort to complete the job. Reid didn't have much stamina. "When we were working on the pole, he was always getting the Parkinson's," Guujaaw recalls. "But he was still working and continued to work for a long time after that." As Nelson remembers, "Bill was sick. When he did that totem pole it just broke your heart. He was moaning. At one point, Guuj, Gwaai and I were sleeping in this little tiny room at the end of Bill's trailer, a little bunk thing, and we got out of there pretty quickly. You could hear Bill moaning in pain and stuff. Working in the cold, he's just going chip, chip, slowly, like that on the pole, but he did it. He was an amazing guy."

So there they were in Skidegate, the gruff, ailing master and his rough and ready apprentice—two headstrong, opinionated and not yet fully realized cultural revivalists, wrestling a Haida story out of a heavy cedar pole. Legend has it that Reid and Guujaaw fought a lot, though Wanagan, a Skidegate elder, remembers a mixture of mutual respect and dependency: "Bill needed Guujaaw, and Guujaaw wanted to learn from Bill." Guujaaw says simply, "We'd have our fallings out and split up for a while, and end up working together again. We had success at most of what we did together. I worked with Bill longer than anyone else, disagreed with him, ate with him, went to Gwaii. Haanas with him, blockaded with him." Guujaaw, questioning everything, at one point noted that there were two female figures on the pole. "And I asked Bill, 'How come we're not making breasts on these ladies?' Bill growled and grumbled but gave no audible answer, so we kept going up the pole. A few months later, we're working on the tail of the shark right on top. There's basically room for one guy to work as it's cold out and there's snow on the ground and it's getting dark, and as I was working Bill said, 'Well, I'm going inside—I feel just about as useless as a tit on a totem pole.' So you see, he always did get around to an answer." In the fall of 1977 the pole was complete, and it was carried out of the carving shed in the village on June 9, 1978, before a crowd of more than a thousand people. The people of Skidegate seemed to have overcome their disinterest in the project, and, according to a chronicle of Reid's life by Maria Tippett, "when they placed the pole in front of the new building, Gary Edenshaw performed a traditional dance. Then, following Reid's instructions, the pole was raised above the heads of the cheering crowd."

Guujaaw would later recall in a speech what he learned from Bill Reid. "With a totem pole...he would just show you a deeper thing to consider than what meets the eye. In his own way, he explained the profound logic that underlies the arrangements and interrelationships of the lines of Haida art, and ways to entrap the tensions. This is one of the world's most regulated arts. A totem pole, when done properly, is an assemblage of planes where the rule does not need to be understood in order to be received as proper by the mind's eye. Bill's mission simply seemed to be to try to maintain the standard that the old people had set and that amazed him so much."

Bill Reid and Guujaaw had completed the Dogfish pole in a temporary shelter. In 1980, Guujaaw received an architectural commission for a longhouse in Skidegate to be used as a carving shed. It is still in use today, including by Guujaaw himself. But before it was built, he was drawn back to the far northwest of the islands, to Kiusta, where his partnership with Thom Henley would take on a dimension that went well beyond protecting the land. One interpretation of the name Kiusta is "at the end of the trail," and the longhouse Guujaaw built there is at one end of a trail that leads across a narrow neck of land to Lepas Bay, a place the Haida call Daalung Stl'ang. It is an often muddy, thirty-minute slog from Kiusta to Lepas Bay, but when you emerge from the forest onto a scallop of sand the colour of a golden retriever, it seems apt that Daalung Stl'ang translates into English as "beach that has everything." Thom Henley had spent a summer there in the early 1970s, building a cabin and, as he recalls it, "exploring the wild west coast and taking a journey of the inner self that proved the greatest single experience of my life." When Henley built his summer cabin at Lepas Bay, he didn't know Guujaaw and he couldn't have imagined the cabin would one day become the first staff quarters for a program called Rediscovery, a youth camp that began in 1978. The idea for the program came to Huck and Guujaaw when they were spending a few days together at Huck's cabin. Among other things, they talked about "how to get kids back in touch with the land and culture and stuff." The goals of Rediscovery, Henley would later write, "were as simple as they were all-encompassing: to discover the world within oneself, the cultural worlds between people, and the wonders of the natural world around us." Three decades later, Rediscovery International supports camps in British Columbia, Alberta, the Yukon, the Northwest Territories, the United States and Thailand.

BY 1979, GUUJAAW was at work on another artistic commission, this time assisting Bill Reid with the carving of *The Raven and the First Men*. It was a big step up from the Skidegate totem pole, not just for Guujaaw but for Reid himself—and indeed for Haida art. "By changing the scale and going beyond just the totem pole—a different scale, different medium—he sorta opened things up," Guujaaw says today. The enormous sculpture had its beginnings in a very small piece, a boxwood carving called *Raven Discovering Mankind in a Clamshell*, which Reid had carved in Montreal in 1970, and which had caught the eye of Walter Koerner, a forest industrialist, philanthropist and noted patron of the arts. It had been the prospect of such a large commission that enabled Reid to leave Montreal for Vancouver in 1973, though it would be several years before he actually turned his attention to *The Raven and the First Men*. First, the material for the sculpture had to be sourced and assembled. The piece was carved not from a single log, as with a totem pole, but from a four-and-a-half-tonne block of laminated yellow cedar. It wasn't until 1978 that the huge cedar block was moved to a carving shed at the University of British Columbia. With the Skidegate pole completed, the next and arguably most ambitious assignment of Reid's career loomed over him. Those who knew Reid wondered if he could pull it off—his Parkinson's was corroding his strength more and more aggressively— but Walter Koerner agreed to support the hiring of a coterie of helpers. "The [then] octogenarian businessman possessed an eye for quality, had a flair for monumental display, and the money and the determination to bring any project he commissioned to fruition," writes Maria Tippett. Koerner also had once held logging concessions on Haida Gwaii, and George Rammell, a non-native carver who joined the project, would later remark that "the lumbermen who clear-cut on Haida land may have been looking for redemption by financing Bill... But what if the Good Liberal Indian Artist suddenly became the Dangerous Native Activist sitting on a logging road and telling the world of the current destruction of Haida Gwaii by Big Business?"

Reid wasn't a forest activist—or at least not explicitly, not yet. When he set out to produce *The Raven and the First Men*, it was to depict the story of human creation, which according to Haida creation stories began at Rose Spit, a long, crooked finger of sand off the northeast tip of Haida Gwaii, where the Raven found himself alone one day. He saw a clamshell and noticed that several human beings were protruding from it. When the Raven successfully coaxed them to leave the shell, they became the first people of Haida Gwaii. *The Raven and the First Men* is breathtaking in size and form, but Reid and his helpers didn't simply create a handsome sculpture in yellow cedar to sit in a purpose-built atrium in a fancy museum. They produced a monumental assertion of the birth of Haida culture and an ironic taunt to those who exploited the land. Bill Reid was adept at navigating the contradictions that arose from having an industrialist patron whose wealth came in part from logging on aboriginal lands. Guujaaw recalls his own interactions with the patron of *The Raven and the First Men* as a mixture of argument and celebration, remembering Walter Koerner as "a friend of mine who frequently visited me at the project—we did talk art and politics, including Gwaii Haanas." Still, there were tensions between the carvers and the curatorial and academic staff at UBC's Museum of Anthropology, and indeed on the carving team itself. The project got off to a slow start with Reid assisted, at first, solely by Guujaaw. Then George Rammell, a Vancouver sculptor, was brought onto the project. Reid gave Rammell a lot of room for artistic interpretation, essentially putting him in charge. It was a tremendously complex undertaking, the intersecting circles of the piece "throwing the French curve into everything," Rammell recalled. Guujaaw was decidedly unhappy at being, in essence, muscled out of a central role by a white guy. As Maria Tippett's book reports it, "Wanting a greater role for himself, Edenshaw moved into Rammell's territory: the figures emerging from the clamshell. When Reid discovered what was happening, 'there was a major blow-up' and, Rammell recalled, 'Gary was suddenly off the job.'" Guujaaw later rejoined the project, becoming central to it. "I basically did the raven," he says, "including figuring how to make the feathers work, and did the clamshell." Two other emerging Haida talents joined in as well: Jim Hart and Reg Davidson. Of the four Haida—Bill Reid, Jim Hart, Reg Davidson, Gary Edenshaw—three were descendants of Charles Edenshaw. The only one who wasn't was Guujaaw. He carried the name Edenshaw, but he didn't want it.

IN 1979, THE name Gary Edenshaw turned up on a courthouse writ for the first time. While Guujaaw had been apprenticing with Bill Reid in Vancouver, the battle for South Moresby had been heating up. The British Columbia government had rammed through legislation in 1978 to create a new Forest Act, and central to it was an automatic twenty-five-year renewal of Rayonier's Tree Farm Licence 24, on Haida Gwaii. The implications for the South Moresby Wilderness Proposal were dire, but calls for a public hearing into the renewal of the licence went unheeded, and the renewal was due to come into force on May 1, 1979. By this time, the Islands Protection Committee had incorporated under British Columbia's Societies Act as the Islands Protection Society, an entity that would have the standing before a court of law that a simple committee of concerned citizens would not. So it was that the IPS petitioned the British Columbia Supreme Court, asking for a declaration that Forest Minister Tom Waterland was under a duty to act fairly in the renewal of TFL 24. The co-petitioners were Chief Tanu, Nathan Young, who was holder of a traditional trapline on Lyell Island in the proposed wilderness area, and Gary Edenshaw, who billed himself as a Haida "Hunter and Gatherer." "Some thought this move was a bit cheeky," writes Wilderness Committee founder Paul George. "But I thought it was brilliant." Guujaaw recalls with some pride, "That was the first time a hunter and gatherer was given standing in court." Essentially, the petitioners wanted to argue that the habitat that supported the wildlife and marine life upon which they depended was irredeemably compromised by industrial logging.

"The day before our court hearing was to commence," George writes, "in February of 1979, Guujaaw insisted that all the documents of the IPS pertaining to South Moresby be put before the court. That way, Guujaaw reasoned, no matter what the outcome, this information would be forever stored in the court's vault and be part of history so that 'future generations could see what happened.'" A thirty-centimetre stack of papers took all night to copy, at one point causing the photocopier at the West Coast Environmental Law Society offices in Vancouver to burst into flames. The papers were filed in court, among them a detailed affidavit by Paul George presenting evidence of Rayonier's persistent overcutting of the forests, an activity sanctioned by the province. The court essentially ignored George's evidence and most of the contents of the IPS exhibit. "The case hinged on whether or not the petitioners had a legitimate interest in the land and whether or not they had been treated fairly by the forest minister," George recalls. "In an unusual exception to the rule that all the testimony of this kind of court proceeding be done entirely by affidavit, Nathan Young, Chief of Tanu, was allowed to orally testify in his Haida language using a translator. The first thing the government lawyer did was to try to destroy Nathan's credibility, asking him about the sea otters that he trapped. Minnie [Croft], a Haida elder, translated the lawyer's question for Nathan. They talked back and forth in Haida and laughed. Then Minnie relayed Nathan's answer correcting the lawyer, saying that Nathan trapped river otters, not sea otters. Sea otters had been hunted to extinction on Haida Gwaii for the fur trade long before Nathan was born. Nathan clearly established he was a trapper and that he knew about the land and the harm clear-cut logging would do to the animals he trapped."

In a court ruling in March, the judge found that Nathan Young was entitled to standing as owner of a traditional trapline, and that Guujaaw had established he had used the land for gathering seafood, fishing and trapping. The judge also ruled that the minister of forests was obligated to treat them fairly. Since the licence was not due to be issued for another two months, though, the judge said the petitioners had not proven the minister would not treat them fairly in the time remaining, and he dismissed their case. When the minister subsequently ignored them, Guujaaw and Nathan Young went back to court with evidence that the government had not responded to repeated demands for a hearing with the minister and were granted a court date: April 30, the day before the licence was to be renewed.

"All of a sudden, the government scrambled to act 'fairly,'" George recalls. "Guujaaw was summoned to Victoria to meet with the top brass in the forest service. He brought me along as an advisor. We spent about four hours in negotiations with the Chief Forester, the Deputy Minister and several other senior people going over the proposed new TFL clause by clause." The government agreed to a number of modifications, conceding that, where information was lacking regarding proper management of an area in the TFL, the company would have to do further studies. But the whole thing was a ruse. The deputy minister swore an affidavit attesting to the fact that the meeting had taken place—that, essentially, the Haida's demand for good-faith consultations had been met—and the next day the affidavit was presented in court. "The justice, accepting that affidavit as evidence the government had discharged its duty to act fairly to the petitioners, ruled against the petitioners," George writes. A few days later, the government scrapped the agreed-upon modifications, and Guujaaw and Paul George got a lesson in "the cynical exercise of raw power" that was a fact of life in British Columbia at the time.

"We lost that round, of course," recalls Guujaaw. But if the power brokers in Vancouver and Victoria thought theirs was a knockout punch, they were to be proven sorely wrong. The Haida's appeal of that court ruling was ultimately lost in 1981, and the tree farm licence was renewed without any greater duty of care on the part of the forest companies than had ever been the case. But far from dissuading Guujaaw and his fellow activists, defeat in the courts just made them all the more determined—and added momentum to a campaign that would be less about affidavits and evidence and more about winning the hearts and minds of the nation. South Moresby was about to become a *cause célèbre* across Canada, indeed internationally, and the drumbeat of the Haida Nation would soon resound with more gravity than the tapping of a gavel on a court bench in the city.

SIX

THE SAME

AS EVERYONE ELSE

IN 1980 "O CANADA," a song first sung a hundred years earlier, was proclaimed as the country's national anthem.

O Canada!
Our home and native land!

Schoolchildren waved little red-and-white paper Canadian flags, and official chests swelled with pride at the thought of an "indigenous" anthem to replace "God Save the Queen." In two more years, Canada would repatriate its constitution, almost entirely freeing itself from—ironically for native people—two centuries under the thumb of colonial rule.

Typically, just the first verse of "O Canada" is sung—home and native land, true patriot love, glowing hearts, True North strong and free. Many Canadians would be surprised to know the original poem included three additional verses, with added talk of pine and maple trees, great prairies, lordly rivers, hope for all who toil, stalwart sons and gentle maidens, and a plea to the ruler supreme to "hold our

Dominion within thy loving care." All four verses end with a refrain that every Canadian knows by heart and sings by rote:

O Canada, we stand on guard for thee!

In 1980, the Haida were little interested in standing on guard for Canada. They had some nation building of their own to do. While they had elected a Haida Nation executive back in 1974 to focus on land claims, in truth not much had happened on that front; off the islands, there was little appetite to engage with any aboriginal entity pressing for title. The Haida, like the Nisga'a on the mainland, were ahead of their time.

Official political discourse on Haida Gwaii and on reserves across Canada was played out in the chambers of band councils, to which aboriginal politicians were elected under a governance system imposed by Ottawa. The band council system was designed to extinguish traditional hereditary power and decision-making, replacing the gift-exchange of the potlatch with a municipal-style system whose rules had little or no relationship to indigenous beliefs or clan systems. Band councils were given onerous and complex responsibilities—to build houses; to keep the lights on and the water running; to deliver or oversee social services, recreation, education, health care and economic development—but they were typically starved for cash, unable to levy taxes independently and boxed in by bureaucratic constraints. Council members were often unschooled in political process and woefully unprepared for what was being asked of them. Elected band chiefs and councillors were senior political leaders in their communities, in the eyes of Ottawa, but they were nonetheless, like all aboriginal Canadians, considered by the federal government to be wards of the state. Although some aboriginal people owned homes on-reserve, the government refused to allow them to own the land upon which those homes stood. On the Queen

Charlotte Islands, transfer payments were funnelled through the Old Massett and Skidegate band councils. The councils took and administered the paltry payments while community members signed onto long lists for subsidized, substandard government housing and submitted to substandard schooling and health care. It was—and in many communities still is—possibly the most egregious example anywhere of the failure of "trickle-down" economics. Huge fortunes were made from plundering resources on aboriginal land, but what reached communities was more akin to a drip than a trickle. Ottawa dispensed just enough money to keep the band councils in thrall and their communities staggering along. There was no money left over to pursue the land question.

Reynold Russ, today Hereditary Chief Iljawass, was the elected chief councillor in Old Massett in 1980. Percy Williams was the chief in Skidegate. "We were having a very tough time with the government not recognizing what we wanted done," Chief Iljawass says now. "Sometimes my desk would be just plugged with papers relating to the land question, but the band council could not touch that." So in 1980, a "re-constructed" Council of the Haida Nation elected Percy Williams as its new grand chief. An initial constitution had been adopted in 1977, setting out a requirement for annual meetings to be an integral part of Haida governance. In 1981, the meetings became known as the annual House of Assembly. In the words of Michael Nicoll Yahgulanaas, the CHN "inherited much of the duty and authorities of the ancient lineage mothers to become the governing entity to address the outstanding jurisdictional dispute with Canada. The CHN is not registered, mandated or otherwise defined or dependent upon the laws and customs of Canada or the United States. CHN authority flows directly from the land through Haida lineage." In other words, the CHN was designed as a *de novo* government body that exists outside the Westminster system but within the bounds of the land and Haida ancestry. This departure from Canada's institutional norms was a return to, and at the same time a modernization of, Haida norms—

the notion that political authority flows from the land itself. Guujaaw and Michael Nicoll Yahgulanaas, who had both been elected to a committee charged with reorganizing the CHN, were not yet at the centre stage of a reinvigorated Haida body politic, but they were no longer stacking chairs in the hall. "Guujaaw and I found a very significant point of entry into the community," Nicoll Yahgulanaas says, "and we took it very seriously. We worked, and when we worked, we walked. Hours of walking at night, walking through the whole community and talking and examining and playing with scenarios, and evaluating who's doing what and what does that mean. Conversations, with brains full of ideas, and we'd go back and write and calculate and we'd say, 'What if that is a protected area? What would it look like?' And I think we established very quickly a relationship with people who were in leadership at that time, that created sufficient trust and basically made space under their wing to do this stuff."

One of the first things the CHN did to flex its authority was to make a pair of declarations about the land. One was directed at the federal government, a formal land claim entitled Declaration and Claim to the Haida Gwaii. Although the land claim was accepted for negotiation two years later by Canada, it was really a feint on both sides, since the Haida and Canada couldn't conclude anything without the Province of British Columbia at the table, and the province was obdurate in its refusal to negotiate land claims that might lead to the surrender of provincial Crown land. Without the landlord's consent to negotiate, a claim to the land by the Haida had nowhere to go other than into a very full filing cabinet in Ottawa. However, Percy Williams made it abundantly clear what the Haida meant by their claim to the land. "These existing Aboriginal rights are limited only by the capacity of what the land and sea can produce, and defined again by the laws of nature and common sense which ensures we sustain those rights through successive generations. Degeneration of the land and sea will further reduce our rights; therefore we have a moral obligation to defend our resources and determine the fate of our tribal territories."

The Council of the Haida Nation made a further claim about its tribal territories, too, this one in the form of a unilateral declaration that it intended to establish and protect a tribal park called Duu Guusd, a swath of about 150,000 hectares that takes in most of the west coast of Graham Island, from Skwakadanee Point in the south, up to Lepas Bay and Kiusta in the far northwest, east to Naden Harbour, and south again in a jagged line that follows the contours of some of the last remaining forested valleys on Graham Island. Duu Guusd was actually a few hundred hectares larger than South Moresby, incorporating fourteen areas of special significance to the Haida. It was an audacious claim given that, as with South Moresby, the Haida had no more *legal* right to declare one square centimetre of Crown land a park than did anyone else. But that's not how Guujaaw or his elders saw it. Guujaaw would later write:

> At the time before people, these islands were under water. The Supernaturals occupied the first rock to come above those waters. Our ancestors came later, from the sea. Our people knew the time when it was like twilight and there was little difference between night and day. Our people told of *Kaalga Jaad* (Ice Woman) hovering in front of a glacier in what is now Skidegate Inlet. When the waters left Hecate Strait, our people hunted and lived there in the treeless landscape. Our relatives saw the first tree and recount floods and tidal waves in their time and before. In one instance, they were saved by the rings on *Kingi*'s hat; in another, the ones who had dogs on their rafts were not upset by the bears; in another, they found salvation in the mountains of *Duu Guusd*.

The ancestors had used the land and found salvation in it, and only the salvation of the land itself would be a sufficient tribute to them.

Michael Nicoll Yahgulanaas recalls, "Duu Guusd was selected for protection at the urging of Guujaaw and myself and others and approved by the nation's highest law-making body, the House of

Assembly, because that landscape is a continuity of Pacific rainforests, undamaged watersheds, and because of the importance of its mountains to our ancestors as a refuge during the last flood." Nicoll Yahgulanaas says that, in 1981, the Haida hosted a dinner on a beach next to a logging camp, "to feed the loggers so their ears would be open as we told them they couldn't log Duu Guusd...Guujaaw worked hard with elders and others to make that feast a success... In spite of their agreeable words that day, [the loggers] went on to work as hard as they could to log those western slopes."

Wade Davis, now a world-renowned ethnobotanist and explorer, remembers working for industry giant MacMillan Bloedel on Graham Island as a forestry engineer, in an area just to the east of Duu Guusd. "My job was to extract timber as efficiently and inexpensively as possible, period. In the year that I spent in a remote logging camp at Dinan Bay, there was not a single decision made that in any way whatsoever took into account environmental considerations. Concern for the cultural heritage of the Haida was not even a remote thought... There were vast timber holdings at stake, and a provincial government in power that was totally allied to industry. The very foundation of scientific forestry at the time was based on the presumption that all old-growth forests were to be cut." Davis has since rhapsodized about western red cedar as "perhaps the most important denizen of the Pacific slope...the tree that made possible the florescence of great and ancient cultures of the coast...Lush and astonishingly prolific, the coastal temperate rainforests are richer in their capacity to produce the raw material of life than any other terrestrial ecosystem on earth." But there was another denizen of the Pacific slope, the logger, who came to make money by "cutting down in minutes trees that had taken centuries to grow." Davis recalls being "completely radicalized" about the industry at the time. "I went to work as a logger because I wanted to know what went on inside these places," he says. "I wanted not only to know what happened to the land, but also feel what the process did to people, to understand the social and psychological motivations and consequences of doing what we were doing to the forests." There was a lot to take in.

At its height in the seventies and eighties, British Columbia's logging industry directly employed up to 25,000 people each year. Industry claimed multiplier effects of three or four times that number in government jobs and ancillary industries. Industrial logging in British Columbia had begun more than a century before Wade Davis entered the woods, and the roots of the liquidation of the coast's vast timber resources were as much strategic as economic. British military might depended on its navy, and British sailors coursed the sea lanes of the globe, buoyed by hulls made from the world's wood and powered by sails unfurled from massive wooden masts and spars. "Up until 150 years ago, a forest of straight, sturdy pine was as valuable as an oil field or a uranium mine today: it was a critical source of energy (i.e., sail power) without which a nation could not fully realize its commercial or military ambitions," writes John Vaillant in his book *The Golden Spruce*. Eventually, traders in British Columbia who had come looking for fur realized there might be just as much value in fir—and in cedar, and in spruce. "It may have been the sea otter that brought them, but timber is why they stayed," Vaillant writes.

For decades, logging on the B.C. coast was constrained naturally by difficult terrain, the sheer impenetrability of the woods and the huge hurdles to transportation to and from remote villages. If you could fell a giant tree into saltwater, then you could raft it up with other trees and tow the lot to a mill. A-frame logging—wherein a tower high on a slope was used as an anchor from which a swath of forest could be cut and the trees then cabled to shore—increased access and impact, but still the trees had to be within reach of water. On Vancouver Island and in some parts of the mainland, railroads offered greater ingress to the woods. Then, as the automobile became commonplace and utility vehicles radicalized the work of farmers, the advent of truck logging triggered a vast network of roads whose capillaries snaked deeper and deeper into the woods. But the real assault on British Columbia's forests began after the Second World War, when the combination of a postwar economic boom, with its attendant appetite for raw resources, and huge advances in mechanization meant that the woods were alive as never before with the harbingers of their death—with loggers.

The industrial enterprise began in capitals and cities like Victoria (policy) and Vancouver (money), but it relied entirely on places like Dinan Bay (wood) and on people (loggers) who were willing to risk their lives, even their sanity, to get the wood out. Wade Davis recalls "the constant grinding of machinery, the disintegration of the forest into burnt slash and mud, the wind and sleet that froze on the rigging and whipped across the frozen bay... With haunting regularity, winter gales swept through the islands, and along the face of the forest exposed by the clear-cut it was not unusual to encounter hectares of timber blown down by the wind. The result was a nightmare of overlapping trunks and roots, thousands of tonnes of wood weighted down with immense pressure and ready to explode with the first cut of a saw. Salvaging blowdown was dreaded work, dangerous and sometimes deadly. To mitigate the hazard and avoid the loss of fibre, government foresters permitted us to expand our cutblocks with the hope of establishing wind-firm boundaries. As a result, openings grew to encompass entire valleys, with the edge of the clear-cut reaching to the ridge line of distant mountains. If a slope was deemed to be too steep to be logged, it was only because machinery could not get to it. Trees left standing by the edge of lakes or along streams inevitably blew over in a storm. So these too were cut... But nobody was worried about what we were doing. It was work, and living on the edge of that immense forest, people simply believed it would go on forever. If anyone in government had a broader perspective, we never heard about it... The priority and focus of every aspect of the logging operation was the extraction of timber... It was a one-time deal, and everyone knew it."

The forest industry didn't always succeed at making money—as in all natural resource industries, its profits rode up and down through the vagaries of commodity prices, market demand, exchange rates, bad management, labour costs and good and bad government policies—but it was unbelievably successful at stripping forests in every region of the province. Vancouver Island has lost almost three-quarters of its original, productive old-growth forest. Even after a couple of decades of park-making, due largely to pressure from environmental groups, massive harvest levels continue across the province. The total volume logged in the five fiscal years to March 31, 2008, was 403,744,699 cubic metres, or an average of 80,748,939 cubic metres per year, a cubic metre of wood being about the volume of a telephone pole. To put that in perspective, the annual B.C. timber harvest could create an unbroken line of fully laden logging trucks that would circle the globe at the equator, and there would still be a 12,000-kilometre-long line of logging trucks looking for a place to park. (This calculation is based on thirty-five cubic metres to the truck load and an average truck length of roughly twenty-five metres.) The total area cleared over the same five-year period was 880,600 hectares, for an annual average of 176,120 hectares. That's roughly equal to the city of Vancouver being cleared one and a half times over each year.

South of the 49th parallel, the primary forests of California, Oregon and Washington have been developed to the point that there is precious little old-growth left anywhere except in parks. By comparison, British Columbia and Alaska are still relatively rich in old-growth. Nonetheless, what has happened—and continues to happen—in British Columbia is an astonishing conversion of the landscape and ecology of a single place by a single industry encouraged by a succession of sympathetic governments. Of all places along the coast of British Columbia, the forests of Vancouver Island and the Queen Charlotte Islands were especially prized by industry, for the same reason they are prized today by environmentalists—their extraordinarily large trees. Vancouver Island and the Charlottes were overrun with thick veins of what came to be known as "green gold"—seam after seam of precious fibre, brought to the ground and thence to market in a process that resembled a sort of open-pit mining for wood. On the Charlottes in the mid-1970s, loggers clear-cut between 3,000 and 4,000 hectares per year, about twelve times the size of New York's Central Park, or ten times the size of Vancouver's Stanley Park. According to the Gowgaia Institute, the total volume of wood harvested on Haida Gwaii between 1979 and 2004 is estimated to have been 48,439,726 cubic metres. So in twenty-five years, almost 50 million cubic metres of wood were cut. According to another analysis, 94 per cent of that volume left the islands as raw wood to be processed in distant mills. The companies paid stumpage to the government, but virtually none of this money was reinvested on the islands. Almost all the logging took place in either good- or medium-quality forest stands. Today, 65 per cent of those stands have been logged. On the Skidegate Plateau, where Wade Davis logged one winter and others logged for decades, 74 per cent of good- and medium-quality forests have been logged. "Which means that 65 to 74 per cent of the best places for salmon, bear, birds, cedar, medicinal plants and people are gone," the Gowgaia Institute says.

As with the fur trade, the Haida were involved in exploiting the forests. Natives and non-natives alike were employed by the logging companies. They bulked up on union-wage jobs that paid better than fishing in all but fishing's very best years and enabled men to work on the islands rather than seek jobs on the mainland or languish on the dole. But a 1994 analysis revealed that, by comparison with the enormous volume and value of the wood shipped off-islands, employment (and pay) for local people had always been modest. For instance, MacMillan Bloedel employed 304 people on-islands, but 1,143 jobs off-islands were attributed to the timber coming off Haida Gwaii, a ratio of 1 to 3.8. Husby Forest Products employed 32 on-islands, 425 off, for a ratio of 1 to 13.2. Timberwest had a respectable ratio of 1 to 1.45, but Western Forest Products employed 6 people on-islands and 132 off, ratio 1 to 22. On average, for every job on Haida

Gwaii related to logging, four jobs were created off-islands. Other than a couple of small local mills, all secondary breakdown of the big logs being downed on Haida Gwaii happened elsewhere. The people of Haida Gwaii were trapped in a kind of postwar industrial serfdom. As Dr. Seuss might have put it, everyone was working for the Once-ler:

> I meant no harm. I most truly did not.
> But I had to grow bigger. So bigger I got.
> I biggered my factory. I biggered my roads.
> I biggered my wagons. I biggered the loads...
> And I biggered my money, which everyone needs.

Ah, but there was no Lorax to speak for the trees. Or at least there wasn't until the Haida realized that their land was being stripped from underneath them, that the land question was being *answered* under their noses and their own caulk boots, and that their uneasy pact with Canada, the Province of British Columbia and the timber licensees was at best a Faustian bargain. Wade Davis left the islands before Duu Guusd was designated for protection by the Haida, but he was aware of the famous "line" that was supposed to protect South Moresby. "At the time, I can assure you, those familiar with the politics of the islands and of the Canadian government in particular saw this delineation on the map...as a purely quixotic gesture."

Quixotic, maybe, but a certain alchemy had begun to take hold on the islands, particularly in the case of South Moresby. Failure to advance their cause with a compromised and corrupted provincial government—"the corporate logging lobby was simply too powerful in B.C.," says the Wilderness Committee's Paul George—pushed the wilderness crusaders to consider a change in tactics. "We needed to shift our efforts to making the protection of South Moresby a national issue," George recalls.

Canada, as in the Government of Canada, has an uneasy relationship with its provinces and territories, as does the central city in any confederation of states—Washington, D.C., Canberra, Moscow, to name just a few. Ottawa taxes Canadians, as do the provinces, and it attempts to govern a country that is often far less than the sum of its parts. The federal government is in constant conflict with provincial premiers, who often govern parties of an utterly different political mien to the national party and who routinely decry interference in their affairs while grubbing for handouts from the central tithe. Resource development issues are complicated by the fact that the province is the Crown when it comes to the land base, but Ottawa is the Crown when it comes to fisheries. There are provincial permit systems unaffected by Ottawa (especially when it comes to logging), but some national standards (especially when it comes to species protection) trigger federal environmental assessments. There are provincial parks and protected areas, but alongside them exists a national parks agenda somewhat akin to that of the United States. Aboriginal Canadians are the responsibility of Canada, which spends $9 billion a year on an array of staggeringly ineffective programs for them, but of course aboriginal Canadians *live* in provinces and territories, and the downstream effects of Ottawa's incompetence are sharply felt in local communities. Finally, there is the constant friction between Members of Parliament, who do duty in Ottawa on behalf of local constituents, and members of the provincial legislative assembly, who seldom are aligned in belief or ambition with their federal colleagues. All of which is to say that there were enough competing agendas that the fact South Moresby was so comprehensively snookered in Victoria meant politicians in Ottawa might give it currency as a national issue. Ottawa and the province had been down this path before—converting provincial Crown logging lands into federal Crown park lands—but every time the feds interceded in an issue with economic consequences for the provincial treasury, the argument boiled down to money.

At first, there wasn't any—money, that is. There was plenty of argument. The first that official Ottawa heard of South Moresby was via a private member's bill (Bill C-454) sponsored by Ian Waddell, an MP with the New Democratic Party. Waddell, according to Paul George, had introduced the bill at the urging of Jim Fulton, MP for Skeena, whose electoral riding included the Queen Charlotte Islands. Fulton, hailing from a resource-rich and logging-centric region of the province, couldn't possibly sponsor a bill that favoured anti-logging forces, so he did it by stealth, getting Waddell, a city boy from suburban Vancouver, to carry his water in Ottawa. The bill was doomed to fail: coming from a third-string party, it had no chance of leaving the order paper and becoming actual legislation. But however underpowered the vehicle, South Moresby was now launched as a national issue. In the face of relentless lobbying, a number of backbench MPs from the governing Liberal Party expressed support for a national park, the whole NDP caucus did likewise and Joe Clark, leader of the Opposition and of the Conservative Party, also pledged support. The enthusiasm with which federal politicians greeted the campaign grated on provincial politicians, who saw it as an intrusion on their jurisdiction. The campaign needed much more than federal political support—it needed massive *public* support. That would come in January 1982, with the broadcast of a documentary on David Suzuki's *The Nature of Things*, a program that held the Canadian Broadcasting Corporation's Wednesday night prime-time TV slot.

David Suzuki is one of Canada's most delightfully and deliberately divisive personalities. In a country that values consensus over conflict and self-effacement over self-promotion, the combative and populist Suzuki is viewed with equal measures of awe and loathing. A CBC show called *The Greatest Canadian* in 2004 listed him as one of ten most important Canadians of all time, and of the people on the Top 10 list, Suzuki, now in his seventies, was the only one still alive. His path to national and international fame began when he parlayed his academic work as a geneticist at the University of British Columbia into a broadcasting career rivalled only, if at all, by the likes of England's Sir David Attenborough or France's Jacques Cousteau. In the mid-1970s Suzuki hosted the CBC Radio science show *Quirks and Quarks*. In

1979, he switched to television as host of *The Nature of Things,* and there he signalled from the outset that he was unafraid to confront conventional wisdom, especially in his increasingly strident broadcasts about environmental issues. Suzuki was just hitting his stride when he travelled to Haida Gwaii for the first time in the early 1980s to catalogue for television the biological treasures of South Moresby and the looming threat of logging at Windy Bay on Lyell Island. The show ran on national television on January 27, 1982. "Suzuki's Windy Bay show pushed South Moresby into the national consciousness overnight," recalls Paul George. It did the same thing for Guujaaw.

Guujaaw is identified on the show by Suzuki as a "Haida carver." Suzuki extols South Moresby's biological virtues—"a priceless inheritance 10,000 years in the making"—and then Thom Henley comes on screen, as fresh-faced and mop-headed as a young Paul McCartney, eloquently articulating the need to stop the logging. Guujaaw is filmed in close up, head and shoulders—a bandana and a black beard, a black-and-red-checked woollen shirt, with just a whiff of menace about him. Suzuki asks him why Windy Bay shouldn't be logged:

"Windy Bay once had a village at the front of it, and in that village, it was almost a self-contained little unit. There was cedar there for them to use, there was fish in the river, and all the game fowl that you imagine. And today it is still virtually the same as it ever was. Throughout these islands now, most of that type of a watershed has been changed for all time by logging, and our people have determined that Windy Bay and some other places in the Charlottes must be left in their natural condition so that we can keep our identity and pass it along to the following generations. A forest like that, the ocean and those things, are what keep us as Haida people today."

Suzuki: "And if they're logged off?"

Guujaaw: "If they're logged off we'll probably end up the same as everyone else, I guess."

Following that exchange, an aerial shot of Lyell Island sweeps across a lush landscape blanketed with old-growth forests, rises up a hillside to a ridge and descends across a morass of mud, roots, slash, slumps and slides that leave the viewer in no doubt about what logging would do to Windy Bay. Those pictures radicalized Canadians, and the interview with Guujaaw jolted David Suzuki himself.

As Suzuki expressed it in a speech in 1999: "I went there [Haida Gwaii] and interviewed a young artist named Guujaaw, now president of the Haida Nation. I said to him, 'A lot of the loggers are Haida. So it's good for your community. You have high unemployment. What's wrong if they are logging? And with MacMillan Bloedel in the islands, millions of dollars come through your communities... Why are you fighting against the logging?' He answered. 'Well, of course, if they cut the trees down, we'll still be here. But then we won't be Haida any more. We'll just be like everybody else.'

"With that simple statement I realized that here was a radically different way of looking at the world. Haida don't see themselves as ending at their skin or their fingertips. To be Haida is to be intimately connected with the land, the air, the water, the fish, the trees, the birds. Their history, their culture, their very reason for existing are tied up in the land. Ever since that interview, I have been a student. I have travelled around the world meeting indigenous people wherever I can. Everywhere it's the same. However impoverished, dysfunctional or oppressed indigenous peoples are, you find a fundamentally different sense of connection with the land. As I reflected on that, I realized they are absolutely right." Today, David Suzuki's First Nations honours include six aboriginal names, including one from British Columbia's Kwagiulth people, who know him as Nan Wa Kawi (Man Who Knows Much); from Australia's Kaurna people, to whom he is Karnumeya (Mountain Man); and from the Haida Ts'aahl Eagle clan, to whom he is simply Gyaagan (My Own). Suzuki returns to Haida Gwaii every summer to visit friends and to fish. In 2008, his daughter Severn married Judson Brown, a Haida from Skidegate.

If David Suzuki's broadcasts from Haida Gwaii—there was another in 1986—helped to vault South Moresby onto the national stage, they also helped to inflame passions on the islands. In the 1980s, there were about 900 logging jobs on the Charlottes (more than double the number now), and harvesting was at an all-time high. Frank Beban, a logging contractor as vocal as he was outsized, also owned the pub in Sandspit, a wind-blown former military base on an eponymous finger of flat terrain that is home to the major air-port on the islands. Loggers would fly in from the mainland and decamp to the Sandspit Inn en route to camps in the woods. Over the years, a lot of hard words were exchanged at the Sandspit Inn after a lot of hard drinking, and the hardest words were for environ-mentalists. In 1979 the South Moresby issue had been put in the hands of a government process—the South Moresby Planning Team—a stakeholder panel that had developed a range of options from business as usual to nearly full protection. No one was under any illusion that business would deviate very far from usual as a result of that or any other government-controlled process. One night, Paul George of the Wilderness Committee and his equally tireless partner, Adriane Carr, walked into the Sandspit Inn, and Frank Beban called them over to a table full of industry types. "We sat down and I said, 'Let me buy you a beer,' purchasing a round for the table," George recalls. "From the talk going down, Frank and all the industry people sitting there were pretty confident that the South Moresby park proposal was going nowhere. The B.C. government must have given them some backroom assurances. As the evening wore on, we kidded back and forth and had more to drink. Frank kept putting me down and tried to hit on Adriane, saying to her sev-eral times (referring to me), 'What's a nice girl like you doing with a four-flusher like that?' (I only learned years later that a four-flusher meant a bowel movement so big that it took four flushes of the toilet to make it go down.) Even without knowing what it meant, it got pretty tiresome listening to him. Frank kept challenging me to arm-wrestle. I knew it was a losing proposition so I kept refusing. Guujaaw was there. Near the end of the evening Guujaaw took up Frank's challenge to an arm wrestle. Guujaaw put him down and won. Shortly after that it was last call and no one at our table ordered anything. We had all had enough. Adriane and I were just about to leave when something snapped inside of me. I said in a loud voice, 'Hey Frank, I always thought you were a generous guy. I bought you a drink tonight and you never bought me one.' It was a royal insult to a guy like Frank. He jumped up from the table, livid with anger. 'A round for the house,' he shouted. Even though it was well past closing time, the waitress brought around drinks for everyone in the still-packed pub. I quickly downed my beer and Adriane gave hers away. We left before anything ugly occurred."

The sentiments voiced in Sandspit against "sissy environmentalists" were anything but pretty. David Suzuki became a lightning rod for reactionary rage, and the Haida were often vilified for daring to lay a claim to their land—never so floridly as by Sandspit logger and self-appointed editorialist R.L. "Redneck" Smith. For ten years, in about a hundred editions of his must-read publication the *Redneck News,* Smith cranked out a double-sided stream of invective using a printer in the basement of Frank Beban's logging office. When Suzuki returned for a second bite at the South Moresby story, the *Redneck News* said: "Everyone on Moresby Island is aware of the activities of the learned Dr. Suzuki, who is here with us again in Sandspit this week. Us rednecks are not in the habit of bad-mouthing tourists when they come here, so I hope Dr. Suzuki has a pleasant stay with us while he spends scads of taxpayers' money to do a smear job on the logging community over the dumb-ass Windy Bay issue." Upon seeing Suzuki's broadcast two months later, Smith wrote, "Those of us who have been watching the weird movies made for the evening television news are finding it hard to believe the snow-job that's going down. Before anyone loses their perspective about all the demonstrations and passionate speeches given by our Haida friends and neighbours in the war paint—keep in mind there is no grounds whatever under Canadian law for our Red Brothers to lay claim to

Lyell Island or any other part of the Queen Charlottes other than established Indian Reserve Lands." And in another issue, "The Haidas are grinding the little people, the working people, into poverty with their lawlessness."

What Smith and his ilk considered to be lawlessness on the part of their "neighbours in the war paint" hadn't actually occurred first on Haida Gwaii but on the west coast of Vancouver Island, where Nuu-chah-nulth people stood up to MacMillan Bloedel on Meares Island. A spectacular congregation of old-growth forest, home to the second-largest known red cedar tree in Canada, the Hanging Garden Tree, and to the native village of Opitsat, the island is a short distance across a stretch of water from Tofino—then a pretty typical logging and fishing village, now a resort town with multi-million-dollar waterfront homes, movie stars, a funky if frigid surf culture and spectacular beaches, including the famed Long Beach. Meares Island provides Tofino with two important things: its view and, from a lake in the centre of the island, its drinking water. On Easter weekend, 1984, the Nuu-chah-nulth declared Meares Island a tribal park in an attempt to thwart the logging planned to take place there. Guujaaw recalls that the Nuu-chah-nulth took their cue from the Haida. "It's worth going back to the original designation of Duu Guusd," he says today. "It started with, 'Let it be known...,' and we gave that to the Nuu-chah-nulth and they used it almost word for word on Meares Island." He and another emerging Haida leader, Miles Richardson, "went there at the urging of our people and sat in strategy sessions with their leaders."

In a bait-and-switch move that would become all too familiar to the Haida, the Nuu-chah-nulth and their supporters in the environmental community were lured into a government planning process on Meares Island, a process impossibly compromised by the company's starting position that it was entitled to log all of the island. On November 10, the B.C. government essentially agreed, ruling that the company could log 90 per cent of the island's 8,000 hectares, leaving a small preserve to protect the drinking water source. The plan included logging the side of Meares that faced Tofino. Just eleven days later, when loggers from MacMillan Bloedel arrived to start cutting, they ran into "the first logging blockade in Canadian history," according to Paul George. It may have been a raggedy group of environmentalists and First Nations activists, but it was sufficient to turn the loggers away in frustration. There followed a long, expensive series of injunctions and counter-injunctions that have never been fully resolved. To this day, a quarter of a century later, Meares Island remains in legal limbo—and undisturbed by logging.

The Council of the Haida Nation took encouragement from events on Meares Island. Guujaaw had been serving on the South Moresby Planning Team since 1979. He knew that the process, as on Meares Island, was fatally flawed—but witnessing it was an essential part of his initiation into the mindset of the logging industry and the government. "It was manipulated, like a lot of other provincial processes," Guujaaw recalls. Elizabeth May, now leader of Canada's Green Party but an assistant to federal environment minister Tom McMillan during the South Moresby denouement, was struck by the meticulous attention to detail that Guujaaw exhibited. He "exercised his scrutiny over details like boundaries and road building plans. He focussed on semantics and subtle issues, like why logging areas were coloured green on planning maps, while wilderness was coloured red."

Miles Richardson, who was destined to become a major political force on Haida Gwaii and nationwide, remembers coming home to Haida Gwaii from the University of Victoria, where he was studying business. "Depending on the outlook for fishing, I would either go commercial fishing or I would go logging. If fishing was going to be a bad year in my estimation I would go logging and at least have some sure income. If it was going to be a good year, I'd go for the bonanza. But anyway I remember this one year I came home and I fished, went fishing for the summer with Dempsey Collinson [Chief Skidegate], and we were sitting on the dock and Guujaaw comes down and gives him a report on Gwaii Haanas [the Haida name for South Moresby] and other parts of the islands. There was lots going on, on the protection front. And I remember sitting there and thinking, 'I can't just be on the outside, I've gotta help these guys.' And I remember saying to Guuj, 'Thanks for what you're doing. Keep it up, I'll be there soon.'" For Miles Richardson, as for many Haida, there was no contradiction between his earning an income from logging and wanting the overcutting curtailed.

When he returned home with his degree one year later, Richardson—known as Buddy to folks on the islands and, eventually, to provincial premiers, cabinet ministers and prime ministers—resisted getting involved with the Council of the Haida Nation at first. "I wanted to be a businessman," he says. But though Percy Williams had righted the CHN ship with the backroom assistance of Guujaaw and Michael Nicoll Yahgulanaas, the council needed fresh legs. An articulate Haida boy with some time logged down south and a university degree to boot... well, Buddy couldn't hold off the elders for long. He was elected vice-president in 1982, served two years and then became president in 1984, a position he would hold for twelve years. Richardson got some of his earliest briefings from Guujaaw, who made sure the environment was top of mind for the incoming head of state.

One issue that had been festering with the Haida was the United Nations negotiation to enact an International Convention on the Law of the Sea. The Haida had formally registered the hereditary boundaries of Haida Gwaii in 1981 with the UN, rejecting Canada's claim to a conflicting territorial boundary that gave it jurisdiction over waters within 200 miles of the Canadian coast, including Haida Gwaii. Richardson remembers Guujaaw calling him one day in 1982: "'Buddy, there's this final UN conference on the Law of the Sea Convention in Jamaica, and we've gotta be represented there. And it's in a week. Canada's going to claim our waters and we've gotta stand up and contest it.' I said, 'Ah, God, we've got no money and I can't go,

I'm too damned busy." And he said, 'I'll go.' So we scraped enough money together to get him a ticket. We got him a return ticket and he said, 'I'll look after the rest.'"

As international diplomatic delegations go, it was a bare-bones affair. A few days after Guujaaw left for Jamaica, Richardson remembers, he got a collect call from Guujaaw who told him he'd lost his return ticket. "He managed to get our protest letter into the convention, which was his mission, but he somehow managed to lose his ticket, his money and everything. He ended up living down there with the Jamaicans on the beach, and he survived by carving. He said they didn't much like Haida art. He told me about these beautiful ravens he was carving and people there looking at them and saying, 'It doesn't look like a bird to me, man.' Anyway, he survived. And we got him another ticket and he came back. But he got the job done."

Jamaica wasn't Guujaaw's first overseas adventure. In 1981, he had travelled to Kobe, Japan, with a group of First Nations singers and dancers led by legendary Squamish Nation chief Simon Baker. Baker—or Khot-La-Cha, Man with a Kind Heart—was at ease being a cultural ambassador for B.C. First Nations, even if that sometimes meant dressing up in the feathered headdresses, buckskins and deer hoofs of a Prairie Indian rather than the Coast Salish dress of his own community. CP Air flew Chief Baker around the world to promote tourism, and if he felt for a second that he was being trotted out as a token Indian, he never said so. "They loved the stories about the Indians of Canada," he reported of audiences in Germany, New Zealand, Britain, Spain and Japan. In Kobe, Baker and Guujaaw were among six dancers who performed at the opening of a new port. In his autobiography, *Khot-La-Cha*, Baker recalled, "As part of our visit we went to many other areas and performed at big shopping centres, the children's hospital, and the opening of a big complex built by B.C. Lumber." Guujaaw would return to Japan as a singer and dancer at Expo 85, but it's fair to say that he hasn't followed up the Kobe trip with any more dances promoting the export of B.C. forest products.

In fact, back home on Haida Gwaii, Guujaaw in 1984 launched a research project into Haida traditional uses of forests, an undertaking that would yield extraordinary results for Haida culture and the ecology of Haida Gwaii. He began what would become a ten-year search of the islands' forests for old and unfinished canoes. He interviewed elders to glean the historical theories and practices of canoe building and tromped through the bush looking for evidence of the importance of the big trees that had given the seafaring Haida an edge among coastal tribes—canoe trees. Though there was no such term at the time, Guujaaw and Wanagan were looking for what would eventually become known as "culturally modified trees," or CMTs. Instead of sifting for pottery shards or poring over ancient texts, Guujaaw's roving archaeological dig was focussed on finding trees that had been altered by his ancestors, proof of not just the Haida's presence on the islands but of their use of its resources. (Today, CMTs are the bane of industrial foresters; they are legally recognized as evidence of traditional use and, if present in sufficient numbers, can render whole tracts of forests off-limits to logging.) Guujaaw wanted to know where these trees were, why particular trees were selected over others, what methods were used to make canoes and how historical methods could be adapted to contemporary canoe production.

As he roamed the woods, Guujaaw was exposed to more and more evidence of the juggernaut destruction of the very trees that had lent such mobility and superiority to his forebears. For him, the new ways of using old-growth forests were offensive, and he shared his disgust with anyone who would listen. The South Moresby Planning Team was one venue. *The Nature of Things* was another. A newly constituted Council of the Haida Nation, with its new president, Miles Richardson, was perhaps the most important audience of all.

"I accepted that preserving the area was the primary, the number one objective, but I also insisted that our rights had to be respected, and they were very tightly related," Richardson recalls. "When I got involved in politics, what went into my mind is, 'I need an issue here.'

Not to make my mark as a leader—that was secondary—but to assert the Haida Nation as a nation...South Moresby was the biggest issue of the day. The challenge then came to take the huge momentum of this environmental issue, which by then was a national issue—*The Nature of Things* had done their piece, the Islands Protection Society had been doing first-class public relations and building alliances as an environmental issue—and as I saw it as a young leader, our job as the Council of the Haida Nation was to restore what had become an environmental issue into a Haida issue." Richardson insists that long before he arrived on the scene, South Moresby "was a top of the shelf Haida issue—but to the rest of the world it was an environmental issue." In effect, he says, the Haida had to rebrand the issue as their own. "We needed a cutting edge. We were fighting the whole economic system of all Canada. That cutting edge was title." And to situate South Moresby as declaration about title, the Haida had to stand their ground. "So you know, the way we did that was with the blockades. And that's why we wouldn't let anybody but Haidas on those blockades. We wanted a crystal clear, unmistakable message that this was a Haida issue—it was an environmental issue, but it was a Haida responsibility. And that's why we did that." And it worked. Dave Porter, a Kaska Nation leader who has held prominent positions in the Yukon and British Columbia governments, says that "for the most part, a lot of us didn't know who the Haida were until we started seeing them on TV every day through that whole struggle."

What led up to the blockades of 1985, the "lawlessness" that Redneck Smith so biliously decried, was a series of egregious political betrayals and double-crosses by politicians who would have made Huey Long look like the pope, in a legislature that would make Tammany Hall seem like a cathedral. For decades, British Columbia was under the almost uninterrupted reign of an outlandishly right-wing administration, courtesy of the Social Credit Party. There were repeated scandals that occasionally dislodged cabinet ministers— hookers paid for with government credit cards, champagne-soaked dinners at taxpayers' expense, insider business knowledge, crooked land deals, influence peddling, railway tracks to nowhere—but what never came unstuck was the grip that the natural resource industries had on the affections of provincial politicians. The South Moresby Planning Team was an exercise in appeasement, but there was no intention on the part of the B.C. government to give an inch to Indians or environmentalists.

By now, there was an increasingly well-established national campaign to save South Moresby. The book Paul George had originally tried to launch, the one about Canada's Galapagos, had come to fruition in 1984 under the auspices of the Islands Protection Society. *Islands at the Edge*—with essays by Bill Reid, Jacques Cousteau, Bristol Foster, John Broadhead, Thom Henley and others and a stunning array of photographs and paintings by Robert Bateman, Toni Onley, Takao Tanabe and more—was a publishing masterstroke. The book referred to South Moresby by its Haida name, Gwaii Haanas, or Place of Wonder, and the book set about demonstrating that the area was all that and more. For all its evocative essays, the book's magic lay in its lush full-colour photos; in the choice between critters and clearcuts, critters win every time. The book landed on the desks of politicians in Ottawa and Victoria. It inspired others to add their weight to the campaign, among them iconic author Farley Mowat. "South Moresby is the last remaining region in Canada that has not been desecrated by the blind avarice of modern man," Mowat wrote in a Wilderness Committee flyer. "It *must* be saved, not just for our time but for all time. It *will* be saved if a shred of honest morality still exists in Canadian society." While some of this support was written off in British Columbia as eastern sentimentality about western issues, it seeped through, even into political back eddies like the office of the B.C. environment minister.

Forestry, health, finance and education—these were the big provincial ministries. Environment was purdah, which is where Austin Pelton ended up in 1985. But in Pelton, for once, British Columbia had an environment minister who seemed to care about the environment and who actually bothered to meet with his federal counterpart to discuss the idea of a park in South Moresby. Environmentalists and the Haida were lulled into optimism when Pelton made reassuring noises about a protection option possibly being acceptable to the province. Six years of work on the South Moresby Planning Team might have produced something after all. Although Western Forest Products was putting intense pressure on the B.C. government to issue a cutting permit for Lyell Island, the government was holding the company at bay. Pelton personally assured Miles Richardson and Guujaaw that no cutting permits would be issued until the government came to an agreement with the Haida. But that turned out to be a promise he couldn't keep.

"Making sure that logging continued in South Moresby was a matter of pride for the industry," recalls Paul George. And the industry rightly feared that any concession on Lyell Island would create a domino effect throughout the woods of British Columbia. So while Pelton cooed cooperation and consultation, saying that no permits would be issued till a formal cabinet decision was made about the fate of South Moresby, what happened was exactly the opposite, as Richardson remembers well. "One Thursday afternoon I'm at a meeting in Prince Rupert and about four o'clock I get a call in my hotel room, and it's Austin Pelton. 'Miles, I'm very sorry, I gave you my word, but I'm only one voice in cabinet. We've just issued a permit over the line on Lyell Island.' And I couldn't believe it. I remember really clearly—the gauntlet's dropped. This is it. We've made our position clear." Richardson remembers telling Pelton, " 'We're going to prepare to defend the area.' I phoned all the key people—Chief Skidegate, Guujaaw, Wanagan. Phoned the Chief Councillors. Unanimous. We had no choice. They're not logging." The Haida had previously warned Pelton that issuing the permit would be seen as an "act of aggression." The Haida had never fought a war for their lands, but they were about to now.

"We didn't have a sophisticated plan," Richardson recalls. "Every-thing started coming together really fast." In Vancouver a few days later, the Haida held a press conference. "We had to put out the call. So we crafted a one-page press release—never done that before—sent it out, booked a hotel room and I remember all the Haidas who were in town turned up, and we went into the room and it was just packed. There was a stack of microphones and, holy shit, I'd never seen anything like this. I'd never even been at a press conference before! And basically all we said was, 'We're going to stop them.' 'How are you going to stop them?' 'Come and see.'"

That weekend, back on Haida Gwaii, Richardson, Guujaaw and others called the band councils together. "Look, we're in a battle, a battle like we've never been in. We need everybody. Put out the call in the communities." In Skidegate later that day, the community hall was packed. "So we made, I dunno, about fifteen committees—a com-mittee for food, a committee for communications, a committee for buildings—you know, it was October, we didn't want to live in tents. We had to get a crew together, because we were going to be there by Monday," says Richardson. "This was Saturday." On Sunday, Guujaaw was sent south in a helicopter to scout a campsite that would locate the blockade in the place where it would cause the maximum disruption. He decided on Sedgwick Bay. It took the Haida till Monday evening to get fully mobilized, by which time the media was in foment and the company had gotten in an extra day's worth of blasting and road build-ing. When the Haida flotilla—three boats—left Queen Charlotte City, people were crowded three or four deep on the dock to show their sup-port. As the boats headed out past Skidegate Landing and the reserve, cars were lined up watching them leave, headlights flashing. "It was awesome," Richardson recalls. "Nobody really admitted it, but everyone was really apprehensive about what we were going to be facing. But we were totally committed. We travelled all night, got there at daybreak and there's only one thing to do: drop anchor and go up to the road. So we left everything, went up to the road and blockaded. Game on."

SEVEN

THEY SAY

ONE OF THE most notorious confrontations in the frontier history of British Columbia was the Chilcotin War of 1864. The word Chilcotin is an anglicization of the name for a nation of people, the Tsilhqot'in, who then and now inhabit a gorgeous, mountain-ringed plateau of forests, grasslands, pristine lakes and clear-running rivers on the B.C. mainland, about 450 kilometres southeast from Haida Gwaii as the raven flies. As ever, this particular set-to arose over access to resources—in this case, the building of a wagon road to shorten the route to the Cariboo goldfields, through remote, steep, hitherto impenetrable country. Native packers assigned to white road crews were said to have realized how the road would affect their land and culture; they were harshly treated by the work party, and they blamed the European labourers for outbreaks of smallpox, writes Alan D. McMillan in *Native Peoples and Cultures of Canada*. Whatever actually happened to turn the Tsilhqot'in on the white intruders, in a short spasm of gunfire in the spring of 1864, nineteen white men were killed. Governor Frederick Seymour, a mere month into his term and fearing an "Indian War," ordered two different armed parties of men into the area to quell the insurrection, which cost another white life before chiefs of the Tsilhqot'in were finally run to ground and allegedly assured immunity if they cooperated with the authorities. Instead, five of them were arrested, charged with murder and transported to court, where in September of that year they came before Judge Matthew Baillie Begbie. There is considerable doubt as to whether all the men in the dock Begbie looked down upon were even present when the road crews were slaughtered, but such was the panic in Vancouver and Victoria that native scalps were much in demand. All five men were convicted and hanged.

Judge Begbie, the first chief justice of British Columbia, went on to be awarded a knighthood. Sir Matthew is memorialized in statuary and historical markers in Vancouver and on a tombstone in Victoria—not far from that marking the grave of British Columbia's first governor, James Douglas. Begbie is popularly remembered—albeit not by the Tsilhqot'in—as British Columbia's "hanging judge." He was tough, at a time when the colony was crawling with unsavoury frontier types hell-bent on finding gold, running roughshod over everything and everyone who stood between them and their personal El Dorado. Begbie's defenders submit that since murder was a capital offence at the time, the judge was just doing his job when he sent convicted killers to the gallows. In fact, the judge was known to admire native peoples, becoming fluent in the Shuswap and Chilcotin languages, earning the name "Big Chief" and even advocating with Governor Douglas for recognition of aboriginal land rights. Begbie was often lenient towards natives, though in the case of the Chilcotin War, he observed convention by hanging the men convicted of the murders. But he didn't accept conventional wisdom as to their motives. The murders were not, in his judgement, crimes of "plunder or revenge." Rather, he concluded somewhat presciently, the real issue for the Tsilhqot'in was rights and title to their land. For the Tsilhqot'in, as for the Haida, it still is.

The intended road, from the head of Bute Inlet up the Homathko River valley, never did get built. Nor was a proposed railroad ever punched through Tsilhqot'in territory, which remains some of the most inaccessible and unspoiled country in all of British Columbia.

The area remained out of reach to all but the hardiest white settlers for more than a century, and those who survived did so in part because they learned to live in unusual harmony with the local First Nations. The region, with its affecting admixture of cowboys and Indians, was made famous by Paul St. Pierre, one-time federal Member of Parliament, sometime newspaper columnist and author of a number of books. (St. Pierre's novella *Breaking Smith's Quarter Horse*, set in the Chilcotin, was adapted into a feature film starring Glenn Ford and Chief Dan George.) People got around the Chilcotin on horseback more than in cars and trucks, ranchers and natives living a sympathetic blend of coexistence and co-dependency. Logging roads penetrated the plateau in the mid-1970s, however, and by the mid-1980s ranch hand and guide outfitter Mike McDonough was quoted in the *Vancouver Sun* as saying, "The future of the whole Chilcotin country is at stake. The logging will be the end of the Chilcotin, and there will never be another Chilcotin. The whole thing is going to be changed forever and it's never going to recover." McDonough was a member of a coalition formed to oppose plans to log an area about half the size of Vancouver Island. The same weekend that boatloads of Haida warriors were girding for confrontation on Lyell Island, a headline in the *Vancouver Sun* read, "Chilcotin anger stalls logging." A "rare coalition of Indians, trappers, homesteaders, ranchers and hunters," the story said, was standing firm against further logging in the region. Of the six Tsilhqot'in communities that would go on to form the Tsilhqot'in National Government, the Xeni Gwet'in First Nation would emerge over the next quarter century as one of the most resolute advocates for indigenous rights and title. As the Haida had done with Duu Guusd, the Tsilhqot'in People of Xeni, also known as the Nemiah Valley Indian Band, would famously and unilaterally declare the Nemiah Valley to be an aboriginal wilderness preserve. They would go on to protect the valley from industrial logging, in some instances throwing up blockades of logging roads. In 1989, they launched what would become a series of legal actions. These culminated in a title and rights case, the *William* case, that matched the Haida's for the sheer breadth of the claim.

Native protests were becoming almost epidemic in the mid-1980s: aboriginal groups opposed logging on Meares Island and herbicide spraying alongside the Skeena River, fought a railroad expansion plan along the Thompson River, laid claim to the Stein Valley. They were "fighting for rights and land as never before," as one headline put it. The Chilcotin story was on page A1 of the *Vancouver Sun* that fateful October weekend in 1985, while a piece on the threat of a Haida protest on Lyell Island was consigned to page A16. But soon the South Moresby fight would come to dominate the news. By standing up to Frank Beban's contract logging outfit, the Haida were calling into question the entire political and economic system that had allowed Beban onto their lands in the first place. That did not go unnoticed in Vancouver, and a furious attack on the Haida and environmentalists was frothed up each night on BCTV by notoriously acerbic Scots broadcaster Jack Webster—the Tartan Torpedo— whose bully pit often set the news agenda in the province. With his glaringly one-sided support for the loggers, Webster helped make Lyell Island a much bigger story than it otherwise might have been. It was clear that, on Lyell Island, a classic morality play was about to be staged. Eventually, the confrontation would lead to the courts, in the form of *Guujaaw v. Her Majesty*. But first, because the Haida didn't care for Her Majesty's laws, they planned to disobey them.

The Haida got to Sedgwick Bay in their boats, based on Guu-jaaw's helicopter reconnaissance. They quickly built plywood bunkhouses and a cookhouse, then lit a fire in the middle of the log-ging road. T.S. Eliot famously wrote that April is the cruellest month, but he had never been to the northwest coast of British Columbia in October, where it can be cruelly cold, windy and wet all at once. So it was when the Haida set up camp and were confronted by Frank Beban and his crewmen. "You're blocking the highway, you're break-ing the law," the loggers told the Haida. "This is Haida land, and there'll be no more logging," Miles Richardson replied. Guujaaw, his face painted black, drummed. So did Michael Nicoll Yahgulanaas, who painted the faces of other young Haida resisters. "If, any time in a person's life, you wanted to display your colours," he later told a documentary filmmaker, "this was the time to do it." The warriors were excited, bouncing about in the cookhouse, full of banter that concealed their anxiety. "There was a huge sense of risk," Miles Richardson recalls. "When we first went to the blockade on Lyell Island, we didn't know if the logging trucks or logging equipment were going to run us over, whether we were going to get into physical battles defending ourselves." In an interview seven years later on the CBC Radio show *Ideas,* Guujaaw revealed something that had otherwise gone unreported: "We looked at all the different options, including armed confrontation...We knew that we would be beat. We were outgunned. We knew that, and we knew that probably there were a lot of people in government [who] would like nothing better than for us to have made an armed blockade—and just done away with us."

Richardson remembers his own role as being that of the "linear guy" whose job it was to keep everyone organized and focussed. Guujaaw's contribution, he believes, was in "the trust that he had then, and still has, for our culture." That, and his resolve, Richardson says. "Our commitment was tested every day through that battle, and Guujaaw never wavered." For his part, Guujaaw remembers distinctly what the Haida were trying to achieve at Athlii Gwaii, or Lyell Island. "We wanted to make it real clear that our culture is our relationship to the land. That's where our songs come from, that's where our language comes from, and the dances are all about the creatures that we share this land with. And so we brought the songs back to the land to express exactly who we are in relation to the land."

Bringing songs back to the land is, for the Haida, as much an expression of ownership as is building a house or putting up a fence for non-native people. But the Haida didn't just bring songs back to

Athlii Gwaii. The blockade there was a significant new chapter in Haida mythology, and it gave rise to a song that today is a kind of national anthem for Haida Gwaii. An old paddle song adapted for the blockade, it is called simply the Lyell Island song, and at major public events on the islands it is almost always performed, as a seminal expression of who the Haida are and how they connect to their land. That first day on the logging road, while Guujaaw drummed and the Lyell Island song fledged in the damp air, the Haida held cedar boughs and shook wooden rattles as a process server's voice boomed out a roll call of their names, among them "Miles Richardson...Gary Edenshaw, John Doe and Jane Doe and persons unknown, defendants..." While the Haida had been setting up camp and establishing their blockade, company lawyers for Western Forest Products had been presenting their request for an injunction in British Columbia's Supreme Court. Now, armed with a judge's order, the company was determined to remove the protesters from the road. "The island was crawling with RCMP," Richardson remembers. Six officers came to confront the Haida, and two dozen more had been spotted around a corner in the road. "We knew they meant business—so did we." But as the young Haida steeled themselves against inevitable arrest, a helicopter could suddenly be heard. "The sound of helicopters meant a lot of things to us," says Guujaaw. "It could have meant that they had come to challenge our buildings on what they were saying was Crown land, and what we were saying was Haida land. It could have been more media coming to see if they could muster up a story. So when the *elders* came out, it was just like, it was just a little moment for celebration—surprise and celebration."

The elders. On a cold, miserable grey day, they had come—Ethel Jones, Watson Pryce, Ada Yovanovich, Adolphus Mark, then in their sixties and seventies, faces etched with the experiences of a century that had been cruel to their people and their land—stepping unsteadily out of the helicopter and, in their own quiet way, taking charge of the blockade. "Blockades are interesting," writes Ted

Chamberlin in *If This Is Your Land, Where Are Your Stories?* "They function like the threshold of a church, or the beginning of a story; and they need to be acknowledged if proper respect is to be paid to those for whom the place is sacred or appropriate contempt shown to those who are polluting it." In coming to Athlii Gwaii, to the threshold of the blockade that the Haida had constructed, the elders consecrated their protest. Guujaaw had spent his youth learning from the elders, recognizing their authority and, most of all, listening. In turn, as Guujaaw and an increasing number of younger Haida had put protection of the land at the top of the political agenda on Haida Gwaii, the elders had listened—and by coming to the blockade, they were recognizing Guujaaw, Richardson and the other young leaders, and they were validating their stand. Miles Richardson: "They basically told us, we've heard what you have to say. We've been silent about this most of our lives. We've wanted to make this stand, and today"—Richardson fights back tears when he recalls what the elders said that day—"and today, we ask you to respect that." The elders had come to assert their right not just to support the blockade but to become its front line—to take charge of the rituals. The warriors were asked to melt away to the sidelines, to quiet their bravado in favour of the gentle but persuasive voices of the elders.

Film footage from the blockade captures their determination. Ethel Jones says: "This is our land and, you know, we definitely aren't afraid of going to jail. Maybe that'll open our government's eyes. Look at this little old lady sitting in jail. For what? For protecting their land? We've slept long enough."

Ada Yovanovich: "We're here to protect our land, and if that's a crime, I'm willing to go [to jail]...I'm over sixty. It doesn't really matter as long as I have some fancywork to do. No, I don't mind at all."

Adolphus Mark: "Well, I'm here to support my younger generation that's here now. And we have good reason to be here. When you ride around and you see the mountains all gone, all the trees stripped clean, and it's not only for us, but for white man's generation to come, too. What are they going to make money from when you've stripped the islands?" And, in an echo of his ancestors seventy years earlier in front of the McKenna-McBride Commission: "We're protecting *our* island. It's *our* island, before white man come only 200 years ago. And how come the government want to make a claim on it, I want to know if the government made this island, or the good Lord? I'd like an answer to that... Did the government make this island, now they claim it? We're fighting for our rights... The government didn't make this island, no way."

As Guujaaw puts it, "The elders clearly represented our linkage to all our history. These are people who had a lot of living behind them and were not just a radical fringe element going out to raise heck with the government for the sake of doing that." Diane Brown, Ada Yovanovich's daughter, was one of the few young women on the line at Lyell Island, and she remembers the importance of the elders joining the blockade. "They brought dignity to what we were doing. They brought validation, they brought history and they brought the future."

Watson Pryce had hoped that, with elders showing up and getting arrested first, "it might do the trick. But it didn't work right away. Lots of others had to block the road before they could stop it altogether." Over the course of several weeks, seventy-two people were arrested on Lyell Island, Guujaaw, Miles Richardson and Michael Nicoll Yahgulanaas among them. But the elders went first. Ethel Jones was led away. Then Ada Yovanovich, reading from the Bible (2 Timothy 4:7)— "I have fought the good fight, I have finished my course"—and Watson Pryce and Adolphus Mark. As Pryce was to discover, four elders getting arrested—an event broadcast on national television—wasn't enough, so the young warriors got their day, too. Or rather, their days. A ritual was established, something that in the years to follow would happen with increasing frequency in Canada during confrontations between developers and environmentalists, industry and Indians: an early morning, workers on the road, protesters blocking their way, a single process server, RCMP officers, sometimes cameras, sometimes not—and just enough arrests for everyone to leave the scene feeling they've accomplished something. On Lyell Island, for almost one month, the process server was there most mornings, offering up injunction papers that fell to the ground when protesters refused to take them, papers that were then used to fan the protest fire. "Got any more?" someone joked at one point when the fire was dying.

Except that it was no joke getting arrested. Each of the seventy-two was taken from the scene, charged under section 387 of the Canadian Criminal Code, then fingerprinted and processed by the police. In late November, B.C. Supreme Court chief justice Allan McEachern sat in chambers in Prince Rupert, the port and pulp mill town on the B.C. mainland due east from Haida Gwaii. McEachern was the province's modern-day equivalent of Matthew Begbie—a stern enforcer of the law—though as British Columbia's First Nations would find later, when he sat in judgement over a landmark land claims case, McEachern, unlike Begbie, had zero sympathy for native land claims. "These are not criminals before you," Miles Richardson, wrapped in a ceremonial blanket, told the chief justice. He gestured to fourteen Haida people cited for criminal contempt of court. "Oh, I know that. You don't have to persuade me of that, that they're not regular criminals," McEachern said. Nevertheless, he convicted ten of them and promised jail sentences of four to six months. "They have challenged the law directly and that challenge cannot go unanswered," the chief justice said. His somewhat apocalyptic conclusion was that allowing the protesters to break the law and go unpunished would give other people an excuse to break the law as well, "and that would be the end of society and civilization as we know it." The *Vancouver Sun* reported that the Haida and lawyers for the logging companies alike were shocked at the severity of the sentences McEachern threatened. The Haida were not represented by counsel in court, but as their spokesman, Miles Richardson was allowed to make a closing statement on their behalf—in which, of course, he raised the land question. To which, of course, the chief justice responded: "Those issues are not before me. I wish they were, but they are not." Those issues did come before McEachern soon after, when in 1987 the Gitksan and Wet'suwet'en First Nations in the B.C. interior brought a land claims case before him, a trial that spanned four years and resulted in the chief justice declaring that aboriginal rights had been erased by colonial legislation. The so-called *Delgamuukw* case, named after a hereditary chief, was infamous too for McEachern's extraordinary paraphrase of Thomas Hobbes to describe pre-colonial native life in British Columbia as "nasty, brutish and short." Some thought that was an apt description of the chief justice himself.

As for the Lyell Island convicts, none of them ended up doing time. Although McEachern had waxed anxious about the end of civilization if they didn't go to jail, others worried about what would happen if they did. The Anglican Church tried to intervene on their behalf. The United Church rallied on the Haida side. Clearly, conservationists everywhere were parties to their cause. More unexpected, and perhaps more important, was the support of the B.C. Federation of Labour, which at its annual convention in November 1985 denounced the provincial government for its "cowardly use of the courts and police in a game of divide and conquer." What was remarkable about organized labour's support for the Haida was that the B.C. Fed included among its members the loggers' own union, the International Woodworkers of America, whose thunderous vice-president Jack Munro told delegates, "It wasn't the Indians who stopped this logging, it was the government...They are directly responsible for this mess." The Fishermen's Union president, Jack Nichol, said, "We as British Columbians ought to be glad that somebody has the guts to defy the law and stand up and say we're not going to allow the rape of our forests any more." A B.C. Government Employees Union delegate, Delphine Trudel, who is Haida, told the convention, "We will not become the victims of cultural genocide. We are loggers, fishermen, office workers and the unemployed. We are a nation forced into civil disobedience to protect the only future we have." At the end of the convention, the federation passed a resolution accusing the government of "creating division between natives and natural resource workers and using that... to cover up their total social and economic mismanagement of this province." On the day after McEachern convicted the first ten Haida protesters of criminal contempt of court, a poll was published that said three out of five British Columbians wanted the provincial government to negotiate native land claims. The Haida warned then premier Bill Bennett that he could throw them all in jail if he wanted, since that would just provoke more protesters to come. Brian Mulroney promised that Ottawa would do its utmost to resolve the "troubling situation" on Canada's westernmost shore.

The Haida didn't have a lot of data then, as they do now, but they were right to believe that the logging industry was gutting Haida Gwaii. It turns out that 1985 was the year when the rate of logging on the islands hit its all-time peak—almost 2.7 million cubic metres that year alone. It was an intolerable assault on the land, and for the Haida there was only one solution. "All we needed them to do was stop," Guujaaw recalls. "That's all we asked of them."

IN DAVID SUZUKI'S second *The Nature of Things* documentary on Haida Gwaii, in 1986, Guujaaw was prominently featured, and he was credited with providing the music for the film. The final agreement to protect South Moresby was still more than a year of horse-trading away, and it was far from a sure thing. Suzuki was determined to add his voice to the clamour to finalize a deal. "Over thousands of years, this remote location has harboured a showcase of evolution," he told viewers. Having escaped glaciation more than 15,000 years ago, it was "an oasis of life," complete with "disjunct species" that are found but rarely, in places like the Himalayas, Spain and Scotland. On and on the good doctor went, waxing lyrical about tufted puffins and sea lions. Guujaaw can be heard in the film before he is seen, though what at first sounds like a drumbeat turns out to be an adze, as the camera finds him chopping rhythmically on a cedar log that is taking the shape of a canoe.

Headband firmly in place, Guujaaw repeated what he had said in Suzuki's first documentary—that without the land, there is no Haida culture and therefore no Haida people. But this time, he went a little deeper. "You have to look right into the Haida mythology, and in doing so it's hard to differentiate between human beings and animals, and the natural and the supernatural things. And that comes from a long-standing relationship with the land, and religion that tells us of respect for those things, and that we are merely a part of those things." The film then leaves Guujaaw's carving shed to find him again, draped in a grey-and-white blanket, jeans rolled up at the cuffs, wheeling around in a clearing in the forest, a large raven mask atop his head. "The raven, giver of life," narrates Suzuki. It is an eerie scene, and to viewers in Calgary or Toronto or Halifax or even in Australia, where Suzuki's films have found surprising resonance and Suzuki himself almost rock-star fame, it must have seemed somewhat surreal to see these goings-on in a prime-time television show about safe, certain, Commonwealth Canada. "Oral cultures understand the world in magical rather than scientific terms," writes Ted Chamberlin. Guujaaw, oracle of a decidedly oral culture, was inviting people to look into Haida mythology and religion—and to consider the supernatural, the magic, rather than to judge the place and its people only on the basis of science—especially a science as dismally imperfect as economics.

"The Haida account of the world begins with the Raven story," says linguist John Enrico, a story "which spreads over the age of supernatural beings and the early part of the human age."

ʔaaniis.uu tangaa ragingang
ʔwan suuga. 'll cidgwaangaas
xuyaaʔaa. tllgu q'aawgyaa
hllngaaygi 'laa qyaangaas.
qawdi.uu gwaay rud gwaa nang
qadlaa q'ayrudyaas 'laagu
q'aawgaay ran 'laa rá 'laa cidaas.
ʔá tl'l sraana qidaads ʔyaahl-
gaagaas riinuus gangaang
'laagu gud gwii xiihlt'ahliyaagaas.
ga sraanarwaa raxaas 'laa
t'isda q'a sq'agilaangaas, tll
gwii xan, hahl gwiiʔad wah
gwiʔaa. radagaas gyaan.uuʔasing
raalgaagaang ʔwan suuga.

This island was nothing but saltwater, they say. Raven flew around. He looked for a place to land in the water. By and by, he flew to a reef [K'IL, or Flatrock Island] lying to the south end of the island, to sit on it. But the great mass of supernatural beings had their necks resting on one another on it, like sea cucumbers. The weak supernatural beings floated out from it sleeping, every which way, this way and that way. It was both light and dark, they say.

Such is Enrico's translation of the beginning of the origin myth of the Haida, as told to anthropologist John R. Swanton by John Sky and published in a book entitled *Skidegate Haida Myths and Histories*. Bill Reid and poet and language scholar Robert Bringhurst popularized the Raven's role in bringing the world into being with their story *The Raven Steals the Light*. "The Raven snapped up the light in his jaws, thrust his great wings downward and shot through the smoke hole of the house into the huge darkness of the world. That world was at once transformed. Mountains and valleys were darkly silhouetted, the river sparkled with broken reflections, and everywhere life began to stir." Just as important a figure was Sea Foam Woman, who gave birth to several Raven lineages. Meanwhile, Eagle lineages traced to mainland British Columbia. As for the supernatural realm, Enrico reports that there were "several sub-realms of spirit beings, those of the sea, the forest and the sky...Most spirits of the sea and forest had earthly forms as sea creatures and forest creatures." There was also a pre-eminent spirit of the atmosphere. "The usual story metaphor for the passage of one of the spirit/animal beings from spirit to earthly realm is the putting on of its skin…humans commonly acquired these transforming skins in stories, were able to 'put them on' and thereby they were transformed into the earthly animals (birds, fish) in question." So it was that Guujaaw danced as a Raven on national television, relaying his belief in an origin that had nothing to do with the God worshipped by colonizers of the Skidegate or Old Massett missions but was inextricably bound to creatures below the water, on the land and in the sky.

In the sky one day in 2004, on a plane from Sandspit to Vancouver, Guujaaw declaims effortlessly about Haida history "lining up" less with Christianity, as in the Bible, and more with the teachings of the Essenes, a mysterious brotherhood—or tribe—that lived on the shores of Palestine's Dead Sea and Egypt's Lake Mareotis for two to three centuries before the Christian era, and perhaps a century during it. The Bible, Guujaaw says, has been "tampered with—there's not much knowledge left in it, not much wisdom to be gleaned from it. But you go to those older books, and there's a lot of good things. The old wisdom is way better, way more prophetic." According to Essenes scholar Edmond Bordeaux Szekely, "The Essenes lived on the shores of lakes and rivers, away from cities and towns, and practiced a communal way of life, sharing equally in everything." They lived according to what was known as the Law, which, as Guujaaw interprets it, "created life and thought." How does the belief system of the Essenes align with Haida cosmology? "Well, it relates to our emergence from the sea. Go to Egypt, or to Peru, one of their gods is a sea foam woman. The mother of Aphrodite and Venus—arguably the same, eh? It was actually Sea Foam Woman. One of the gods got his cock cut off and thrown in the foam, and maybe there was some cum there…" At this point, a flight attendant says something loud over the plane's PA system, and the thread is lost.

When the announcement is finished, Guujaaw continues. "Take human beings and take their equal weight in sea water, and break it down into how much copper and how much other stuff and it's almost one-for-one, just put together differently. Anyway, there are some pretty big connections out there." There is a strong connection between the beliefs of the Essenes, considered by some historians to be authors of the Dead Sea scrolls, and those of Zoroaster, the Brahmins, the yoga systems of India and even Buddha. In a review posted to amazon.com on July 15, 2001, written by "Guujaaw (Skidegate: Haida Nation)," *The Gospel of the Essenes* is given five stars, alongside which Guujaaw has written: "If you knoweth these things you knoweth enough. This book gives us back the wisdom that was taken from us in the interests of priestcraft. The logic and science of the Essenes should be put in the hands of every preacher, rabbi, politician, teacher and human being who has been affected by western civilization and organized religion." Michael Nicoll Yahgulanaas talks of a "Haida blood connection to the Jewish Peoples," and it could be said that the Haida's concern for the land bears a strong resemblance to the Jewish concept of *tikkun olam,* or "repair of the world."

In the foreword to *Haida Gwaii: Human History and Environment from the Time of Loon to the Time of the Iron People,* a book on the archaeology of the islands, Guujaaw expands on the Haida origin myth and its parallels with those of other ancient tribes. He goes on to mention a song about a grizzly bear that came to kill people, even though there are no grizzly bears on Haida Gwaii. There was also a story of a young hero who slew a mountain lion, another species not present on the islands. "This was all myth, of course," he writes, "comparable to fairytales put together to make some sense of things— at least until a few years ago." Now, Guujaaw notes in his foreword, science has concluded that perhaps there were grizzly bears on Haida Gwaii, and the ice age came to an end more abruptly than previously thought. "We can now look beneath the waters at the sea floor and appreciate the effects of the great meltwaters and the havoc unleashed upon our people as the lands were swallowed by the sea. We all know that in addition to floods, tsunamis had been, and will continue to be, a reality of coastal life. It isn't science, however, but the Tibetans who also remember the time when they lived in twilight. As we have known Sguhlgu Jaad (Sea Foam Woman), the Egyptians and people of Peru know of a 'god' called 'Seafoam' in their own languages. The Hopi talk about their people coming out of the earth; we told them it was Nangkilstlas who stomped his feet to call the different tribes from the Earth.

"Science is coming of age, and while there is a convergence and a reconciliation of science with our histories, scientists may have to take our word on certain facts. It was because Raven fooled around with his uncle's wife that Gaahlins Kun (his uncle) spun his hat and caused the water to rise, accounting for one of the floods. Scientists are still trying to figure out how the sun and the moon got up there, and while they have theories, give them time and they will come back to us. And we can tell them, because it was told."

"The grammar of aboriginal hopes and fears," writes Ted Chamberlin, "the logic that informs their stories and songs, is a spiritual grammar; it's not a social or economic or political or even a cultural one. It is grounded in a knowledge and belief in something beyond easy understanding, expressed in the stories and songs as well as the dances and paintings that speak about the spirits. And it pushes back against both the pressure of reality and the rhetoric of other people's imaginations. It is a blockade too, saying no to other ways of being in the world." Guujaaw's practice of Haida culture, his use of a spiritual grammar through constant references to the land, and the supernatural, is a constant manifestation of resistance. "Today, mythological thinking has fallen into disrepute; we often dismiss it as irrational and self-indulgent," writes religion scholar Karen Armstrong. Yet for people whose beliefs predate the scientific era, Armstong continues, "the 'gods' were rarely regarded as supernatural beings with discrete personalities, living a totally separate metaphysical existence. Mythology was not about theology, in the modern sense, but about human experience. People thought that gods, humans, animals and nature were inextricably bound up together, subject to the same laws, and composed of the same divine substance... The very existence of the gods was inseparable from that of a storm, a sea, a river, or from those powerful human emotions— love, rage, or sexual passion—that seemed momentarily to lift men and women onto a different plane of existence so that they saw the world with new eyes."

Guujaaw, as he oscillates between what is expected of him as a political negotiator—to be linear of thought and deed—and his life as a teller and maker of Haida mythology, can leave people puzzled, frustrated or intimidated. In meetings, he can be as rational, detail-oriented and argumentative as the next person, but then quickly slip into hortatory and sometimes disjointed idiomatic speech. Bureau-crats stop taking notes. Guujaaw, for his part, never uses them. He draws on a "spiritual grammar," as Chamberlin calls it, that confuses some people and can unsettle them.

"People like to get scared of the word 'spirituality,'" says Diane Brown. "It conjures up some kind of fear—that people who are spiritual aren't right in the head or whatever." Guujaaw's spirituality, according to Michael Nicoll Yahgulanaas, is also evident in the way he approaches conflict. "Guujaaw sees no advantage in insulting our opponents, in goading them on. He approaches people and situations with gentle and genuine interest. For a good heathen, he would make a great Buddhist." Of course, this offers a steep discount on at least two incidents when Guujaaw went beyond good-natured arm wres-tling, or Buddhist equanimity, or Christian forgiveness, and actually punched a couple of people who took him on over South Moresby. But that was in his formative years, before he learned to turn the other cheek.

Diane Brown grew up around Guujaaw when he spent time down in Skidegate, though she's a few years older. Her adoptive mother and his grandmother were sisters, daughters of Susan Williams. In her early sixties now, Brown is the youngest Haida person to be totally fluent in the language, which she teaches. She remembers a childhood much like Guujaaw's. "In the summer, you're on the beach all day, every day, and towards the fall you start moving into the forest. It was a huge thing to chase cows," she recalls with a laugh. "I spent a lot of time going down south in March to Burnaby Narrows to gather food—taken out of school—stay there for a long time and come back in May, just in time to throw everything off and go to Copper Bay for spring fish. Then I'd come in and go to school the last week or something to pick up the bad report card. A lot of families were like that." Brown, whose Haida name is Gwaganad, is a powerful figure in Skidegate. She travels across indigenous time and space in a way that few do. She goes to sun dances and to traditional elders' circles, and she has entrée into traditional teachings and rituals that don't get written about in books and are seldom, if ever, shared with non-native people. She is quick to state that she is not a medicine woman—"not yet, I don't know enough"—but she does "do" four medicines, traditional remedies that help people battle cancer, HIV, hepatitis C and general malaise. Guujaaw, she says, does a couple of medicines himself. Guujaaw is referred to as a "medical practitioner" in his online biography, and "making medicine" is something he does even as he makes mischief with the bureaucrats and their political masters. But the medical practitioner doesn't come with any letters after his name, he hangs out no shingle and he doesn't send patients to the pharmacy. The medicines he uses come from the only laboratory he knows—the land.

David Suzuki credits Guujaaw with giving his father, Carr Suzuki, enormous relief when he was suffering from cancer. "When he got liver cancer, he was actually yellow with the effects of it," Suzuki recalls. "The surgeon said, 'Go home and die,' and gave my dad three to four weeks to live." It was 1992, and Suzuki took his father to Quadra Island, where he prepared to face death, unafraid. "Guujaaw heard he had liver cancer and sent down two bottles of medicine and instructions for how to use it." That first night in the cabin on Quadra, more out of respect for Guujaaw than any real belief it would do anything, Carr Suzuki took the medicine. In the morning, he reported that the pain had gone away, and it never came back. Eventually he died of a related ailment, but "he got two and a half high-quality years that Guujaaw gave him," Suzuki recalls. Guujaaw did the same thing for Suzuki's sister a few years later. The doctors, Suzuki said, were shocked. Guujaaw's only concern was that the identity of the plants remain a secret; he was terrified of a potential gold rush on medicinal plants that could soon be made extinct. Diane Brown, citing the frenzied cutting of yew wood before a synthetic version of taxol was created, concurs. In any event, she says, "people could kill themselves" if they don't know how to use plants properly. "Very powerful stuff. It'll kill you if you take it wrong."

AROUND THE SAME time that the Haida were blockading Lyell Island, Guujaaw found time to build a scale model for a Bill Reid–designed canoe, and at about the same time Guujaaw designed a longhouse in the Haida style to be constructed at Windy Bay. The *Loo Taas,* or Wave Eater, was one of Bill Reid and Guujaaw's more remarkable achievements, a fifteen-metre-long cedar canoe that has achieved talismanic status among admirers of Haida art and culture. The Windy Bay longhouse, built on the site of a traditional village, was a deliberate move by the Haida to establish a presence on the land they were trying to protect. (Predictably, the B.C. government labelled it a "trespass cabin.") But the building of the *Loo Taas* had a much greater effect on the public imagination. "For the local and national press, every stage of the *Loo Taas's* making was a newsworthy item," writes Maria Tippett. The attention was due in large part to the fact that the canoe was commissioned as part of Vancouver's impending world's fair, Expo 86, whose theme was transportation and communication. A Haida canoe built by master artist Bill Reid was a highly anticipated feature of the fair and, as with most things Reid touched, it was controversial. There was trouble finding a suitable log, although a 750-year-old cedar on Haida Gwaii was eventually felled and the log brought to Skidegate. There was trouble getting funding, but the Hong Kong Bank of Canada eventually stepped in. Then there was the carving itself. According to Maria Tippett, "After work commenced, there was trouble with Reid's assistant, Gary Edenshaw. He was unhappy, as he had been during carving of *Raven,* because Reid was employing non-natives to help him carve the canoe. Edenshaw also wanted to carve intuitively, in the traditional Haida manner, rather than follow Reid's carefully worked-out calculations. Unable to carve in this way, Edenshaw left the project in a huff. Reid found himself in the news once again." The canoe itself was a remarkable creation, so much so that more than two decades later it would be rhapsodized in *Canadian Geographic* as "arguably the most beautiful vessel ever devised by a sea-going people." After the *Loo Taas* was completed, Guujaaw's abilities as a canoe carver were in demand among other coastal peoples. The Heiltsuk Nation on the central coast was preparing for a huge canoe festival and needed advice on building canoes the old way. Guujaaw visited Bella Bella, where he was billeted by a young schoolteacher, Marcie Watkins. He would later return the favour, he and Jenny having separated, and Guujaaw and Marcie have been together ever since.

Expo 86 was shaping up as an enormous opportunity for Canada and British Columbia to tout their virtues, but there was risk as well. In December 1985, a powerful coalition of American conservation groups met with Canada's ambassador to the United States, Allan Gotlieb, to inform him that South Moresby was an international conservation priority—so much so that Canada risked getting a black eye at the world's fair. Paul Pritchard, president of the National Parks and Conservation Association, told reporters, "The coalition is urging visitors to see both sides of B.C. if they visit Expo 86... [including] the unparalleled destruction of South Moresby." In a wonderfully ironic expression of "transportation and communication," the wilderness campaign took to the rails on March 5, 1986, in St. John's, Newfoundland, when the Save South Moresby Caravan began its 7,500-kilometre sojourn across Canada. A brainchild of Thom Henley's, the whistle-stop tour was timed to arrive in Vancouver before a pivotal B.C. government report on South Moresby was due to be released. The trip took ten days, with overnight stops in Halifax, Montreal, Toronto and Winnipeg. In Ottawa, federal environment minister Tom McMillan met the train to say he favoured saving "as much of South Moresby as possible, including Lyell Island." In Toronto, the train was met by Guujaaw, drumming loudly in Union Station as he and other Althii Gwaii blockade veterans—including elders Ada Yovanovich, Ethel Jones and Watson Pryce—joined the caravan for the rest of the trip. That night, at Toronto's St. Paul's Cathedral, almost 2,000 people showed up to hear one of Canada's foremost popular historians, Pierre Berton, describe clear-cut logging on Lyell Island as "an act of vandalism, a national disgrace." Elizabeth May, at the time an Ottawa-based environmental lawyer, recalls, "The high point of the evening was the arrival of the Haida elders. Wearing the traditional black and red flannel of the Haida, Ada, Ethel, Watson and Grace [Ethel's sister] walked slowly to the altar. Most of the people in the church had seen them on the evening news being led away to police vans. Seeing them in the flesh, their dignity and stoicism evident, caused an unexpected wave of emotion. The entire audience spontaneously rose to its feet. Much to their amusement, the elders were introduced as 'criminals' to cheers and prolonged applause."

The caravan rolled west, along the way hearing that British Columbia's Wilderness Advisory Committee had proposed a compromise that would save much of South Moresby, but not all of it, and not much of Lyell Island. No one was in a mood to compromise, emboldened as they were with 27,000 new signatures on a petition to save South Moresby and a huge rally to look forward to at the Pacific Central railroad terminus in Vancouver. The train crossed the Rockies into British Columbia. "As the train rolled on through the night," May writes, "Guujaaw kept a group of passengers awake teaching them the song he had sung on the logging road at Lyell." More than 2,000 people were on hand to greet the caravaners, and together they marched noisily through the city to a rally at the Canada Place pavilion, built especially for Expo 86.

Amid the hubbub about Expo and the politicking about South Moresby, a documentary film released in 1986 was something of an oasis, a calm reminder of what the Haida were about, not just what they were fighting for. *Islands of the People,* a British Broadcasting Corporation production, documents Guujaaw's work and travels on Haida Gwaii. There is only a passing reference to the Lyell Island controversy. Instead, the film focusses on Guujaaw and his second-born son, Jaalen, the old master at the oars of his tiny bobbing boat, two peas in a small and unsteady-looking pod. They hook a squid together, and on land, Guujaaw shows his son how to harvest the roots of a yellow water lily, how to skin a deer, how to net a salmon and tend to the smokehouse. The film is narrated by May Russ, a Haida woman who went on to run the Haida Tribal Society (since renamed the Secretariat of the Haida Nation). In the film, Russ says, "It was important for Haidas to live life to the full, so that when you grow old you could sit and tell your stories and the children would stay and listen because it's interesting. And if you didn't have a story to tell by then, then you didn't have a place. Without knowledge to share, you're not of much use to anybody." The film shows Guujaaw rowing Jaalen into the bay at Ninstints, a remarkable old village site at Skung Gwaay near the southernmost tip of Haida Gwaii. There stands the largest collection of totem poles in their original location in North America, a collection so important that Skung Gwaay is listed as a UNESCO World Heritage Site. Guujaaw walks with Jaalen among the poles, a father sharing knowledge of the land just as his father and his Uncle Percy had done with him. It is very much a picture of a man in full.

Despite all the positive media, the international coalitions formed to press for the protection of South Moresby and the desire of thousands of Canadians to see the area preserved, the B.C. government was having none of it. In the summer of 1986, it approved new logging plans on Lyell Island. In frustration, nine Haida—including Miles Richardson and Guujaaw—sent a telegram to Prime Minister Mulroney saying they were renouncing their Canadian citizenship. "The Haida were never given the opportunity to voluntarily become Canadian citizens," Richardson told the press. "We had it imposed on us." To the prime minister, he wrote: "As Canadians, your courts ruled that we have no right to protect our land." (Three years later the Haida issued their own passports, and Guujaaw tried to use his on a trip to Hungary. "We travelled with Bill Reid to Budapest," recalls Diane Brown. "We were there at the invitation of the president of Hungary. And there Guujaaw is, held up at the airport in Budapest, insisting that they stamp his Haida passport and they won't. We're all checked into our hotels and no sign of Guujaaw. I'm getting kinda worried. It was something like five hours before he pulled out the Canadian one." It is probably safe to say that Guujaaw's stubborn assertion of Haida sovereignty was lost on the immigration officials at Ferihegy Airport, but the president reportedly liked his singing and drumming.)

From around the world, wilderness advocates gathered in Ottawa in June 1986 for a Fate of the Earth conference. The capital's Congress Centre was packed to capacity, recalls Elizabeth May, and the lineup of speakers included actress Margot Kidder, folk singer Pete Seeger, Ottawa mayor Marion Dewar and Nobel Prize winner and antiwar activist George Wald. "But for all the celebrities and fanfare, for all the movie-star glitter, Guujaaw stole the show," May writes. "When Guujaaw rose to speak, without warning, he opened with a long, compelling war song in Haida. He sang a cappella, for he was even without his drum. Some quick-witted lighting technician instantly killed the house lights and put a baby spotlight on the long-haired Haida. When the song was over, he had the audience in the palm of his hand. He spoke of the history of the Haida Nation when his people roamed the seas and were masters of the coast, when food was plentiful within the waters of Gwaii Haanas. He told of the deaths of thousands of Haida, felled by white men's diseases. He talked of the Haida's long search to regain their culture and traditions. 'We're trying to rebuild our numbers,' he told the transfixed crowd. 'Us young fellas do all we can.' And then he laughed, and hundreds of people roared with him. He went on to describe the fight for Lyell Island, and he won over the whole conference to the cause."

But still the chainsaws bit into the forests of Lyell Island. In the fall, another blockade took place, one that was little noticed other than on the islands. The federal and provincial governments agreed to fast-track negotiations for a federal park, but on the ground, the only thing that seemed to be going fast was the logging. The Haida had once threatened that no matter how many people got arrested, more would follow, and over the winter plans were laid for another major blockade in the spring of 1987. As another flotilla of protesters headed south from Skidegate to Lyell Island, the B.C. government unexpectedly announced a moratorium on issuing new permits to log on Lyell, though existing permits meant there were still three or four months of harvesting on the books. Guujaaw flew down to Vancouver to speak at a sold-out public meeting organized by the Western Canada Wilderness Committee. He opened with drumming and a song. "That was a Haida war song," Guujaaw told the crowd. "We are at war to protect our lands."

And then they won.

On July 7, 1987, nearly thirteen years after the battle lines had been drawn, Canada and British Columbia announced that they had struck a deal to establish a national park that would take in 138 islands, including Lyell Island, and embrace the full 147,000 hectares below the Tangil

Peninsula line that Guuj and Huck had drawn on the kitchen table in Tlell the night they met. "Moresby park deal reached; cost and details under wraps," ran the front-page headline in the *Vancouver Sun*. The cost turned out to be $138 million, which Canada paid to British Columbia to remove the land from the province's predatory maw.

On the day of the announcement, Guujaaw and Huck were in the *Loo Taas*. The magnificent canoe had appeared as planned at Expo 86, where it was positioned in front of the Royal Yacht during the opening ceremonies. By the summer of 1987, the Skidegate Band Council had wrested the canoe away from the bank that commissioned it, and the council and Bill Reid had asked Huck to work on an expedition to return the canoe to Skidegate—not on a barge, which was how it had been transported to Vancouver for the world's fair, but under Haida power. So it was that as a prime minister, a premier and their legions of bureaucrats worked the phones between Ottawa and Victoria to arrive at a price for South Moresby, as loggers direly predicted the end of logging altogether, as conservationists worked the corks out of champagne bottles and as journalists scribbled and scribed through another day's news cycle, the two men who had started it all, Guujaaw and Thom Henley, were among a crew of Haida nearing the end of an exhausting 900-kilometre paddle home in a cedar canoe.

In her book *Paradise Won,* Elizabeth May says Guuj and Huck heard the news that South Moresby was saved at a stopover in Hartley Bay, a tiny Gitga'at village on the mainland. Henley isn't too sure. "I can't recall where we actually got word that an agreement had been reached," he writes. "Elizabeth May may well be correct that the decision was made by the time we reached Hartley Bay. There had been so many false promises over the years that Guujaaw and I probably didn't really believe it anyway." Huck does remember that when the *Loo Taas* left Vancouver, "things were looking quite desperate for South Moresby...Miles Richardson said at the launch site on False Creek that the expedition would terminate on Lyell Island, where we would all face arrest at the logging blockade. It was a dramatic moment, and given the high media coverage of this historic canoe journey, it seemed to really get the politicians scrambling to come up with some sort of resolution during our journey. The *Loo Taas* expedition had taken on a life of its own for us. The paddlers were hearing drum songs on the waves and practising new dance moves on the beaches where we camped. The expedition was such a powerful personal journey for all of us that the Moresby issue became secondary to it."

But somewhere near the end of the journey—whether in Hartley Bay or not—word reached the paddlers that the bite of each paddle-stroke was taking them closer to a celebration at home, not to another protest. "We actually arrived two days too soon on Haida Gwaii," Henley recalls, "and had to hide out in a cove on Moresby Island so we could arrive in Skidegate as scheduled for the welcome feast. I was put ashore from the support vessel, along with the film crew, to photo document the arrival. Guujaaw was in the canoe drumming and leading the singing, with Bill Reid on the bow." As the crew bore down on a joyous crowd on Second Beach in Skidegate, another song was brought back to the land.

"The Skidegate feast that night was the most powerful moment I ever experienced on Haida Gwaii," says Henley. "Of course there was absolute elation at South Moresby being saved, and the cake cutting with the federal environment minister was cute, but the real highlight was having the paddlers sing the song that came to them on the waves and they put to dance. The entire hall was on its feet cheering. Elders were weeping. Haida culture was fully in the moment, no longer grasping for memories or remnants of a fragmented culture from the past. 'The land still speaks to our youth,' I heard an elder say. That night was far more significant than the signing of the South Moresby agreement. It marked the rebirth of a nation."

EIGHT

PUSHING BACK

IN THE LATE 1950s, Bill Reid began using a technique known to the art world as repoussé. *Repoussé* is a French word meaning "to push back." In silver, gold and copper, this occurs with the formation of a negative image made by hammering out a design on a sheet of precious metal, imbedding it with pitch, reversing the piece, scraping off the pitch and then hammering out the contours to give a naturally rippled texture to the design.

In the Museum of Anthropology in Vancouver, it is possible to find dozens of examples of Bill Reid's mastery of repoussé. So too in the Haida Heritage Centre at Ḵaay Llnagaay, in Skidegate. A short drive away, in the offices of the Council of the Haida Nation, there are many more examples of repoussé, though in this case the artist is not Bill Reid, but Guujaaw, and his material is not silver, gold or copper, but paper. At the CHN offices, filing cabinets bulge with well-wrought examples of the Haida pushing back against governments, industry, developers and a range of other interests bent on eroding the Haida's hold on their land. The correspondence comprises a clear evidentiary trail through the Haida's claim to their rights and their title. It is an extraordinary body of work, much of it under two signatures—Miles Richardson and Guujaaw. But long before he was writing under the authority of the Council of the Haida Nation,

Guujaaw was writing under his own authority as a Haida hunter and gatherer.

In an eloquent letter to the Skidegate Band Council in 1978, written on behalf of the Islands Protection Society, Guujaaw warned that the Haida could not afford to remain silent about South Moresby, since "Rayonier appears to be winning…Blasting can already be heard from Hot Springs and Tanu, and the papers are shuffling in Victoria and New York." The letter was copied to all Skidegate households, to the Old Massett council and to "other key tribespeople." There was the issue of Riley Creek, which had been logged to oblivion, causing landslides and the destruction of salmon habitat. Constant prodding of federal fisheries officials had resulted in the arrest of fifteen loggers, "whisked out of the woods and into jail" by the RCMP, according to the *Province,* a short-lived reversal of fortune for the forest industry that briefly caught the attention of Prime Minister Pierre Trudeau. After the International Woodworkers of America threatened to shut down the entire logging industry in British Columbia if the loggers weren't released, fisheries officials caved in to pressure to drop their charges, and timber extraction once again took priority over salmon.

Guujaaw lived in Vancouver for a time while he and Reid were working on *The Raven and the First Men,* and he wrote a series of letters in late 1979 from his address on the city's West Side. The Haida had earlier that year lost the legal action launched by Guujaaw and Chief Tanu opposing the renewal of Tree Farm Licence 24, but one positive result of that action was that Guujaaw was given standing by the court to seek access to information relating to the authorization of the licence. This unheard-of scrutiny by a mere citizen into the mechanics of the government's relationship with the forestry industry was perhaps a greater victory than blocking the licence renewal would have been. Guujaaw wasted no time in pressing home this new advantage.

On the evidence of those early letters, it is fair to say that Guujaaw was not a skilled writer or typist, and he couldn't spell to save himself. But he had the help of lawyer Garth Evans and the Wilderness

Committee's Paul George, so that by the time the letters left 3705 West Sixth Avenue they were polished and demanding. To Forests Minister Tom Waterland: a request for all information regarding mammals, migratory birds and fish resources that the forest service intended to use in developing its plans, along with requests for independent studies on soils and slope stability, guidelines to improve Rayonier's forest practices, a formula for determining the rate of cut and so on. "Mr. Minister, we would rather work with you than against you, but so far it seems that everything has been against us...Chief Nathan Young and myself have strong ancestral and emotional ties to South Moresby and our interests will not terminate." Guujaaw ends by requesting a face-to-face meeting with the minister, signing his letter "humbly and sincerely, Gary Edenshaw." A few days later, a flurry of letters— to the fish and wildlife branch, to recreation and conservation, to federal fisheries, to Rayonier itself and soon another letter to the forests minister. The minister rebuffed Guujaaw's request for a meeting, pushing him down the chain of command to the chief forester. The chief forester, in response to a specific question from Guujaaw about whether any constraints would be placed on Rayonier to protect recreation and wildlife, responded with bureaucratic opaqueness: "While the allowable annual cut determination does not afford protection for those purposes in an 'area' sense, it does attempt to make allowance for the anticipated effects of such constraints." Oh, and in future, Mr. Edenshaw shouldn't bother the chief forester, but should communicate with the regional manager instead. Mr. Edenshaw, of course, persisted in his petitioning of ministers and minions alike.

By the time the *Loo Taas* made landfall in Skidegate in 1987, Guujaaw had about a decade of letter writing under his belt and had witnessed much dissembling and outright dishonesty by elected and appointed officials. If Guujaaw had learned not to trust political types, he had come by that knowledge honestly. In fact, many Haida were brought up being told white people of any stripe couldn't be trusted. "My mother was suspicious of everybody white," says Diane Brown. "I didn't get immunized until after she died. She hid me as soon as she saw the nurses. They had a navy uniform and a black bag, and we'd pile upstairs to hide and she would answer the door. She understood English but she never spoke it, she'd just pretend not to understand a word. She said the stuff they'd put in you, it would probably kill you, because that was everyone's goal, to get rid of us." Thom Henley remembers a hike on the west coast of Haida Gwaii with Guujaaw. "He and I were doing it alone, and then we came to a creek. We were both really thirsty, and I just bent to drink and he went way, way up river. And I said, 'Guuj, where are you?' And he said, 'Drinking up here. My grandpappy told me never drink downstream from a white man.'" Henley also remembers one time when Bristol Foster visited the islands. Foster was director of ecological reserves for the provincial government, and the recipient of at least one of Guujaaw's letters about TFL 24. Foster was a great advocate for conservation in an administration that didn't much like them, but he was untested at the time on Haida Gwaii. He was seeking to land a boat when Guujaaw threw rocks in front of him. "It was kind of a joke," Henley says. "'Go away, go away, get off our land,' but it's a kind of Haida-style thing, too. Haidas do like to test people. What they want to see is a warrior response... they want to see the gutsy response."

A story, possibly apocryphal, that has made the rounds on Haida Gwaii over the years suggests that Guujaaw refused a white man's hand from about the earliest time his hand was big enough to shake one. Governor General Vincent Massey was on a ten-day tour of Western Canada in July 1956, which would make Guujaaw three years old. Massey's first stop was the Queen Charlotte Islands. According to a March 2002 account in the *Vancouver Sun*, "When about 100 school children greeted the governor-general on the dock at Queen Charlotte City to sing *O Canada*, the young Guujaaw...allegedly approached Massey and told him he was on Haida land. Guujaaw isn't sure that's what he really did. But he does admit he gave Massey a cold reception. 'Aw, I think it might be a bunch of bull. All I know is that I didn't shake his hand. I refused to,' the Haida leader says now." (Relations improved between Rideau Hall and the Haida in the years since Massey was the Queen's representative in Canada. In 2002, Governor General Adrienne Clarkson camped out at Daalung Stl'ang—she vows never to camp again because of the discomfort she suffered there—and the vice-regal Christmas card that year featured a photograph of Her Excellency, her husband, John Ralston Saul, and Guujaaw, sitting on a log at Lepas Bay.)

A vein of resistance, of sheer stubbornness and mischief-making, goes way back among the Haida, and it is made perfectly manifest in Guujaaw. In 1990, he was at the centre of another dispute on Haida Gwaii, this time concerning fishing. He had never been afraid to stand up for Haida rights to fish—he'd been arrested in 1986 and jailed two days for catching twenty-nine salmon from the Yakoun River without a licence. (Commercial fishermen took 750,000 salmon from the same source that year.) "I told the judge, 'This has nothing to do with con- servation, this is subjection,'" he said to the *Globe and Mail*. "It was natural for me to be [at the river]. You don't bring the sea lion into court for eating salmon. Why has the sea lion got more rights than me?" The Haida, he said, wanted to be freed from government rules limiting their traditional rights to fish. "Some of these guys spend all of their time thinking about nothing but licences. I haven't got a licence and I'm not ever going to get one. Not ever." Early in 1990, about twenty Haida headed to Langara Island in the far northwestern corner of Haida Gwaii to confront a festering issue that had mostly gone unnoticed in the flurry to protect Gwaii Haanas. A fishing lodge owner who operated a floating resort in Henslung Bay—right across the channel from the old village site at Kiusta—had gotten provincial approval to build a permanent lodge in a location that the Haida claimed as the site of another old village, and thus an important archaeological site. The site was also within the boundaries of Duu Guusd, the unilaterally declared Haida tribal park, so the Haida set out to shut the lodge owner down. Years of skirmishes ensued, including dangerous exchanges between Haida protesters in the *Loo Plex* canoe (a fibreglass replica of the *Loo Taas*) and float planes trying to land guests at the lodge. In one incident, a float plane propeller clipped the front of the canoe. On a return trip in 1991, while enforcing what they called a "Haida injunction" against a growing profusion of fishing lodges in the area, twelve Haida were arrested by the RCMP, Guujaaw included. Despite their strong avowals to rid the area of sports fishing lodges, this is one battle the Haida still haven't won—there are so many lodges crammed into Henslung Bay now that on change day, when one set of guests ends their stay and new ones arrive, the bay is as busy as Times Square on New Year's Eve. According to Guujaaw, "It's way out of control, it hasn't been managed. The problem is they wipe out the ling cod, the bottom fish, the halibut...If you are killing a thousand coho a day, that's not acceptable...It's a matter of picking priorities, and they are pretty tough [to battle] because they are rich people." But, he vows, "they are going to get managed."

The Haida had more success in the late eighties with a gold mine that was proposed for the headwaters of the Yakoun River, the largest river on Graham Island and producer of five species of salmon. The proposal dated back to 1981, when a pilot plant and tailings pond were plagued with technical problems. The price of gold dropped in 1982, and the development was discontinued. Now here it was again, gold prices having rebounded, and here were the Haida. Ernie Collison said at a public meeting, "Long after...the mining people have gone with the gold and the profits, we'll be dealing with the pollution and the sickness, we'll have to answer for it to our people." The Old Massett chief councillor showed the B.C. government's mine development steering committee the door: "You have your guidelines, we have ours. We will not let the mine operate. Your society has taken away our rights and resources, but we won't let you take away our food. Right from the start there will be confrontation. Come back in 300 years and try again." The mine proposal died soon after, and it remains dead to this day. (Tragically, Ernie Collison himself—described by

Guujaaw as "co-conspirator" in the Haida's battles for their title and rights—died in a car crash in September 2001.)

Although they were busy fighting fishing lodges and gold mines elsewhere on the islands, the Haida hadn't taken their eye off South Moresby, and they didn't like what they saw. Their rejoicing in the decision to protect South Moresby was short-lived; almost immediately they embarked on a new round of resistance, this time objecting to the way in which senior governments proposed to enshrine the new protected area. Some environmentalists were ready to declare victory and consider their work done, but the Haida pushed back.

"We didn't stand on the line on Lyell Island to have a national park shoved down our throats," thundered Miles Richardson barely six months after the announcement that South Moresby would be saved. "Our objective—preservation—has been won. In the meantime, it's our responsibility to manage South Moresby. Anything they [Parks Canada officials] do, they do with our consent. It's that simple." Soon after, Richardson stunned a blue-chip audience of more than 250 people in Toronto when he refused to accept a Governor General's Conservation Award for his part in saving South Moresby. He said he couldn't accept the award until the Haida felt at home in Canada. This, from a leader who had already renounced his Canadian citizenship.

Richardson's public posture was that the Haida had to dictate the rules for any new park in their territory. But it wasn't simple getting Ottawa to agree. The federal government had said it would pay the provincial Crown to transfer the area to the federal Crown, but the Haida saw that arrangement as yet another erosion of their title. Through the winter of 1987–88, negotiations about the exact nature of the management of South Moresby reached an impasse. According to Elizabeth May, "The starting Haida position had been that they must have an equal say in all decisions affecting Gwaii Haanas. Ottawa's position was that the minister of environment had a statutory responsibility under the National Parks Act to be the ultimate authority. Fine, said Guujaaw, but the minister is not the ultimate authority over Haida Gwaii. It was difficult to develop a framework for cooperation without touching on the more fundamental question: 'Whose land do you think you are standing on?'"

By the spring of 1988, with Miles Richardson's blast still ringing in their ears, federal bureaucrats thought they had a workable deal. A statement of "Interim Purpose and Objectives" was reached, and a promotional booklet was produced. "The booklet was beautiful. With a dramatic border of black, the cover photograph of a fresh water lake, high in the San Cristoval mountains, offered a view of South Moresby that was rarely featured. Inside, the text was evocative and richly illustrated...It seemed that, perhaps, we were finally back on track," writes May. That is, until the Department of Justice saw a copy of the interim statement of purposes and objectives. "Justice saw our beautiful little booklet, South Moresby—Gwaii Haanas, and didn't like it one bit. The booklet contained ominous references to the 'hereditary activities of the Haida.' There were dangerous suggestions that the Haida considered the area to be 'a vital part of their spiritual and ancestral home.' The booklet and its interim statement confirmed that both Canada and the Haida recognized that the Haida Nation had lived on the islands for thousands of years, in harmony with nature. What's worse, it suggested there might be some 'right' to continue traditional activities. Justice lawyers said we could not risk saying such things. It might eventually compromise our land claims negotiations with the Haida." May, who as senior policy adviser was paid to think about these things, foresaw trouble. "I was totally disgusted when this latest roadblock was put in our way. Guujaaw had had to get every syllable approved by the elders and by the Council of the Haida Nation. This was not a simple matter of cancelling one publication; this risked undermining our whole relationship with the Haida." But the Department of Justice prevailed, and the booklets, $20,000 worth, were shredded—"every single one of them."

Matters were hardly helped when British Columbia decided to issue a permit for a mining company to drill in the proposed protected area. That issue soon faded, and in the summer of 1988, a federal-provincial agreement was signed that established a national park "reserve" in Gwaii Haanas. (A "reserve," rather than a park, because Haida title was still in dispute.) But Richardson immediately attacked the 108-page document for failing to even mention aboriginal title or to prescribe any special role for the Haida in the operation of the reserve. The Haida threatened to declare the area off-limits to visitors. "Gwaii Haanas will be closed in 1989 until we've come to agreement with the government of Canada. There will be no general tourist traffic. Without an agreement, there is a good chance of conflict between the federal government and the Haida Nation and there's no need for people to come up here and get in the middle of that," Richardson told the press. By early 1989, the Haida had begun issuing Haida passports. At the annual House of Assembly meeting of the Council of the Haida Nation that year, a Haida flag—depicting a red raven and eagle in a red circle—was consecrated with much less debate than Canada went through when it agonized its way to agreeing on a red maple leaf in the 1960s. That image now adorns Haida Nation letterhead as well as the Haida national flag, and it appears on decals found all over the islands that declare, "I support Haida Title."

The Haida and the federal government finally signed the Gwaii Haanas Agreement in 1993. Guujaaw had been assigned the role of chief negotiator for the Haida, even though he was, in his own words, "an unelected appendage, mostly without pay." Guujaaw's statecraft set a new standard for how protected areas are managed in Canada. Not for the Haida a park that subsumed their title and gave authority over to uniformed bureaucrats from Parks Canada. "We look at that area as a source of culture, a source of food, and a place where people have an opportunity to connect with the unspoiled Earth, not as a place where picnic benches are the norm," Guujaaw is quoted as saying on the Gwaii Haanas website. "The priority is for the well-being of the land. The overall goal is that in 20, 50, or even 200 years, someone could go down and enjoy the land as we see it today." The Gwaii

Haanas Agreement presumably got a read from someone in the Department of Justice, and presumably it gives a few bureaucrats heartburn to this day. In some ways, the agreement presages how the Haida—if or when they win title—and the Government of Canada might learn to live side by side in the same country. It squarely lays out the "convergence" of viewpoints regarding protection of the area and the "divergence" of views over sovereignty, title and ownership. The first page of the agreement looks like this:

The Haida Nation sees the Archipelago as Haida Lands, subject to the collective and individual rights of the Haida citizens, the sovereignty of the Hereditary Chiefs, and jurisdiction of the Council of the Haida Nation. The Haida Nation owns these lands and waters by virtue of heredity, subject to the laws of the Constitution of the Haida Nation, and the legislative jurisdiction of the Haida House of Assembly.

The Government of Canada views the Archipelago as Crown land, subject to certain private rights or interests, and subject to the sovereignty of her Majesty the Queen and the legislative jurisdiction of the Parliament of Canada and the Legislature of the Province of British Columbia.

"Notwithstanding and without prejudice to the aforesaid divergence of viewpoints," the agreement goes on to articulate the workings of an Archipelago Management Board with equal representation from the Haida and Canadian governments and a mandate to govern by consensus. Guujaaw, as one of the principal negotiators of the Gwaii Haanas Agreement, sat on the AMB in the early years and made sure it actually worked. Haida values are deeply embedded in the agreement; it allows for Haida cultural activities and traditional resource harvesting. An AMB planning document issued soon after the agreement was signed acknowledges the presence of more than 500 Haida archaeological and historical sites in the designated area and references studies that suggest "that human occupation of the islands has occurred for 10,000 years." It is a stunning reversal of previous statements from the federal government. Remarkably, by 2006, the Parks Canada website would offer this: "Although the fledgling partnership that sprang from the *Gwaii Haanas Agreement* did not immediately win the support of all Haida people, there were several turning points that increased public support among the Haida community. In one instance, human skeletal remains were found while the construction of a visitor information centre was in progress: work was halted while elders and community leaders were consulted. The Haida leaders told Parks Canada work could resume if they held a special ceremony for the disturbed burial site. This became the first ever federally hosted potlatch." A federally hosted potlatch! You can be sure that no mandarin from the Department of Justice turned up at that ceremony.

THE TECHNIQUE OF repoussé has an opposite technique, called chasing. Repoussé is done from the back of a metal work, to produce a raised design; chasing is done on the front of the work, to produce a depressed design on the surface. The term is derived from the noun *chase,* which refers to a groove, furrow, channel or indentation. The adjectival form is *chased,* as in "chased work." Throughout the eighties and nineties, Guujaaw's "chased work," if you will—the opposite to his fierceness and obstinacy—could be found in the time he spent with his family, in his construction projects, in his art, in his performances and in his growing stature as a diplomat.

There were three more longhouses that he built near Kiusta and a second longhouse at Windy Bay, along with his family residence in Skidegate, where he and Marcie live with their three children, daughter Niisii, son Kung St'aasl and another daughter, Xiila T'aayii Guujaaw. There was a succession of new commissions—the carving of a Gaagixiit mask that was traded for sea otter pelts; a six-metre Sea Grizzly totem pole for a private collection in Ontario; the carving of a two-metre pole with master carver Masimito in Japan. In 1997, the Government of Canada commissioned Guujaaw to carve a nine-metre Thunderbird pole for presentation to President Suharto of Indonesia. Guujaaw refused, but he did agree to carve a pole for "the President and the people of Indonesia." Guujaaw attended the pole-raising ceremony in Jakarta, accompanied by, among others, his two eldest sons, Gwaai and Jaalen. He performed at the unveiling at the Canadian Embassy in Washington, D.C., of *The Spirit of Haida Gwaii: The Black Canoe,* Bill Reid's largest and most complex work of sculpture, and at totem pole raisings in Birmingham, Alabama, and San Francisco. Guujaaw also turned up on a popular CBC television show, *On the Road Again,* filling host Wayne Ronstad in on the intricacies of drumming and dancing "in the Haida style." He even appeared on *Sesame Street* with a Haida children's dance group, the Hlgagilda Dancers.

Guujaaw's travels took him far and wide: to Venezuela, Brazil, China, Hungary and, repeatedly, to Japan. There, he developed a particular affection and affinity for the Ainu, the indigenous people of northern Japan. And they for him. "He has an aura about him, he's been taught the old way," says Kelly Brown, a leader from the Heiltsuk Nation on the B.C. mainland, with whom the Haida share a marine boundary and a history of sometimes violent confrontation. Brown accompanied Guujaaw on a trip to Hokkaido, and, in addition to their being dunked in a shallow river by an Ainu who lost control of his canoe, he particularly remembers the regard the Ainu showed the man from Haida Gwaii. "The Haida people, for whatever reason, are seen almost as *the* aboriginal people of British Columbia," Brown says. "They haven't been afraid to show who they are. Guujaaw makes me proud to be an aboriginal person."

Guujaaw also went to the Amazon in solidarity with the Kaiapo Indians there. Paiakan, a Kaiapo warrior who achieved international fame for standing up to gold miners, loggers and ranchers in his territory, had been interviewed by David Suzuki when Suzuki was shooting a documentary on the destruction of the Amazon in 1988. In February 1989, Paiakan flew to Canada thanks to the efforts of Suzuki's wife, Tara Cullis. His painted face and coloured headdress were irresistible to the media and to the people in Toronto and Ottawa who attended gala events featuring author Margaret Atwood, singer Gordon Lightfoot and others. Within a few short days, the organizers had raised more than $70,000 towards Paiakan's most urgent cause, which was to stop a series of dams from being built starting in the Amazon's Xingu valley, near the frontier town of Altamira. Soon after Paiakan returned home, a group of almost forty North American activists followed. Tony Pearse, who had been a technical adviser to the Haida in 1985 in a fight against offshore oil and gas drilling, was among them.

Pearse remembers that at a meeting in Altamira between industry, government, environmentalists and Amazon Indians, the Brazilian military turned out in force. But the soldiers looked nervous in the face of about 700 Kaiapo tribesmen, a few of whom brandished bows and arrows and machetes. It was tense, Pearse recalls. "These guys [the Kaiapo] kill people. They don't fuck around." In his autobiography, David Suzuki recalls an "electric moment" (presumably no pun intended) when an official from Eletronorte, the power company that wanted to dam the nearby river, was speaking and an elderly Kaiapo woman jumped to her feet, whipped up the crowd of Kaiapo warriors, then raised her machete and slapped the official on the cheek with the flat side of her weapon. Paiakan stood to defuse the moment, holding out his arms and calming the crowd. Pearse recalls that when Guujaaw was asked to speak, he talked about the universal struggle of indigenous peoples: "It was a speech of unity, you know, 'we're here to help' and all that." Later, the Canadians decamped to Paiakan's village on the outskirts of town, built there to reduce the chances of the indigenous people contracting diseases with non-Indians in Altamira. "It was wonderful," Suzuki writes. "We were fed traditional foods cooked on fires, and Guujaaw and Simon [Dick, a Kwagiulth dancer from Kingcome Inlet on the B.C. mainland] created a sensation when they appeared in full First Nations regalia, dancing, drumming and singing." Guujaaw takes obvious delight in the bond that was formed with the Kaiapo. "They're still singing some of our songs down there," he says today with a grin.

Going to the Amazon, and indeed travelling among indigenous peoples all over the world, enabled Guujaaw to appreciate more deeply that the Haida aren't alone in their struggles. "When you start looking around, you see the pattern, the fact that it's not just here that it's important for the industrial nation to put down the people, it's necessary everywhere. Necessary in the Amazon to kill them off or assimilate them in order to get at those resources." Travelling also awakened Guujaaw to just how rich in many respects Haida people are. "You know, you live here, and catching a fish is just that. You catch a fish and eat it, and that's normal and it *should* be normal. But when you travel around the world, you realize that it's not ordinary to be able to catch something or go sleep out on the land where there's nobody around, and to have the kind of freedom that we have here."

Still, even with Gwaii Haanas protected, neither the Haida nor the non-native residents of Haida Gwaii were content to sit back. As Guujaaw says, "Drawing the line is the easy part, holding the line is the challenge." In the same year, 1993, that the Haida and the federal government were finally signing off on the Gwaii Haanas agreement, British Columbia was rocked by a summer of massive civil disobedience in Clayoquot Sound. The Nuu-chah-nulth's earlier vow to protect Meares Island had set off a chain reaction of running skirmishes between environmentalists and industry, which resulted in more than 16,000 people from around the world descending on Clayoquot Sound. More than 800 people were arrested for blockading bridges and logging roads in a nonviolent but utterly determined stand that was highly reminiscent of what the Haida had done at Athlii Gwaii almost a decade earlier. But a strong industry-supported backlash also occurred, in the form of a virulently anti-environmentalist group modelled on U.S. "wise-use" groups; the province-wide group called itself Share B.C., and a local group on Haida Gwaii was known as Share the Rock. The group was determined to ensure that the victory in Gwaii Haanas did not spread to further threaten logging jobs.

Then, in 1994, the provincial forests ministry released a timber supply review that projected a rate of harvest for Haida Gwaii's remaining unprotected forests of more than twice the long-run sustained yield of all of the islands' forests. The alarmed response on the islands led to the formation of the Islands Community Stability Initiative, or ICSI. That initiative included every community and rural electoral area on Haida Gwaii. It soon disarmed the Share the Rock movement, whose members began to realize how their own long-term future would be made insecure by such an egregious assault on the forests that offered them their livelihoods.

The ICSI Consensus, which emerged in early 1996, was the first of a number of foundational documents that would articulate a radical new vision of community control over resource harvesting. Leslie Johnson, a signatory to the Consensus and a long-time resident of Haida Gwaii, said that after the Gwaii Haanas fight, "Some people felt like losers, but the winners didn't feel good either. And the companies said essentially, 'You've got your park, but we have to keep making the cut, so we're going to hit the islands harder. We still had a problem, but people didn't want to fight like that any more." So they had stopped fighting—the Haida, Share the Rock, environmentalists, business owners, loggers, even government officials—and hammered out the Consensus. The document argued that the overall cut on the islands should be reduced to a sustainable level and proposed a plethora of other reforms that put community interests first. "We had to come together," Johnson said. "We knew we couldn't go on like this. We realized that the companies didn't have the interests of the employees or the community at heart. We saw the trees disappearing. We finally understood that community needs are more important than any of our special interests. And we found that if we let people speak, rather than tell them what they should be thinking, the answers will come."

NINE

THIS BOX OF
TREASURES

SKIDEGATE HAIDA MYTHS and *Histories*, published by the Queen Charlotte Islands Museum in 1995, is a groundbreaking book in which stories collected by John R. Swanton between September 1900 and August 1901 have been edited and translated by linguist John Enrico. "For the Haida," Enrico writes, "a 'myth' is any story that is not about this world as we know it." In his introduction to the book, though, Guujaaw cautions against reading too much into what is written down. "Open this box of treasures and know that our story has always been the spoken word, animated with subtleties and emotions that don't translate into print...Look past the written word and you will find yourself in the world of a people whose fate is intimately tied to the ocean people, the sky people and the forest people." This theme was later employed as the introduction to a seminal exhibit of Haida art, *Raven Travelling: Two Centuries of Haida Art*. Guujaaw continued:

> ...and know
> that Haida Culture is not simply song and dance,
> graven images, stories, language, or even blood.

It's all of those things and then...

        awakening on Haida Gwaii,

        ...waiting for the herring to spawn.

It's a feeling you get when you bring a feed of cockles to the old people,

        and fixing up fish for the smokehouse

        ...walking on barnacles, or moss.

It has something to do with bearing witness as a falcon gets a

        seabird...

      and being there when salmon are finishing their course.

Along the way, you eat some huckleberries,

        watch the kids grow up...attend the funeral feasts.

    It's a matter of dealing with the squabbles within

and the greater troubles that come to us from the outside.

      It is about being confronted by the great storms of winter

and trying to look after this precious place.

As he concludes in *Skidegate Haida Myths and Histories:*

"All that we say is ours is of Haida Gwaii. This is our lot, our heritage, our life."

Although the Haida's story has always been spoken, for almost two decades a great deal of thought went into defining in writing all that they say is theirs. A revised Constitution of the Haida Nation was adopted in principle by the Haida's parliament, the House of Assembly, in 1985. Such is the care the Haida took with articulating their lot, their heritage, their lives that it was 2003 before the constitution was ratified. According to it:

"The Haida Nation is the rightful heir to Haida Gwaii.

"Our culture, our heritage, is the child of respect and intimacy with the land and sea.

"Like the forests, the roots of our people are intertwined such that the greatest troubles cannot overcome us.

"We owe our existence to Haida Gwaii.

"The living generation accepts the responsibility to ensure that our heritage is passed on to the following generations.

"On these islands, our ancestors lived and died, and here too we will make our homes until called away to join them in the great beyond."

Canada's own constitution is more prosaic and predictable. It talks about the desire to form a union that mimics the government of the United Kingdom, indeed to promote the interests of the British Empire. There are references to private property, to Indian reserves and to provincial rights to "the management and sale of public lands...and of the timber and wood thereon." There is provision for the provinces to make laws in relation to resource exploration, development and conservation. But there is little to suggest that the land is viewed as anything other than a source of "primary production." Canada got a second bite at the constitutional cherry in 1982, with the repatriation of the Charter of Rights and Freedoms, but the new wording starts out sounding as antiquated as the 1867 version: "Whereas Canada is founded upon principles that recognize the supremacy of God and the rule of law..." The Charter devotes sixty-one sections to describing the rights and freedoms of the people, the duration of their legislative bodies, their freedom of movement, their freedom to make a livelihood, their legal rights, equality rights, language rights, aboriginal rights, the rights of schools, multicultural rights and so on. But never once does it mention the land or the sea, and certainly not "the great beyond." The United States Constitution makes little mention of land either, other than as something to be defended; the same is true for Australia's constitution and New Zealand's, and for the letters patent, so to speak, of the United Kingdom, which is the fount from which most modern democracies have crafted their laws and structured their governments. The foundational language of these societies restricts itself to how people are governed and their rights protected. It takes no account of how the land or the sea or the sky are protected. The framers of most national constitutions had no words for the land or people's relationship to it.

But the Haida do. They have something called Haida Gwaii Yah'guudang, "our respect for all living things." It is an ethos that, in theory at least, informs everything the Haida do on and to the land, and with and to each other. They are not alone in basing their governance on guidance from nature or embracing the notion that there is something more to good governance than managing people. The Nuu-chah-nulth tribes on the west coast of Vancouver Island subscribe to what they call Hishuk ish tsa'walk, "everything is one." The Nisga'a Nation have their Ayuukhl, a set of laws to protect their land and culture. The Heiltsuk Nation cleave to what they call their Ǧvi̓'ilás, which "directs us to balance the health of the land and the needs of our people, ensuring there will always be plentiful resources." It is a very different way of codifying people's relationship to their land, and not surprisingly, it yields a very different view of how that land should be used.

When the surveyor Newton H. Chittenden produced his *Official Report of the Exploration of the Queen Charlotte Islands for the Government of British Columbia* in 1884, he quoted "an Indian" as saying the region was "only mountains, forests and water." Chittenden went on to inventory what he considered to be useful on the Queen Charlottes, listing its bays and sounds (but bemoaning its lack of harbours); its lakes and rivers; its climate, soil, agricultural and grazing lands, forest growth, animals, birds, fish, minerals, coal, copper, cereals, vegetables and fruits. While unimpressed by the people— "The Indian generally, is an ill-mannered brute"—Chittenden realized that he had happened upon a cornucopia of resources. "No country which I have ever visited affords greater natural resources of food supply from the sea and forest." His report, along with anecdotal accounts from explorers, missionaries and traders, brought on more than a century of largely unchecked exploitation of those resources. Even today the B.C. government's website points first to Haida Gwaii's offshore oil and gas potential, then to pronouncements from the ministry of forests and range, before extolling Haida Gwaii's tourism values. The government is simply incapable of articulating the value of Haida Gwaii in other than reductive, mercantile terms. The provincial Integrated Land Management Bureau is charged with producing land-use plans in which "needs are identified, land use zones are defined, objectives are set, and strategies for managing resources in those zones are developed." There is language about the needs of communities "now and in the future," but the government is hidebound by a need to get the wood out, the fish processed, the ore dug and the tourists roaming over the untrammelled bits with dollars falling out of their shorts.

The Haida also want access to resources. It's just that they value them differently. According to the Constitution of the Haida Nation, "Every Haida citizen has a right of access to all Haida Gwaii resources for cultural reasons, and for food, or commerce consistent with the Laws of Nature, as reflected in the Laws of the Haida Nation." To ensure that such access doesn't perpetuate the ruinous ways of recent times, that all commerce is reflective of the laws of nature, the constitution directs the Council of the Haida Nation to "establish land and resource policies consistent with Nature's ability to produce." The Haida have gone to some lengths to express what that means.

They say:

"The common name for these islands is *Haida Gwaii* meaning 'people island' or 'island of the people.' In earlier times this place was more commonly known as *Xaaydlaa Gwaayaay,* meaning 'taken out of concealment.' At the time of the supernaturals and *Nangkilstlas* it was *Didaxwaa Gwaii,* meaning 'shoreward country.'

"Our oral history traces the lineage of our families back to our ocean origins. We've witnessed the ice age, two great floods, changes in the sea level, the arrival of the first tree and many other earth-changing events. Together with all living things we've grown and prospered through the ages, nourished by the wealth and generosity of the ocean around us.

"Our physical and spiritual relationship with the lands and waters of Haida Gwaii, our history of co-existence with all living things over thousands of years is what makes up Haida culture. *Yah'guudang*—our respect for all living things—celebrates the ways our lives and spirits are intertwined and honours the responsibility we hold to future generations.

"*Haida Gwaii Yah'guudang* is about respect and responsibility, about knowing our place in the web of life, and how the fate of our culture runs parallel with the fate of the ocean, sky and forest people.

"Our people are satisfied and thankful with our place in the world. Our stories, songs, dances and crests are displayed through the ancient traditions of feasting and potlatching, where prestige is gained through the distribution of property. Told through the spoken word, animated and fulfilled by inflection and nuance. Handed down in private or displayed in the formal way of our traditions, they weave together through time the historic fabric of Haida Gwaii."

In their 2005 land-use vision, known on the islands either by its acronym, HLUV, or more popularly as Haida LUV, the Haida aren't shy to count their art forms as "among the world's great intellectual accomplishments," nor to deride industrial resource exploitation as a "corporate bonanza [that] has come at the cost of culture and communities. There has been no comprehensive planning or regulation other than the extraction of resources and revenues to feed the insatiable appetites of people who don't live here and are not concerned with the consequences of their actions. Today we recognize that the resource industries have gone too far too fast, and that important cultural, economic and environmental issues need to be addressed."

The HLUV is arranged in two parts. The first is a description of "the key things about the land and waters that have a special place in Haida culture," including the condition of the island's resources. The second addresses "what must be done in accordance with *Yah'guudang* to bring land and resource use into balance." In assessing the well-being of land and waters, the Haida turn their attention to key features, including *tsuuaay* (cedar), *tsiin* (salmon), *taan* (black bear), *kil* (plants), *xiit'iit* (birds) and *sk'waii* (beach).

TSUUAAY—Cedar

Our stories begin in the time before cedar, when living conditions were more basic. They tell of the intervention of supernaturals in the birth of canoe technology, and of the first totem poles being seen in an underwater village. *Tsuuaay* arrived on Haida Gwaii about six thousand years ago. In time it became an essential part of Haida culture, and the products of our cedar technology fill many volumes of books, display cases and collections around the world. Today as ever, the cedar tree is essential to Haida well-being—which includes material things and cultural affairs as well as growing economic opportunities in forest management, logging, carving and construction. The renewal and strength of Haida culture is intimately linked to the well-being of *tsuuaay*.

Cedar trees are important to many other living things great and small. They provide habitat for forest creatures, some of which are an important feature of Haida crests and histories. The biggest one is *taan,* the black bear, taking shelter and giving birth in hollow, dry cedar trees. Smaller, but as important to the forest, are the birds, bats and others that nest and perch in cedar trees. As insect-eaters and seed-spreaders, they help to maintain healthy forest conditions, which include hunting opportunities for predatory birds and mammals.

When a Haida person goes for bark, a pole or a canoe, the trees are approached with respect. Their spirits are hailed in a song and thanked with prayer. A bark gatherer takes care that the tree will go on living. A canoe builder *looks into the heart* of a cedar (test holes) so that trees with unsuitable qualities will be left standing alive much as before. The Culturally Modified Trees (CMTs) and canoe blanks that you find in the forest are the sacred workplaces of our ancestors.

TSIIN—Salmon

> "Salmon are creatures of the forest, they're born there and they die there." —Charles F. Bellis

Salmon are integral to all life on Haida Gwaii and to Haida culture. We express this understanding in our art forms when the salmon-trout-head design is placed in the ovoid joints of other creatures. There are races of salmon and other fish on Haida Gwaii that are ancient and unique in the world. The sockeye return much earlier than other parts of the mainland coast. There are land-locked salmon in various lakes, the outcome of changing sea levels. Every year the salmon swim into the forest to spawn, carrying in their bodies thousands of tonnes of nutrients gathered in ocean food webs, back to the land. They feed everything on the way upstream and down. They are the single most important source of nourishment in our diet, and over the years we have developed many ways to prepare, store and serve them in family meals and ceremonial feasts. Many others also rely on *tsiin* for food. Over time, black bears snatch tens of thousands of salmon out of the streams and bring nutrients to the forest floor. Many times they eat choice parts and leave the rest to be eaten by birds, small mammals and insects. Eventually the nutrients within their bodies pass into the soil and from there to the roots of trees and plants. The salmon feed the forest and in return receive clean water and gravel in which to hatch and grow, sheltered from extremes of temperature and water flow in times of high and low rainfall.

TAAN—Bear

Our Bear Mother Story, which is often depicted as a crest figure on family poles, explains our long and close relationship with bears. We are also similar to them in material ways, such as our reliance on salmon and cedar, and we learned a great deal from them about plants and their various uses. Bears play a key role in the well-being of the land. When they lift salmon out of the streams each year, they transfer a great load of nutrients from the ocean to the forest floor, much to the benefit of many other kinds of life. The best kind of forest for a bear contains lots of cedar trees of the right size with cavities for dens and daybeds, succulent plants for spring feeding, berries and salmon streams. This kind of forest grows at lower elevations in valley bottoms and neighbouring slopes. The best bear mother dens are in larger cedars with a cozy chamber inside sheltered from wind and rain, and a small well-hidden opening, easy to defend against intruders. Daybeds used in warmer times by male, female and young can be found near streams and other places where different foods are in season. A bear mother has five or six trees in her territory, and moves between them from winter to winter, birth to birth. If she feels threatened in her den by a roaming male or disturbed by human industry, she will pick up and move her cubs to another den tree.

KIL—Plants

Haida plant technology is ancient and complex. Many medicines were shown to us by a supernatural woman and others by the birds and other animals such as *taan*. The first tree to arrive in Haida Gwaii was the pine tree, which was taken as a crest by the X̱aagi K̲iigawaay who wore a pine branch in their hair. Science has recently confirmed that the pine tree was the first to arrive, about 14,000 years ago. Everyone depends on plants—people, fish, birds, animals and insects—for the same sorts of things, for nourishment and shelter, and everyone has a role to play in their well-being. Our uses include a wide variety of things made from different parts of different kinds of trees and plants—root, bark, stem, flower, berry, leaf and branch. They provide us with medicines, food and teas. Pigments and dyes. Materials for the smokehouse, cooking and weaving of clothing, hats, mats and baskets. From them we can make spears, arrows and bows; string and rope; fish hooks, nets and weirs; tool handles and clubs; whistles, rattles and ceremonial adornments. The wide range of plants we use grow everywhere from deep forest to open muskeg, meadows and shorelines, but the old growth forest contains many important things, including some of the most powerful medicines with proven effects. Plants and trees are nourished and affected by the ocean. Depending on its proximity to the ocean and exposure to its influence, the same kind of plant has different qualities for food value and medicinal effect. Alder plays an important ecological role in the forest. It's one of the first things that grows on the most disturbed sites, and brings nitrogen out of the air and into the nutrient cycle that makes new soil. When alder sees a landslide she exclaims: "I'm going to have that place!" Modern drug companies are always searching for natural medicines to create new commercial opportunities. This commercial enterprise has caused many problems for traditional medicine practitioners in many parts of the world, for which reason we hold our knowledge of these things in secrecy. They cannot be explained here or shown in any detail on maps.

XIIT'IIT—Birds

Many different kinds of birds fly the airways of Haida Gwaii, coming to ground to swim, bathe, perch, eat, rest, sing and nest. Their families include seabird, songbird, shorebird, falcon, hawk, owl, crow, duck and goose, sapsucker, woodpecker, kingfisher, heron, swallow, crane, hummingbird, grouse, loon, gull and cormorant. Through the ages, birds have played an integral role in building and maintaining the well-being of the land and Haida culture. As seed-spreaders, insect-eaters, predators, scavengers and fertilizer carriers, they play a key role in tending the plants in the forest, muskeg, estuary and shoreline what [sic] they are. Seabirds, like salmon, come in from the ocean in great numbers every year to birth their young. They nest in burrows in the ground or mossy platforms in the treetops. Their umma [guano] is rich in nitrogen, and over the ages the forests where they nest have grown wealthy with large trees. They are also a part of our traditional diet, an important source of nourishment in the time before the salmon return when stored supplies are running low. From watching the birds we learned the properties of plants, what is good for nourishment and medicine. Their songs and doings are expressed many different ways, many of which are family crests. Two of the most prominent birds in Haida culture are the eagle and the raven—which are the crest figures for the two main branches of Haida lineage and social structure. Eagle down is held sacred and is used in ceremony to signify peace and good intentions.

SK'WAII—Beach
Island dwellers are ocean-going people. In the beginning we came out of the ocean, and like everything else that inhabits the land we are nourished and shaped by it—in terms of food, the supernaturals, many stories, the cycle of the tides, currents and weather, and our use of cedar canoes for travel, trade and adventure. In river estuaries large and small, Creek Woman meets the ocean, releasing the young ones into the beds of eelgrass and kelp forests where they begin the saltwater stage of their lives, then welcoming them on their return. The sand and gravel beaches are inhabited by razor clams, butter clams, horse clams, cockles, geoducks and crabs. On rocky shores are barnacles, mussels and a multitude of periwinkles, and nourishing seaweeds rich in minerals and trace elements. Hiding in the seaweed are the abalone, urchin, scallop and octopus. The places washed by the ocean's tides are where we go to gather sea foods of all kinds—animal, vegetable and mineral. With every tide comes the nourishment of all living communities.

Alongside their lyrical descriptions of the attributes of their land and marine resources, the Haida mince few words in describing what has happened through more than a century of industrial assaults on those resources:

TSUUAAY—Cedar

For several decades the Haida have voiced growing concerns that the high rate of cedar logging is threatening the continuity of Haida culture, both today and especially for the coming generations. Cedar of high quality for canoes, poles and longhouses are disappearing from Haida Gwaii within *our* lifetime, cut down and floated away on log barges at a rate out of all proportion to their number. The needs of future artists, communities, bears and other forest dwellers are not respected by government planners and professional foresters. The problem is compounded by the large population of introduced deer, which has reduced the ability of cedar to grow back after logging, and even in the old growth forest that remains. The young cedar stands in the 19th century burn area between the lower Yakoun and Tlell rivers need special consideration. Some of them grow in very rich soil, and three hundred years from now they'll be one of the few remaining sources of accessible monumental cedars—if they aren't logged out in the next decade.

TSIIN—Salmon

Years of habitat disruption and overfishing is evident in all our streams. Sockeye in particular are in dire straits compared to their historical abundance. Every year we have to carefully limit our catches in different rivers so as not to endanger them. At times we find there's not enough to go around to provide for the needs of single families, let alone [for] large public feasting. As a watershed becomes progressively logged, the qualities that make for a healthy salmon stream become degraded. In many places the riparian forest that surrounds the streams and lakes has been laid bare. Because the hillside forests have been taken as well, seasonal floods run faster and higher, ripping away the structure of logs and spawning pools and the shelter of small side channels. Roads and bridge crossings funnel sediments into the streams. Landslides and debris torrents are catastrophic events that effectively erase a stream's capacity to provide habitat. One of the worst examples is the Ain River, once a major system and important food source; today barren of sockeye. The Copper River is not much better—almost 90 per cent of the watershed has been logged. Where the sockeye are a shadow of their former abundance, Creek Woman's wealth has been diminished. Other major salmon systems in trouble include the Davidson, Naden, Awun, Mamin, Yakoun, Deena and Mathers, with many smaller streams becoming increasingly degraded. It is clear that the provincial Forest Practices Code is a case of too little, too late. It provides no protection for the thousands of small stream habitats, or the vital headwaters of streams where much logging is happening today.

TAAN—Bear

A great many bear den trees and the forest places around them have been cut down. Experienced local loggers say that for most of the past 50 years the common practice has been to cut them. Sometimes loggers are allowed to leave occupied dens until the bears depart. When a mother with cubs feels threatened by a disturbance, she packs up and looks for another den. When bears are stressed this way, or by developments such as fishing lodges located in the best places for their foraging, they come out of the forest—thrashing around and trashing things in anger. The pattern of change can be seen by looking at the age of second growth forests. The places where the old forest has been logged have lost whatever big standing cedar trees for bear dens and daybeds they once contained, and their disappearance from the land has been extensive. This forces the bears to concentrate in old growth remnants, bringing them stress from crowding and depriving the land of the role they play in the salmon nutrient cycle. In the recent past, the troubles facing bears were compounded by the Department of Fisheries' misguided and now discontinued policy of killing bears because they eat fish. Most recently, their lives are further threatened by a rapid increase in commercial sport hunting, which, like catch-and-release sport fisheries, are unforgivable exercises in disrespect and disregard for the lives and spirits of creatures we hold to be our relations.

KIL—Plants

The single-minded focus of the logging industry pays little regard to the many kinds of plants it calls "non-timber forest products." No respect is shown for plants which are sacred to us for their proven medicinal powers and food values. Where we might approach a yew tree in a ceremonial manner, the industry takes them for building temporary roads, bucked into pieces for the heavy steel-tracked machines to travel on, then left behind on the ground. Many of the most powerful medicine plants grow in the old growth forest, especially under the canopy in riparian areas within one hundred metres of the streams. So much of this kind of forest has been clearcut that plants like devil's club—also an important medicine for the bears who taught us to use it—have become very difficult to find. Other kinds of plants for food and medicine have become scarce, and we have to travel further and further to find them. Recently, more people have become interested in harvesting plants for personal and commercial use in off-island markets, and this is a growing problem that needs to be addressed. Plants and trees are nourished and affected by the ocean. Depending on their exposure to the ocean's influence, the same kinds of plants have different nutrient and medicinal properties. Because of this they need to be protected in various places from the shoreline to more sheltered inland places.

XIIT'IIT—Birds

Many kinds of birds depend on old growth forests with their high canopies and understories of fern and shrubs such as salal and huckleberry, and plenty of insects to eat. Those who live inside the forest are very vulnerable to disturbance by logging. Clearcuts and the "variable retention" openings are barren of the conditions that birds need to live there, and so their numbers decline. The problem is compounded by introduced species. Rats, raccoons and squirrels are alien predators of adult birds, eggs and hatchlings. The growing flocks of starlings are vigorous competitors for the foods that remain. The deer have had the greatest effect, and while we respect that they have become an important part of many people's diet, we need to realize how their heavy browsing of bird and insect habitat has impoverished the plant communities. Some birds adapt to the new openings and edges that logging creates, but after several years the young conifer forest draws together into a tight canopy that blocks most of the light out from the understory. When this happens, the forests are unsuitable habitat for many birds for up to 60 years, a condition that exists over an ever-increasing portion of the land. Goshawks have declined in number such that they are listed by the government of British Columbia as a threatened species—the reason given is the logging of the forests where they nest and forage. *Ts'alangaa* (Marbled Murrelet) is listed by the province as a threatened species. Heron and saw whet owls have become increasingly rare, dependent as they are on old forest conditions for nesting and foraging. In effect, the loss of birds is depriving the land of their essential role in insect control, seed dispersal and nutrient loading, a condition that will surely become worse if logging continues in the pattern of recent years. Shoreline birds are easier to observe, and those who count them say that the falcons and eagles are still high in number here, in comparison to the other parts of the mainland.

SK'WAII—Beach

The beaches are vulnerable to disturbance by pollution from human sewage, oil and the many products made from it, by seepage from mining sites, and by timber industry activities at log sorting and dumping sites. Log dumps are usually located in sheltered bays, where bark and debris sinks to the bottom and decomposes, starving the water of oxygen and smothering clams and other life forms. Wherever streams have been heavily logged and damaged by landslides and erosion, in periods of heavy rainfall the estuaries are loaded with silt and huge quantities of gravel are washed out of the stream channels and into the sea.

And so, given all that, there is the need to decide "what must be done in accordance with *Yah'guudang* to bring land and resource use into balance—to ensure the continuity of Haida culture and the economic well-being of the entire island community." In other words, how the rubber will hit the road. The Haida have mapped out what protection of *tsuuaay, tsiin, taan, kil, xiit'iit* and *sk'waii* would ideally look like. They go on to say that the *Haida Land Use Vision* is not just about the protection of natural areas. "It is also about understanding economic conditions, and providing a vision of a sustainable economy in which the forest continues to play an important role in the well-being of the island community. The forests have fuelled an industry that has provided jobs to Haida and other island communities for a few short decades. Families have been fed and sheltered, and relationships among our communities have grown. But the forest was logged too fast, and without provision for the stability and sustainability of the island community as a whole. There is room enough for forestry and other commercial activities on Haida Gwaii, but in order to be sustainable they must be managed with more respect and greater responsibility—in other words, in accordance with *Yah'guudang*.

"In Haida culture, wealth is a different thing than money, which is a currency for doing business in the modern economy. Wealth flows from the well-being of the land, and from having the opportunity, knowledge and capacity to support our families, raise healthy children, and organize the individual collective efforts of our clans and society. Wealth is to be shared and distributed—prestige is gained through the ability to do so."

The Haida haven't yet figured out what a new economy will look like on the islands. That's a work in progress. What they do know, as the HLUV says, is that "the land and waters of Haida Gwaii can and must be made well again. Our economic needs can and must be brought into balance with the capacity of the land to function and provide. We have the political will and we accept the responsibility to see that this is done."

TEN

A RECOGNIZABLE
CULTURE

IT IS SOMETIMES said that when the Haida don't have
an enemy, they turn on themselves. "Over the years," Guujaaw once
told CBC Radio, "we fought with our neighbouring tribes and then
we fought on this island among the different villages, and within the
villages we fought amongst the clans." In the 1990s, with the battle
for Gwaii Haanas won comprehensively, Miles Richardson recalls
that the Haida "kind of lost our rudder for a few years." Richardson resigned the presidency in 1996 to take up a posting with the
B.C. Treaty Commission, formed earlier that decade when Mike
Harcourt's New Democratic Party came into office and agreed—a
hundred years too late, give or take—that the province would participate in treaty negotiations. For awhile, says Richardson, things at
home "got a little out of whack." Then in 1999 Guujaaw stepped up—
or rather stepped down—to take on the role of president of the
Council of the Haida Nation. He's been down there ever since. "Pres-
idents and all elected people in the Haida Nation are not elevated
into a position," Guujaaw said in an interview with an on-island
journal, *SpruceRoots*. "They are lowered into a position. I'd be happy
doing other things, like getting out on the land more often, but we

have to make sure we aren't the last generation to enjoy that birthright." Miles Richardson was surprised when Guujaaw agreed to run for president. "I never even approached him," Richardson says, "because of what he'd told me before, that he would never be interested in running for elected office." Guujaaw had always downplayed his role in Haida political life, once calling himself "one of the guys who would set up the chairs and drag people out to have meetings about land claims and stuff." As offhand as that sounds, there was nothing casual about Guujaaw's descent into high office.

As with everything political on Haida Gwaii—and on Haida Gwaii, everything is political—Guujaaw didn't simply throw his hat in the ring to declare his candidacy. The elders played a role in putting him there, and they play a role in keeping him there. "We talked about Guujaaw for about a year, and we decided to give him a try, let's see what happens, because the candidates that were running at the time were, in our minds, not capable of the kind of work that had to be done," says Hereditary Chief Iljawass, Reynold Russ, the senior chief in Old Massett. "Chief Skidegate [Dempsey Collinson] and I talked Guujaaw into running, so Dempsey filled out the nomination form and I seconded it. That was the first time, that's when he got elected to be president of the Haida Nation." While other candidates have since come and gone, none have brought with them the sponsorship of the head chiefs of Old Massett and Skidegate. Early in 2008, Guujaaw was acclaimed as president, the first time that had ever happened in the history of the Haida national government.

Guujaaw is deadly serious when he talks about high office being a lowly pursuit. The only thing that makes it bearable is that, as Miles Richardson discovered, the "accomplishments [of the president] can't be separated from the people. It's the people who do it." Guujaaw phrases it this way: "The trick isn't what I can pull off, you know. I cannot pull anything off by myself. It's required that people are behind me and back me along the way. And they are quite involved in the effort to protect the land. They are totally behind me, every stripe of people. There's no one who disagrees that we have to protect the land. Getting to the common cause, that's really the trick." As for the chiefs and elders, "they watch pretty hard and they pay close attention to what goes on. Where you find dissent is where there is self-interest. Any place where somebody's looking out for their own interest, that's where you run into dissent."

In fact, Chief Iljawass *has* been watching pretty hard, and not everything is to his liking. The morning after Jimmy Hart's doings in Old Massett in August 2006, Reynold Russ sits in his living room in a bungalow that faces onto Masset Inlet. He recounts the troubled history of Haida governance, stretching back before the CHN's founding convention in 1974. He recalls thwarted attempts by successive administrations, including his own as elected chief in Old Massett, to address the land question. Although he nominated Guujaaw as CHN president in 1999 and has supported him ever since, his face darkens as he recalls Christian White's potlatch on the Saturday night and Jimmy Hart's on Sunday. "I don't agree with what he [Guujaaw] is doing right now in the hereditary system, like he's favouring one hereditary chief over another, and it's not his place to do that. He can't do that." At issue is a simmering dispute between Chief Thasi (Ken Edgars) and Chief ʔIdansuu and others about plans for a new fishing lodge in Naden Harbour. Chief Thasi claims hereditary authority over territory that Chief ʔIdansuu says is within *his* domain and, indeed, falls within the boundaries of Duu Guusd, the tribal park. What's worse, Chief Thasi intends to partner with Rick Bourne, owner of Langara Lodge. The place still sits in Henslung Bay like an abscessed tooth, in the opinion of many Haida, who remember the sports fishing battles of twenty years before. In Chief Iljawass's view, the issue should be hashed out at clan meetings, not before "the general public" at a potlatch, which is what he feared would happen at Jim Hart's doings.

He went to the potlatch full of trepidation, he admits. "I couldn't stay away from the do last night. Some of the chiefs stayed away." If the issue of territories had been raised by Hart at the potlatch, he says, "people were going to stand up and turn their blankets inside out and stand there till he changed his mind, that's the way I understood they planned it. I didn't want to see that happen…This is leading up to the title case, and to have this happen, boy, you could see the split in the whole community if this happened." In the end, the issue of the territories didn't arise at Hart's potlatch, and a potentially explosive issue subsided from view. Robert Davidson has equated the potlatch, in its importance to the Haida, with the Supreme Court of Canada. Along with the House of Assembly, potlatches are where the Haida transact their most important business. The House of Assembly is open to the Haida alone, though, while potlatches are very public affairs. Like the swirling waters of Masset Inlet just outside the chief's window, last night's doings had back eddies full of dark portent. In Canada's high courts, judges don't turn their robes inside out; they write dissenting opinions to the majority judgement. At Hart's doings, the chief had detected a hint of self-interest in the air and with that, as Guujaaw himself allows, comes the prospect of dissent. Chief Iljawass still supports Guujaaw, but he is watching him. Unreservedly, however, he cites the ample proof that Guujaaw is "a leader that can make a presentation to the courts."

WHEN GUUJAAW BECAME president of the Council of the Haida Nation, high on the list of things to attend to was a court case concerning a proposed licence renewal of TFL 39. In 1995, during Miles Richardson's second-last year as CHN president, Richardson and the CHN had filed a petition in the B.C. Supreme Court to block renewal of MacMillan Bloedel's TFL on Haida Gwaii, on the basis that the licence was "encumbered" by the Haida's unresolved claim to title. MacMillan Bloedel was entitled under TFL 39 to cut more than one million cubic metres of wood a year from what it called its "Haida Tree Farm Licence." But according to Greg McDade, counsel for the Haida, "the land ownership dispute and the title held by the Haida Nation clearly constitutes an encumbrance on these forests." Miles

Richardson, not yet a treaty commissioner, told the CHN's journal, *Haida Laas,* "If we really want to make treaty negotiations work and provide some economic certainty and options for our common future, we have got to get old mistakes out of the way." MacMillan Bloedel was an iconic name in Canadian forestry and had been one of the biggest companies in the history of the province after the glory days of the Hudson's Bay Company. They were a very large "mistake" to get out of the way. The Haida lost the case.

Back when the Haida had blockaded Rayonier on Lyell Island and been dragged into court before the chief justice, they relied on Miles Richardson to speak for them. When they argued against the renewal of TFL 39 in 1995, they were assisted by Greg McDade of the Sierra Legal Defence Fund, which took on the case on the Haida's behalf. By the time they attempted to overturn yet another renewal of TFL 39 in Masset in 2000, three things had changed—MacMillan Bloedel had sold out to Weyerhaeuser, the Haida now had Haida legal representation and there was a landmark Supreme Court of Canada case for the Haida to rely upon.

In 1997, the Supreme Court of Canada had found, in *Delgamuukw,* that aboriginal title had *not* been extinguished in Canada, despite Canada's and British Columbia's claims to the contrary. *Delgamuukw* was named after a petitioner, Hereditary Chief Delgamuukw, Earl Muldoe, who was one among many of the Gitksan and Wet'suwet'en First Nations people on mainland British Columbia who had launched a land claims case in 1984. It took three years for the case to get to court, and the trial itself spanned 374 trial days between May 1987 and June 1990. The sitting judge was none other than Chief Justice Allan McEachern. In 1985, when he tried the protesters from Lyell Island, McEachern had said he wished the land question was before him. Well, now it was. Different natives, same question. But McEachern could not have been more ill-disposed to the petitioners as elder after elder entered his court, giving oral testimony that the judge claimed to find—even in translation—utterly incomprehensible. Some elders sang at one point to try to convince the judge that the Gitksan and Wet'suwet'en had a viable culture and an unbroken link to their land. McEachern's notorious ruling in 1991 gave no weight to the oral histories that had been presented to him, and he dismissed the Gitksan and Wet'suwet'en claim as a quaint affectation of a bygone era. The natives, he said, could not possibly succeed on their own merits, and they should "make their way off their reserves" and assimilate with the larger Canadian whole.

McEachern essentially found that a "tide of history" had swamped Canada's First Nations and thereby sunk their claim for title and rights. He never actually used that term, but on the opposite side of the world, Justice Gerard Brennan of Australia's High Court did— except that Brennan found in favour of aboriginal rights. In the *Mabo* case, Brennan said that the "tide of history" could not be cited to justify the washing away of indigenous rights. The High Court in *Mabo*, named for Eddie Mabo of the Meriam tribe, found for native title in Australia at almost precisely the same time McEachern was ruling against it in British Columbia. Australia and Canada have, over the past few decades, conducted a legal version of checkers when it comes to aboriginal rights, each jurisdiction leaping over the other on issues of title and rights. So while Australian aboriginal people were celebrating *Mabo*, Canadian First Nations were lamenting *Delgamuukw*, which they appealed. Inevitably, the case ended up at the Supreme Court of Canada, where McEachern's rulings were overturned.

Canada's top court, in *Delgamuukw*, did not give blanket title to aboriginal Canadians. It didn't even give title to the Gitskan and Wet'suwet'en. What it did say was that aboriginal title is a unique right in the land itself arising "from the prior occupation of Canada by aboriginal peoples." First Nations may have aboriginal title if they can prove that their ancestors had exclusive occupation of the lands at the time when the Crown asserted sovereignty, which in British Columbia is 1846, and that there is continuity between present and pre-sovereign occupation of the land. The court also said that title has limits, in that the land cannot be used in a way that destroys the people's relationship to the land. It was a judgement rendered in Ottawa, but one made in heaven for the likes of the Haida. What the decision said, in effect, was this: prove that you were here before 1846, that you've continued to be here since then and you've continued to use the land to the exclusion of others, demonstrate that you can exercise a duty of care for the land, and you have title. The court also said that, even before proof of title, the government has a duty to consult First Nations. "There is always a duty of consultation," the court said, and in most cases the government's duty "will be significantly deeper than mere consultation. Some cases may even require the full consent of an aboriginal nation."

Clearly, someone had neglected to tell the Province of British Columbia, or at least the forest service, about that Supreme Court decision, because when it came time in March 2000 to renew Tree Farm Licence 39, Block 6, the government merely convened a conference call the day before and told the Haida that the renewal was going ahead. This, for a licence that covered about one-quarter of Haida Gwaii's land mass. The Haida saw red.

"What's at stake here is Haida Gwaii and our culture," said Guujaaw at the time. "Over the last 40 years industry has run the government on an election-to-election basis. Corruption is institutionalized throughout the entire forest industry. The very licence that gives them the 'right' to cut has always been illegal, and this is what we have set out to prove." It wasn't just the Haida who were rebelling against the assault on traditional lands. In June 2000 in Vancouver, an event billed as a "Turning Point Conference" was held among First Nations of the north Pacific coast. Thirteen First Nations and councils, including the Haida, signed the declaration, which said that "the connection of land and sea with the people has given rise to our ancient northwest cultures [and]...this life source is under threat like never before and all people must be held accountable." The Turning Point declaration laid a foundation for the eventual protection from industrial forestry of more than 30 per cent of the Great Bear Rainforest. It also gave rise to a powerful coalition known as the Coastal First Nations, which became an unusually influential and durable negotiating forum and is currently presided over by Guujaaw. In the summer of 2000, however, the Haida's immediate concern was with the renewal of TFL 39, Block 6. Cue Terri-Lynn Williams-Davidson, a Haida woman who had recently married Robert Davidson, had recently graduated from the University of British Columbia's law school and is as forcefully graceful as Guujaaw is gruff. Williams-Davidson led the Haida's legal argument against the TFL renewal. She relied on *Delgamuukw,* which, to her reading, as she told *SpruceRoots,* "held that Aboriginal title could be an encumbrance, and said the whole purpose of the Forest Act is to prevent the illegal distribution of timber. A lot of us thought that would change the way things are done." But they were wrong.

After a hearing that summer, the Haida lost. But on appeal, they won, and it was a stunning victory. Justice Douglas Lambert, writing for the majority, found that both the province and Weyerhaeuser had an obligation to consult with the Haida. What's more, the B.C. Appeal Court judge went so far as to say there was a "reasonable probability" the Haida would be able to establish title on at least some of the lands in question, and a "substantial probability" they would be able to establish an aboriginal right to harvest red cedar trees from those lands. The ruling in February 2002 struck terror into the hearts, or at least the balance sheets, of corporate Vancouver. Companies had always assumed that, at the very least, they could safely hide behind the process: "Well, we've got a licence from the government. If it's illegal, that's the *government's* problem, not ours." But what this ruling essentially said was that the licence issued by the B.C. government was no good, and the company was in possession of fenced goods, if a timber licence rather than a stolen stereo. Guilty by association, in other words.

Then, one week after the Court of Appeal decision, the Haida struck again. Guujaaw remembers provincial bureaucrats warning him that regardless of the Haida's victory in the courts, they would not be allowed to "fetter" the authority of the forest minister. According to Guujaaw, "We advised that we'll fetter him, all right. In fact, we'll tar and fetter him." The next day, with fanfare, the title case was launched. The ceremony on March 6, 2002, took place on the Squamish First Nation reserve in North Vancouver and was even more theatrical and stylish than the customary displays of Haida strength. There were the ritual dances, songs, drumming and spreading of the eagle down, but this time there was something else. In his hand, Guujaaw held a writ, and in the presence of two young Haida runners, Nika Collison and Amos Setso, he handed it to Terri-Lynn Williams-Davidson. Williams-Davidson held the writ aloft in front of a cheering crowd, before she and the runners made their way to Vancouver's downtown courthouse to file suit against British Columbia and Canada, claiming all of Haida Gwaii. The next day, and in the days that followed, a cascade of headlines rained down. "Haida sue for Queen Charlottes" (*National Post*). "Haida lay claim to lucrative B.C. islands" (*Canadian Press*). "Haida claim emphasizes need for serious negotiations" (*Vancouver Sun*). "Native claims: Back to the courts" (*Province*). "We'll consult: Premier" (*Province*). "Guujaaw hints at break with Canada if Haida can't work things out" (*Province*). "Haida claim a wakeup call" (*Times Colonist*). One headline invoked the title of Rohinton Mistry's wonderful novel, with its universal themes of searching and belonging: "Such a long journey: The Haida's struggle for justice."

All the Haida did was file a claim. Nothing was proven, nothing had been decided, but coming as it did on the heels of the TFL 39 appeal victory, the meaning of the claim wasn't lost on many. Nor did many observers miss the fact that this was no longer just about forests. This was about all of it—or as Chief Iljawass told the *Province*, "We own Haida Gwaii lock, stock and barrel." He might have said "lock, stock and 10 million barrels," because what some in the media seized upon was the Haida's pivotal role in any future oil and gas development in Hecate Strait—something the ruling Liberal government had been eyeing for a while. The *Calgary Herald's* coverage focussed on that: "Haida grab for offshore oil has a chance." In the *Province,* "Haida fear environmental disaster if drilling comes." "Offshore oil is ours, say Haida," warned the *National Post.*

None other than the *Washington Post* tracked down Guujaaw in downtown Vancouver, "this concrete and glass city," as the newspaper called it. "'Look at them,'" the *Post* quoted him as saying. "A window separates him from people walking on sidewalks in suits, carrying briefcases and umbrellas to protect them from the empty sky." "Most people haven't ever killed anything for their supper and haven't dirtied their hands to get something to eat, so each of them in the city feels they're innocent," Guujaaw said. "They don't seem concerned that the ocean has lost its richness," he said, "that fish are being depleted and the land is being wasted. They cannot hear the cries from the bottom of a disturbed seabed pierced for oil." The *Post* report referred to a 1972 federal moratorium on drilling off the shores of British Columbia and the subsequent provincial moratorium, put in place in 1989. But it noted that B.C. premier Gordon Campbell had recently commissioned a study on the impact of drilling in the Queen Charlotte basin and pointed to statements indicating that Campbell would support drilling—the lifting of the moratorium—if it was proven the drilling could take place safely. Guujaaw told the *Washington Post* the Haida could bring the economy of the province to a halt. "And it wouldn't hardly affect our people at all, because we're used to being broke," he said. Although the Haida had been almost eradicated by white men's diseases, "they made the mistake of leaving some of us alive."

As well as news stories, the filing of the writ prompted in-depth features, some of them focussing on Guujaaw himself. In one piece in the *Province,* he dodged a question about his age and chuckled,

"I'm like Conan the Barbarian, an ageless savage. Still strong," he added, "everything works." More seriously, he framed the Haida struggle as being about much more than their claim to Haida Gwaii. They were fighting what he considered to be a "deliberate attempt to destroy the Earth," he told the newspaper. "It's going to take humanity to stop it and most people are so far removed from the natural world they don't feel any sense of responsibility toward it. They hunt and gather in the malls. Live in compartments...Civilization itself is measured by how far from the natural world you can be brought. The more pavement and synthetics you can pack around you, the more civilized they say you are."

On the radio hotlines, all sorts of noisy chatter was heard, including a particularly delicious encounter between Guujaaw and one of the noisiest mouths in British Columbia at the time, CKNW Radio host Rafe Mair. Mair had been a cabinet minister in Bill Bennett's Social Credit administration, and British Columbia's environment minister in the late seventies. Before he welcomed Guujaaw onto the show, he spouted out an editorial, in which he could not help taking a swipe at the legal system. "The courts, especially since the Charter of Rights and Freedoms came upon us, are doing social work at a high level, with occasional bits of law thrown in. Since that is the world we live in, we had better find ways to make the best of it...The pickle we're in today is because governments have not done what native leaders have been suggesting for eons: settle these issues."

In introducing Guujaaw, Mair referred to him as, among other things, an actor and a comedian. Guujaaw said he preferred to be known as a hunter-gatherer. "What brought you into politics?" Mair asked his guest. "Because that is sure as hell where you are now." "No," Guujaaw told Mair. "Actually, as a carver, or as an artist, or anybody interested in culture, you have to be political, otherwise you lose that culture...Everything has to be associated. Every artist is political, and in fact most of our people are." He went on to repeat something he had said to Mair the politician in a letter twenty-three years earlier, a point his ancestors had made a lifetime earlier than that: "We don't actually claim the land. It's the government who claims *our* land."

British Columbia's ruling Liberal Party knew it would take years for the Haida claim to get to court. But government and industry had a live issue in the courts with the ruling in the Haida's favour regarding TFL 39. They had been knocked so far back on their heels that they took the extraordinary measure of requesting a special hearing of the Court of Appeal to "clarify" the meaning of the ruling. Normally, you just appeal a judgement you don't like if there is a legal basis to do so. But the government and Weyerhaeuser were dumbfounded by the ruling. Surely, the court could not have meant to rule the way it did? And surely it wasn't legal, in any event. Weyerhaeuser shared its concerns with other industry players, who were equally terrified by the implications of the ruling. When Weyerhaeuser got the highly unusual "clarification" hearing it sought, the company was supported by intervenors from the Council of Forest Industries, the B.C. Business Council, the Chamber of Commerce and even the B.C. Cattlemen's Association. By a two-to-one majority, the Appeal Court sustained its opinion that the ruling included the company. Government and industry got their clarification and, in the words of Terri-Lynn Williams-Davidson, "I think they're sorry they asked for it."

The case was clearly headed for the Supreme Court of Canada. But in the meantime, remarkable things were happening on Haida Gwaii. All these visits to court were reactions to someone else's agenda. The government or industry would act, the Haida would react and the courts would be asked to sort it out. Hardly a way to build a national consensus, no matter who was winning. So in 2001, the Haida House of Assembly had directed the CHN to create a thousand-year plan for cedar. "The success that our people have had in the courts and in the public arena can be attributed largely to a recognizable culture," Guujaaw wrote in *Haida Laas*. His government was instructed to create a plan that would ensure "a long-term supply of red and yellow cedar for Haida cultural needs." In a story headlined "Tsuuaa 'kiing ja, or Looking into the heart of the cedar," Guujaaw wrote,

> For thousands of years the people went into the forest for cedar.
>
> Among the living trees we find some with strips of bark removed to make clothes, hats and baskets.
>
> We find cedar with planks split off—planks for a baby's cradle, a cooking box, a drum, a house and a coffin.
>
> In the remaining forests we find stumps marking the remains of trees crafted into canoes, houses and to display the crests.
>
> Some tluu will be shaped in various stages of construction.
>
> We will look into the heart of cedar and walk in the majesty of the great magician.

Guujaaw was at the same time working some magic of his own. It has long been assumed, with ample justification based on the decades it has been true in British Columbia, that loggers will side with companies when it comes to access to wood. On Lyell Island, Frank Beban's boys were angrily opposed to the Haida blockade, stoked by Redneck Smith and fuelled by fear that if the companies lost control of the woods, the workers would lose their livelihood. Unions and companies often bashed heads over wages, benefits, safety, market slowdowns and mill closures, but the core compact remained the same: the companies brought capital, the workers provided labour and the government cleared the way of all obstructions to the constant supply of timber. Environmentalists were a threat, and, increasingly, Indians were, too. But labour at least acknowledged that First Nations had rights. On Haida Gwaii, labour also came to realize that the Haida, not the companies, might soon control the access to timber.

Somewhere in the Haida's commitment to a thousand-year plan for cedar, in their persistent court battling, in their constant support for

people over profit and in the fact that the Haida were *from* this place—
somewhere in all that, and in the fact that a B.C. company, MacMillan
Bloedel, had sold out to an American giant, Weyerhaeuser...well, a
few months after the Haida won their case in the Court of Appeal,
local loggers mutinied. They threatened a wildcat strike against Weyerhaeuser but instead took part in a salmon barbecue to celebrate a
new coalition between the Haida and as many as 135 of the 155 Weyerhaeuser workers on the islands. The workers' new-found fealty to
the Haida came less from any dewy-eyed conversion to the aboriginal cause, than their conclusion that the fate of the forests of Haida
Gwaii was in better hands with the Haida than with distant offshore
companies in collusion with dishonest off-island governments.
"They take everything, and they put nothing back," one young non-
native logger said. "I used to work for the company, but I don't trust
them...I'm on the Haida's side now." Said Bernie Lepage, a Weyerhaeuser weigh master, "We also know that the Haida are likely to get
title to these islands. We said, 'Heck, they're going to be our land-
lords, anyway. Let's do this thing right and start working with them
right away.'"

Buoyed by local support, the Haida upped the ante even further.
They sent registered letters to every tenure holder on Haida Gwaii,
warning them they were breaking the law if they failed to consult the
Haida and accommodate aboriginal rights before they went about
their business. "Like Weyerhaeuser, your company has been granted
a tenure from the province which interfaces with Haida rights and
title," the letters said. Small business owners, fishing lodge owners,
mineral claim holders, offshore oil and gas interests, bureaucrats and
others gathered at a meeting in Skidegate to hear what the Haida had
in store for them. Not a lot of tenure holders felt much like Weyerhaeuser. A lot of them were feeling pretty vulnerable. Guujaaw,
speaking as president of the CHN, reassured them that the Haida
were seeking accommodation with tenure holders, and for the most
part expected to achieve it. But inevitably, he said, some activities, by

their very nature, would be incompatible with Haida rights and title. "In the end, I think anybody who is using these lands has to look after them in the kind of way that we are expected to and within the definition of what aboriginal title is. There are certain licences, tenures and activities going on that we don't expect we'll be able to make compatible with our use and enjoyment of this land, and in which our core action is to get rid of those tenures." In other words, fishing lodges and bear hunters, watch out.

If the tenure holders were feeling spooked, the B.C. government was beside itself. It had already held an ill-advised referendum into native treaties that was widely condemned as a clumsy attempt to scuttle the treaty process. The referendum was boycotted by progressive groups, and far from being what government called "an experiment in direct democracy," it was described by Canadian public opinion polling guru Angus Reid as "one of the most amateurish, one-sided attempts to gauge the public will that I have seen in my professional career." The referendum served further to antagonize First Nations the province over. The Haida now had the government on the back foot with the TFL 39 case. Its core constituency, business, was in state of high anxiety. Then, a masterstroke! Attorney-General Geoff Plant, on record as having called the Haida "particularly obstructionist," in September 2003 offered them 20 per cent of Haida Gwaii if they would put the title case into abeyance and return to the treaty table with British Columbia and Canada. Responding for the Haida, Guujaaw was nothing if not predictable, and indeed obstructionist: "The government is just posturing, this is nothing but a PR game. This offer was designed to be rejected...We think [the government is] up to some kind of mischief...The Haida are really being told to surrender 80 per cent of the Haida claims." To a man who had slept in all the old villages, who had buried the remains of his ancestors to keep them from scavenging tourists, the offer was a bald insult. In fact, it was an insult to all Haida. Guujaaw had no choice other than to reject it. "If Guujaaw had accepted the 20 per cent of the islands that the province of B.C. presumed to offer," said Arnie Bellis in a speech in 2004, "he would have ceased being president the second he did, because it's in violation of our constitution."

The government's offer reverberated well beyond the shores of Haida Gwaii. There was the government negotiating treaties on the mainland and telling various First Nations not to expect their land settlements to go higher than 5 per cent of their territories—yet they were offering the Haida four times that. "Plant later had to explain to the First Nations Summit why they were negotiating at 5 per cent while we were rejecting 20 per cent," Guujaaw says. The former Attorney-General's recollection is that the offer was designed by the government "to take the conversation with the Haida to a higher level." Plant says that the Haida "were generally bent on doing things their way, and insisting on respect for their title and rights at a pretty high level. It was difficult to get them to engage with us on any of the public processes that *we* had designed." So the government, tired of "seemingly endless additions" to the areas off-limits to logging that Guujaaw kept asking for, "decided we would do things quite differently [through] a unilateral offer to the Haida." When the offer was made public, the attorney-general was called to account by other First Nations who wondered why the Haida were getting a better deal. But Plant disputes the notion that the Haida's rejection of the 20 per cent offer "had quite the paralytic effect that Guujaaw would like to think it had" in terms of negotiations with other First Nations. Then again, he concedes the offer didn't achieve its goal of taking the conversation with the Haida to a higher level. "Not particularly, no," Plant says.

If the government was taken aback by the Haida's outright rejection of its "offer," it could hardly have anticipated the quarters from which further resistance would come. Soon, it was not just loggers mutinying, it was whole communities. The municipality of Masset— the town where the military had once marched and where the liquor and punches were plentiful at the Seagate pub—signed a protocol with the Council of the Haida Nation in 2004, pledging "common cause" in seeking security for peoples' families and their homes, and recognizing that "harmonization of Haida and Crown titles need not be divisive or exclusive and can be taken as an opportunity to make things better." The municipality and the CHN pledged to work together to "design an all island governance model," at the core of which would be commitments to stewardship and sustainability. Port Clements, the loggers' town, signed on as well. This remarkable rapprochement might have had merely local effects but for the fact that the Haida were headed to the Supreme Court of Canada on the final appeal of the TFL 39 case. They would go to Ottawa with two non-native resource communities on their side.

In March 2004, a couple of months before leaving for Ottawa for the Supreme Court hearing, Guujaaw was in Vancouver at Simon Fraser University's Morris J. Wosk Centre for Dialogue as a keynote speaker at a B.C. Treaty Commission conference on business and treaties. He sat alongside Jerry Lampert, president of the B.C. Business Council. Lampert gave the usual business line about the need for certainty. Certainty. Certainty. Certainty. The more business said it, the less likely they were to get it, because as one First Nations leader later remarked, *uncertainty* was the only asset natives had. But Guujaaw didn't say that. Sitting there surrounded by business types, he said: "I believe real strongly, there's a conscious effort to spoil this world, and when you come down and find out who it is, you find it's nice people who are spoiling the world." He then looked directly at Lampert and asked, "Is that you?" It was a moment that fairly dripped with menace, evoking in real time U. Utah Phillips's famous observation, "The Earth is not dying—it is being killed. And the people who are killing it have names and addresses." There was uneasy laughter in the Wosk Centre. Guujaaw didn't smile; he pressed his case. The B.C. Business Council was an intervenor in the appeal of the TFL 39 case, lined up in opposition to the Haida. "I'd like the B.C. Business Council to withdraw," Guujaaw said, again looking straight at Jerry Lampert. Lampert offered to do no such thing. With resigned disgust, Guujaaw said it was hard to accept the "nice words" of the B.C. Business Council; the Haida had no choice but to use the courts to expose the "soft underbelly of the economics of this place."

When it came time to argue the appeal in Ottawa, there, at the base of the steps leading into the highest court in the land, stood Guujaaw, flanked by Haida hereditary chiefs on one side and, among others, the mayors of Port Clements and Masset on the other. After being photographed among his allies, he entered the court. The usual suspects were aligned against the Haida: the B.C. government, the Canadian government, the company. But such were the implications of this decision that the provinces of Alberta, Saskatchewan, Manitoba, Ontario, Quebec and Nova Scotia had all joined the party, along with cattle interests, mining companies and a variety of "business intervenors" (the B.C. Business Council prominent among them) who were worried that the B.C. Court of Appeal judgement would be allowed to stand. On the Haida's side, along with the towns of Masset and Port Clements, were the Dene Tha', the Haisla, Squamish, Lax Kw'alaams and Tenimgyet First Nations and the First Nations Summit. A summary of Port Clements's written argument in support of the Haida said the village supported "the balancing of Haida rights and title, the public interest, and the interests of industry. The village submits they share the same concerns as the Haida related to the unsustainable rate at which logging has occurred."

Armed with support from such an unlikely quarter, Haida counsel Terri-Lynn Williams-Davidson told the panel of judges, "An incredible amount of Haida Gwaii has been logged by Weyerhaeuser and its predecessor companies. It's clear from this map that the old-growth forests of TFL 39 will not survive Weyerhaeuser's logging plans." She then presented to the court a photograph of Skidegate from the nineteenth century that showed longhouses, totem poles and canoes. "One is struck by the indisputable Haida use of the forest," she said. "The cedar tree is our sister, providing for and sustaining our culture. Among the rights at issue in this case is the right to use the forest—which includes the right to leave the trees standing." Co-counsel Louise Mandell, who had appeared before the Supreme Court of Canada years earlier as counsel for the First Nations in the *Delgamuukw* case, would later note that having a Haida woman argue the case was a remarkable precedent—legal or otherwise. "I don't think the court has ever had the facts rendered the way she did," Mandell told *SpruceRoots*. "It was very much done from a Haida perspective and not from an aboriginal law, non-aboriginal perspective. Which is what I and others have argued before because we're not aboriginal. She did quite an unusual thing when she referred to the Haida in the personal sense, as in 'I,' and 'we,' and 'our.' She rendered the facts from her perspective rather than the way the court is used to. I thought it was a first-time beautiful moment for advocacy. To see the way in which an aboriginal person speaking about their own rights and their own territory and their own people would try and get the court to see it from their perspective." About the only thing Williams-Davidson didn't do was present the Haida case to the court in the Haida language, but that day may yet come.

Mandell herself knew perfectly well what was weighing on the court's mind, because of what had been ably brought to the court's attention by government and business interests: siding with the Haida would be disastrous for the "certainty" that business needs to invest and governments need to govern. She said that shouldn't concern the court, invoking Mark Twain when she told Canada's top judges: "My life has been filled with terrible disasters, most of which have never happened."

THE SUPREME COURT of Canada reserved judgement in order to weigh what were, in effect, competing claims for certainty. Back on Haida Gwaii, the master craftsman of *papier repoussé* exhibited no uncertainty at all in pressing the Haida case. By now, his signature was a confident swish, a *G* that looks like a capital *S* with its tail tucked in, followed by an *uj*. As in, "Thank you for your attention," *Guj*. Or in some instances, more dramatically,

I am,

Guujaaw.

That he was writing on Council of the Haida Nation letterhead gave him a lot more authority than in 1979, when the hunter-gatherer was rattling off missives on his own recognizance. But what was telling about this new round of correspondence was that Guujaaw was no longer trying to create a legal precedent: he was citing it. "Weyerhaeuser's TFL suffers a fundamental legal defect," he had written to government and industry in 2003. "It is our contention that all tenures issued unilaterally by the province are unlawful." His authority? The TFL case, albeit under appeal. To Weyerhaeuser, which had sought a "partnership arrangement" with the Haida, no dice: the Haida did not want to become "part of the problem." To the federal Department of Fisheries and Oceans: "Regaining access to a livelihood from the ocean is an honourable objective of our people." To the B.C. Ministry of Forests: Show us that what you deem to be an "undercut" is supported by any sort of surplus "and that the resulting harvest level will be sustainable." To Premier Gordon Campbell himself, more talk of the "fundamental legal defect" afflicting tenures in the province's name.

The letters were longer now. What had once been perhaps six paragraphs was now six pages. "We cannot continue to compromise the archaeological forests based on recommendations of industry," Guujaaw wrote in a lengthy harangue addressed to a low-level provincial ministry manager. "Until we are able to get beyond the rehashing of our differences, there is no point in getting together," he told a negotiator with the B.C. Treaty Commission. To the RCMP, a lengthy impact statement about the removal of culturally modified trees from Kumdis: "Every tree utilized by our people tells us something of the history and the movement of our people. Every tree removed erases traces of the existence of our people." To the forests minister, in response to an offer of revenue sharing and a forest tenure: "You have made an 'offer' whereby you would give us a few of our own trees and a few dollars, which are generated through the exploitation of our forests. In exchange, you suggest that we accept your authority on all counts, including dominion over and management of our culture." A non-starter.

Then, a clear favourite of Guujaaw's: a letter to Premier Campbell in which he pointed out that through the Haida's "multi-billion-dollar lawsuit for recognition of title to Haida Gwaii, the surrounding waters and seabed and compensation for occupation and exploitation of our lands... [the Haida] are confidently challenging the very foundation upon which the Crown claims these islands... More than one deal has already gone cold in consideration of our interests. The Canadian Association of Petroleum Producers has also stated that they have no interest in investing in offshore oil and gas while these legal and jurisdictional issues remain unresolved. In your Public Accounts, 'Summary Financial Statements' ending March 31/02, Aboriginal issues appear far down the list of provincial concerns, liabilities and potential risks. You are well aware of your obligation to your creditors to fairly disclose the true status and stability of your financial position. We believe that you are deliberately downplaying and misrepresenting the reality of the province's precarious legal and financial situation and that we deserve a far more prominent place in your prospectus. We will be paying close attention to this year's Financial Statement."

In response to an invitation from the minister of forests to participate in a trade mission to China? "As I understand it, the mission is to find new markets for B.C. wood, including Haida Gwaii. While I am flattered, we believe your invitation may have been misdirected. We remain open to discussions, though we do not presently enjoy the good relations with your government to support this mission." Then, possibly the best letter of them all, addressed to Claire S. Grace, Corporate Secretary, Weyerhaeuser Company, Federal Way, Washington:

> Re: Notice of nomination for election of Guujaaw to the Board of Directors of Weyerhaeuser Company
>
> Dear Ms. Grace,
>
> I understand that Sharon Smith, a shareholder of record of one share, has submitted a letter nominating me for election to the Board of Directors of Weyerhaeuser Company. I further understand that Sharon Smith is entitled to vote at the annual meeting of shareholders to be held at the Corporate Headquarters Building, Federal Way, Washington...
>
> This letter will confirm that I consent to serve as a director of Weyerhaeuser Company if so elected.
>
> Sincerely,
>
> Guujaaw

Many are called, but few are chosen. Guujaaw, while acclaimed on Haida Gwaii, went unelected down in Federal Way.

IT WAS NOVEMBER 18, 2004, and in Ottawa, the Supreme Court of Canada had just handed down judgement in the TFL 39 case, ruling seven to zero that British Columbia must engage in meaningful consultation with the Haida before renewing the licence. Chief Justice Beverley McLachlin's majority judgement could not have framed the issue better if it had been written by Guujaaw himself. "Put simply, Canada's Aboriginal peoples were here when Europeans came, and were never conquered," McLachlin wrote. "Where the government has knowledge of an asserted Aboriginal right or title, it must consult the Aboriginal peoples on how exploitation of the land should proceed."

The court rejected the arguments of Canada and the provinces that acceding to First Nations would create untold turmoil across the land. McLachlin roundly criticized British Columbia in particular for presenting "an impoverished vision of the honour of the Crown... When the distant goal of proof is finally reached, the Aboriginal peoples may find their land and resources changed and denuded. This is not reconciliation. Nor is it honourable. The Crown, acting honourably, cannot cavalierly run roughshod over Aboriginal interests where such claims affecting those interests are being seriously pursued in the process of treaty negotiation and proof."

Curiously, in the days that followed, media sources were full of the fact that Weyerhaeuser, and by extension private businesses everywhere, were off the hook themselves in terms of a duty to consult and accommodate First Nations. It was an odd reaction, because even though the court had relieved companies of some of their duties to First Nations, it had emphatically stated that governments have a moral and a legal duty to negotiate with aboriginal communities—a ruling that in the words of the *Globe and Mail* "slammed the brakes on governments unilaterally handing out logging licences or mining rights for vast tracts of land that are tied up in land-claims litigation."

The *Globe* story was accompanied by a photo of Guujaaw and his drum, Terri-Lynn Williams-Davidson in full voice and Robert Davidson singing and drumming alongside them. The photo was taken the day of the ruling at a gathering at Vancouver's Native Friendship Centre, a meeting place for Vancouver's large urban First Nations community, and home away from home for visiting aboriginal people. Guujaaw brimmed with excitement as he addressed the jubilant crowd. "The ruling that came out this morning is very much about honour," he told them. "It is a victory that will be felt throughout the indigenous world," said Dave Porter, one of three political executives of the First Nations Summit. "Thanks, Guujaaw, for your courage and commitment," said Grand Chief Doug Kelly of the First Nations Summit. "The decision of the Supreme Court of Canada today is a real 'title wave,'" Louise Mandell told the assembled group.

British Columbia's Attorney-General, Geoff Plant, however, sought a way to twist the ruling in British Columbia's favour, saying that the judgement left the government as the final decision-maker in resources issues and did not confer a veto to aboriginal people. "It's a funny thing for him to say," Mandell told the *Globe and Mail*. "I don't think it's a question of veto or no veto. For governments to come running back, saying 'We've got the upper hand' just reiterates the colonization they've benefitted from." Guujaaw saw something even more sinister in what Plant had to say. In a statement that would prove prophetic, he warned: "This victory is only going to be real if we go out and get it."

ELEVEN

HOW THE WORLD
GETS SAVED

THERE IS A field in high country on the B.C. mainland that has seldom felt the tread of humans, and then only lightly. Folded around the field is a rim of mountains that in summer are still flecked along their ridges with cornices, hard carapaces formed by the remains of winter snows, imperceptibly melting and trickling downwards towards a field where Robert Quock once made his camp.

Quock was Tahltan, and while non-natives call this place the Klappan, the Tahltan call it Klabona. "Kla" for headwaters, "bona" for open country, according to Jimmy Dennis, a Tahltan elder and an old friend of Robert Quock.

It was to this field in the shadow of Mount Klappan, this natural amphitheatre in Klabona, that Robert Quock came in the summer of 2002. He sought the serenity it could offer a dying man. Quock had long ago named the place "Beauty Camp," this in a land where every camp the Tahltan ever made was in a setting of breathtaking beauty, a land where rivers rise in some of the most spectacular wilderness in North America. It is a veritable Serengeti of grizzly bears, black bears, mountain goats, moose, caribou, salmon, trout, eagles, loons and countless other species that prosper here, much as the Tahltan have done since time out of mind.

When Robert Quock came here for the last time in 2002, the country looked much as it always had, but for a railbed laid down by a development-minded government in the 1960s in expectation of a resource boom that never made it this far into the hinterland. The railbed became a dirt road, which made getting to Klabona easier for Robert Quock and for his family members, some of whom have returned to Beauty Camp in the summer of 2006 to honour Robert's memory and declare his beloved territory sacred.

And not a moment too soon, given signs that commodity lust is once again targeting Tahltan country, this time with more capital behind it than had the would-be railwaymen of yore. Just below Beauty Camp, the road widens for a stretch that is big enough to double as an airstrip. A windsock indicates a gentle wind blowing from the west. Nearby, a metal railing surrounds a coal-bed methane test pump and a series of gauges and taps. A sign attributes owner-ship to Shell Canada. Right now, Shell has just a few coal-bed methane test sites in Tahltan country but, if it is allowed to proceed with its development, it will eventually have between 1,500 and 10,000 drill pads scattered over a vast area, all serviced by roads and whatever subsequent infrastructure is required to get the gas to market. A coal mine proposed by another company, Fortune Minerals, is one of fourteen active mine proposals for Tahltan country, one of which, the Red Chris mine proposed by Imperial Metals, is just eighteen kilometres southeast of the community of Iskut and promises both environmental and social devastation. Looking up at Mount Klappan, it is possible to see a thick tongue of black "overburden" poking down from a ridge towards Beauty Camp, waste from a test dig for anthra-cite coal by Fortune. Testing, testing, testing and provoking, on this day, a quiet vow of absolute resistance from Rhoda Quock, Marie Quock and about a hundred other people who have gathered at Beauty Camp to listen as five matriarchs from the Klabona Keepers Society drum a song of defiance and call out the names of ancestors who have gone, in their words, to the spirit world, Robert Quock neither first nor last among them.

Into the centre of the circle of people steps Gerald Amos, long-time leader of the Haisla people from and around Kitamaat, several hundred kilometres to the southwest. "The symbolism of what you are about to see should be treasured for a long time," Amos says. "The mixing of the waters from Haida Gwaii, where Guujaaw is from, to the Sacred Headwaters, and all points in between. This is a catalyst for a historic moment in the history not just of British Columbia, but in North America."

With that, Tahltan elders line up at a small bentwood box made by Huey Carlick. One by one, each elder holds a small glass jar high in the air, rotating it unsteadily while invoking in Tahltan and in English the names of ancestors and animals that have crossed this land for generations, then tips into the box an ounce or two of water from the Stikine River. In the same way, they then add water from the Klappan River. Next chiefs and elders from a neighbouring nation to the south, the Wet'suwet'en, stand, and add water from the Bulkley River, a tributary of the Skeena River. Water from the Skeena is deposited into the box by members of the Gitksan Nation, the land of *Delgamuukw*. To this mixture, Sandra Jack, newly elected spokes-person for the Taku River Tlingit First Nation north and west of Tahltan country, adds water from the Teslin River. Finally Gerald Amos steps forward again to mix in water from the Kitlope River, which runs through the land of milky blue waters that the Haisla and Henaksiala people call home.

Guujaaw steps into the circle at this point. Beside him are his daughter Niisii, and his son Kung St'aasl. "I'm from the Ravens of Gak'yaals Kiigawaay of Skedans, and my kids, like their grandmother Diane Brown, are from the Ts'aahl people of the Eagle Clan," he announces. There is rapt silence among the onlookers. Guujaaw owns this moment, commanding centre stage, dressed in his trademark cedar bark headband trimmed with animal fur, his ponytail hanging down over his signature Haida vest with a Raven motif on the back, one hand comfortably weighing his trademark drum. Niisii and Kung St'aasl are both dressed in headbands and aprons, awaiting their father's signal to proceed.

"I am the political representative of the Haidas, so I am sent by my people to support you," Guujaaw says, nodding towards the women of the Klabona Keepers Society. "I am not just representing myself and my family, but the Haida Nation." He gestures to the surrounding mountainsides. "The waters that start up here in a little trickle and go down, creating the great rivers that we know today and supply so many people with their sustenance and well-being, they carry on and mix with the ocean around our islands. We took water from the sea to bring to this ceremony today."

Guujaaw begins to drum, and as he gives powerful voice to a Haida canoe song, Niisii and Kung St'aasl circle the bentwood box, pouring sea water from Haida Gwaii into the mixed waters of the rivers that owe their provenance to this place. As Niisii and Kung St'aasl empty their jar, a discordant noise rises from the south, the spoiled ridge of Mount Klappan, as a Fortune Minerals helicopter thuds into view trailing a sling—fuel, is the speculation—and circles a few times before bearing away. A young Tahltan man looks up and mutters, "Where's my gun? I wanna shoot that sucker."

But the chopper retreats unharmed, and the dignity of the moment is regained. Guujaaw ends his song to loud applause, and Rhoda Quock stands and reads a declaration: "The First Nations of this land stand united today at the birthplace of the great Stikine, Skeena and Nass watersheds. We celebrate and reaffirm our stewardship of these sacred headwaters and all that flows from here." There is a loud cheer, and Jimmy Dennis musters into a celebratory circle the hundred or so witnesses to the Tahltan's declaration of defiance against Shell, Fortune and others who would defile their lands. Then a chill breeze picks up, and people quickly disperse. Down below

Beauty Camp, a big, healthy grizzly bear provides a momentary distraction as it feeds near the road, but soon the camp is struck and the field is empty again.

This is how the world gets saved, not with a bang but a whisper. Around a fireplace the night before the Sacred Headwaters Gathering, there was a meeting to familiarize travellers from afar with the issues confronting the Tahltan and their neighbours, and to strategize about how best to amplify their concern for the Klappan. The meeting was devoid of bombast, and you had to strain to hear speakers as they offered encouragement and advice. Once people were clear about the logistics for the next day and the protocols that governed who would get to speak and when, attention turned to the Sacred Headwaters Declaration. A draft was circulated, its exact wording was parsed and changes were read aloud. Around the fire were Tahltan members, neighbouring tribal and political leaders, environmentalists, campaign funders and a few stray supporters of indeterminate origin, all drawn to a cause. The declaration initially began, "The First Nations of northern British Columbia stand united today," but Guujaaw took exception to the phrase "northern British Columbia" and offered an amendment: "In saying that [northern British Columbia], you are conceding to them [the federal and provincial governments] as being the authority. I would change that just a little bit to say what *you* want to call British Columbia, rather than saying it is British Columbia, because they have no treaty with your people to say this is British Columbia, or with any of us in the north here."

The point was classic Guujaaw. To concede that Tahltan land was part of British Columbia would be to accept the colonists' nomenclature, allowing a name that was barely 200 years in usage to trump the ownership and traditions of thousands of years of Tahltan presence on their lands. There were quiet nods of approval around the campfire. Wade Davis, owner of a summer camp just a few kilometres away, offered up a simple alternative: "This land." Guujaaw gruffly assented. And so the next day at Beauty Camp, when the declaration is read aloud after the mixing of the waters, it is "the First Nations of this land" who stand united. Guujaaw's quiet statecraft has made its way into another campaign to curb the commodity cravings of people in lands so far from here as to seem on another planet.

"We really don't want development here," Chief Marie Quock of the Iskut Band tells a *Globe and Mail* reporter covering the gathering by phone from Vancouver. "There are certain areas sacred to the Tahltan and this is one of them. This is not to say that we are against all development, but certainly we don't want to see it in the Klabona." She expresses a hope that the stand the Tahltan are making here resonates not just locally, but "globally maybe." "Is it only a native fight?" Guujaaw asks the same reporter. "No. It's got to be everybody's fight… all of us have got to be concerned about what's happening to the Earth."

Guujaaw, here in solidarity with the Tahltan, comes with a special regard for this place. Distant as it is from his Haida homeland, it is to these Sacred Headwaters that the Haida trace their origins. "This piece of the Earth is part of our history, as well as the history of the people from this region. The Raven took the light from this area, from the headwaters of the Nass is our story, and in their [the Tahltan's] story it is the headwaters of the Stikine. The story is pretty much identical, and I argued with one of the Tahltan people about where it occurred, but he took me up here and it's in fact the same place."

Guujaaw stands ready, with others, to defend the place that gave birth to one of the central and enduring creation myths of the Haida people. Is it only a native fight? No, but to native people it sure seems that way sometimes. Is it a global fight? Absolutely.

IN FARAWAY AUSTRALIA, there is a land that could not look less like the Sacred Headwaters or Haida Gwaii, a dry, desolate but gorgeous place that white people call the Coorong. It is the territory of the Ngarrindjeri Nation, who will tell anyone who asks, "They took our land and then our children." When the state of South Australia was established in 1834, the land was referred to in British Parliament as "waste and unoccupied." Britain told the local colonial administrators to negotiate with aboriginal people and to compensate them for the loss of their land. But the colonialists were too busy colonizing to pay attention, so they didn't negotiate. Instead, they did everything they could to wipe out the aboriginals. When that failed, they set about "civilizing" them by building a Christian mission, and then they took away the children—the Stolen Generation.

One hot afternoon in 2008, tribal elder Tom Trevorrow is sitting in a boardroom in the Ngarrindjeri's office complex near the town of Meningie. "I met a Haida, in Auckland," he says. He had met Vince Collison, as it turns out, both of them in New Zealand for a conference about repatriation of aboriginal remains. Collison is one of a number of determined Haida cultural restorationists who have travelled the globe in an effort to repatriate, to Haida Gwaii, ancestral remains from the likes of Chicago's Field Museum, New York's Museum of Natural History, Toronto's Royal Ontario Museum and London's British Museum. "We believe the souls of the dead don't rest in peace if their bones are not left in their homeland," Collison told a conference at the Museum of London in 2007. The repatriation of remains is a vital part of the Haida's rebuilding process, and it is also "a massive issue" for the Ngarrindjeri, says Trevorrow. After Collison and Trevorrow met in New Zealand, Collison visited the Ngarrindjeri in their homeland, which they call the Kurangk—Place of the Long Neck of Water. Except these days there isn't much water; the Murray-Darling river system is drying up in Australia, thanks to a debilitating drought. With the onset of global warming, things aren't likely to get any better, and the Ngarrindjeri have already begun to see significant declines in fish populations and the health of the indigenous swan grass.

Elder Matt Rigney, one of thirteen children, tells of being sent away to residential school. Even when he found his way back to his community, Raukkan, he and the other aboriginal kids weren't allowed to go to Meningie, a white town. Until the seventies, in Meningie, "blacks" were not welcome under any circumstances. Rigney talks about totems, *ngaitji* as his people call them. Their totems aren't carved poles but rather living creatures placed in the peoples' care. Rigney, from an early age, was put in care of two totems—the black swan and the huntsman spider. It is not hard to think about having stewardship responsibility for a swan, but a spider? Indeed, all the spiders? Such is Rigney's lot, and he undertakes it willingly. For swans and spiders *and* aboriginal peoples to survive, of course, they need land—or what indigenous Australians call "country."

In 2003, some Ngarrindjeri, including Matt Rigney and Tom Trevorrow, along with Ellen and George Trevorrow, went to Government House in Adelaide to present the "Crown"—in this case Marjorie Jackson-Nelson, the state governor—with a proclamation demanding that the government recognize Ngarrindjeri dominion over their lands, enter into a social charter with the tribe and present a bill in Parliament for a treaty between the Ngarrindjeri and South Australia. The governor agreed to place their petition on the public record "for posterity," but she didn't promise anything else.

Matt Rigney and his fellow elders are being herded towards what the government calls "indigenous land-use agreements." After the heady days of *Mabo,* the huge title and rights win for Australian aboriginal people back in the 1990s, a massive fear campaign was waged by mining and farming interests, encouraged by John Howard's federal conservative administration, and Australia spent a decade going backwards. In 2002, the year the Haida won their Court of Appeal case in British Columbia, the Yorta Yorta people, who live upstream from the Ngarrindjeri in the neighbouring state of Victoria, lost a title and rights case in the High Court of Australia because the court decided there had been an "interruption" in their observance of traditional laws and customs. That the interruption came at the hands of murderous colonizers wasn't the point, in the court's view, and so now Australian aboriginals operate under a Native Title Act that offers them many things, but not native title. In the view of Matt Rigney and Tom Trevorrow, the land-use agreements on offer extinguish rights and title. The Ngarrindjeri aren't biting, but they don't seem to be winning, either. The Yorta Yorta case illustrates the precariousness, still, of aboriginal peoples—be they in the states of Victoria and South Australia or, indeed, in the province of British Columbia—who need to prove their prior existence within a system that will always assign more weight to the written records of settlers than to the oral history or the songs and dances of ancient cultures who took up neither arms nor the pen. "One step forward, two steps back," in the words of Lenin. Or as Canadian poet Dorothy Livesay would phrase it, "Shove the lever / push it back."

Down at Raukkan where Matt Rigney was born, the place the missionaries and the maps named Point McLeay, the aboriginal housing is about what you'd expect, from the neglected to the merely abject. But one building, a gorgeous little stone church, is undergoing renovations with what would seem to be plentiful government funds. It is the Point McLeay mission, and Rigney points out that it appears—along with one of his ancestors, David Unaipon—on the Australian $50 banknote. David Unaipon was an aboriginal inventor who in 1914 anticipated the helicopter, based on the principle of flight of the boomerang. For that, and inventions like an improved handpiece for mechanical sheep shearing, he was known at the time as "Australia's Leonardo." As an aboriginal man of standing in white Australia, a rarity, Unaipon presented his views at a royal commission into aboriginal affairs in Australia in 1913—the same year, coincidentally, that the McKenna-McBride Commission was paying a visit to Haida Gwaii. Unaipon wanted his people to be understood. On the Australian $50 banknote, he is quoted as saying, "As a full-blooded member of my race I think I may claim to be the first—but I hope, not the last—to produce an enduring record of our customs, beliefs and imaginings." Curious, isn't it, that the government that put that on a banknote won't acknowledge the *actual* rights of the full-blooded people who inhabited the land as long as 40,000 years ago?

The Canadian $20 bill features the Queen and the Centre Block of Parliament on one side and four images from Bill Reid on the other: *The Raven and the First Men* and *The Spirit of Haida Gwaii*, flanked by *Haida Grizzly Bear* and *Mythic Messenger*. As in Australia, every day Canadians go to their bank machines to load up their wallets with the currency of the realm. Australians may not think about this every time they proffer a $50 banknote to buy Vegemite and a nice red from McLaren Vale, and Canadians may not think twice as they peel off a $20 bill at Tim Hortons, but the distance between not just the picture but the honour of the Crown on one side, and not just the pictures but the reality of Raukkan or Haida Gwaii on the other, is very much greater than the thickness of a banknote.

ORDINARY CANADIANS CAN be forgiven for thinking that if the Supreme Court of their country renders a unanimous judgement on a question of national importance, the system will somehow snap to attention. Not so. A case like that of the Haida and TFL 39 is guaranteed to spawn learned papers that dissect the judges' ruling, parsing their comments and asides, turning them this way and that like forensic archaeologists examining the remains of the Kennewick Man. Oh, and conferences, lots of conferences, where people can talk about the implications of the court's ruling: What does it *imply* for the province? What does it *imply* for Weyerhaeuser and other timber companies? Heavy on implications, strangely light on action. And typically devoid of any substantive discussion about the implications for the people who brought the case in the first place. The fact is, judges do not render decisions, then throw off their robes, pull on their working skivvies and head out into the field to examine their handiwork. Judges rely on governments to respond to their rulings and, if necessary, change the laws. In the end, the distance between the bench of the Supreme Court of Canada and a workbench in Masset or Skidegate or Sandspit is a very great distance indeed.

In the case of TFL 39, the B.C. government *had* actually leapt into action after the Court of Appeal found in the Haida's favour, but not in the way that taxpaying, law-abiding, decent Canadians might have suspected. Prominent native leader Dave Porter recalls that on the heels of the Haida victory in the fall of 2004, the entire provincial cabinet met with British Columbia's First Nations leadership in a Vancouver hotel in what turned out to be a "slugfest." John Ward, of the Taku River Tlingit, and Guujaaw went nose to nose with Attorney-General Geoff Plant. "'Listen to your own courts!'" Porter recalls them saying, dressing down the Attorney-General for refusing to recognize, still, that First Nations' rights were real. "The temperature certainly did rise." Porter says the Haida decision caused "a fundamental shift in the provincial approach—that was the moment when the pendulum completely swung over." He believes that was also the moment when Premier Gordon Campbell realized he had to move negotiations with First Nations into his own office and out of a ministry, that of the Attorney-General, whose reflex instinct was almost always litigation. But the shift took time to occur. In the meantime, true to historical form, the government tried to dodge the bullet of the Haida ruling by yet again changing the rules. After being told it had the primary duty of consultation with First Nations, Campbell's government drastically rewrote the Forest Act, offloading most of those duties onto the companies. By the time the Supreme Court of Canada upheld the province's requirement to consult, absolving Weyerhaeuser of the same duty, and by the time the court set out a clear direction that "the honour of the Crown cannot be delegated," the province had done precisely that. Such that when Weyerhaeuser decided to sell its coastal forestry operations in British Columbia to Toronto-based asset managers Brascan in early 2005, something that would normally trigger a review, under the new rules of the Forest Act it did not.

After the *Delgamuukw* decision, Wet'suwet'en Hereditary Chief Satsan, Herb George, said: "What our chiefs don't understand, what they have difficulty with, is that when we compare the case law that is put forward in *Delgamuukw* with our own laws, our chiefs say, 'That's really funny. Look at that. They can just change the law anytime they want. Where our laws have remained unchanged for centuries.' They can't understand that." Put another way, think of the Sufi tale of the master archer renowned for always hitting a bull's eye. "What's your secret?" the novice demands to know. "It's easy," says the master. "I shoot my arrow, and wherever it lands, I draw a bull's eye around it."

So the B.C. government had moved the net, effectively, in the TFL 39 case. Neat, but in the end, not clever enough. "Massive Haida blockades shut down Weyerhaeuser," said one headline in March 2005, in what Yogi Berra might have described as déjà vu all over again. Certainly, there were overtones of Lyell Island. But in a number of ways these blockades were very different. They were on Graham Island, a more populous part of Haida Gwaii. Two blockades were set up, one at a log sort yard near Queen Charlotte City, the other at Juskatla; both were accessible by road, which meant it was easy for people to turn out in force. In order to block the $1.2 billion asset sale, which people on Haida Gwaii were convinced would lead to even more aggressive harvesting by Brascan, islanders simply blocked Weyerhaeuser and Ministry of Forests personnel from going to work. There was little of the outright confrontation of the eighties. Neither the company nor the provincial government sought an injunction, almost a reflex action in times past. Weyerhaeuser, upon hearing of the blockade, turned an incoming log barge around and sent it back to Prince Rupert to avoid a standoff. The Haida seized some logs that were already down, and they vowed to sell them off and spend the money on community projects.

Once again, the elders stood their ground. Chief Gaahlaay, Watson Pryce, who had recently celebrated his one hundredth birthday, looked spry—a veteran of Lyell Island, back for more of the same. Chief Niis Wes, a mere ninety-two, was there most days. And Guujaaw was there, saying something about how, when reason and diplomacy fail, the spirit rises. That's what the blockade was called— Islands Spirit Rising. Robert Davidson told folks the action wasn't about winning, it was about who they were becoming. Irene Mills from the Council of the Haida Nation said, "We're helping the Crown restore its honour." Just in case the Crown wasn't listening, Guujaaw wrote to then Governor General Adrienne Clarkson.

Excellency:

We respectfully request your attention in the matter of the Honour of the Crown.

The history of the Haida Nation will show that for more than a century we have attempted to resolve the longstanding issues of Title dispute through diplomacy, negotiations and appeals to your highest Court.

Likewise, we have attempted to resolve the immediate issues of the use and exploitation of the resources of these lands vis-à-vis the Province of British Columbia. We have also worked diligently with our neighbours to design the conditions which would provide for the well-being of these islands as is necessary for a continuing culture and a sustainable economy.

While Courts have made efforts to compel the Federal and Provincial Governments to sit down and resolve these matters through a fair process of reconciliation, British Columbia has responded with attempts to absolve itself of that responsibility. While we sought legal guidance through the Courts, British Columbia enacted legislation to divest itself of the legal authority and public duty to regulate the forests, and practically eliminated every public mechanism to oversee industrial and environmental accountability.

The Province has always put economic interests before the well-being of the land, and continues that pattern.

We note that the Supreme Court of Canada in its wisdom had opted for moral persuasion as the potential solution, and we agree, Honour should lead to the resolutions of this dispute.

On the basis of the moral authority of your office and the sovereign responsibilities vested in you, we formally request your intervention in the delivery of the Honour of the Crown.

Respectfully,

Guujaaw,

President of the Haida Nation

The Governor General had shown herself willing to get her feet wet and her hands dirty—visiting remote communities all over Canada was a hallmark of her time in office, and during her tenure she visited Haida Gwaii twice. But if she intervened in this instance it wasn't in person, and the Haida never learned of it.

Instead, the Islands Spirit Rising insurrection succeeded because a vast majority of the islanders supported it. "Something that's different this time around is that people from every island community and walk of life are standing with the Haida," wrote John Broadhead, veteran of the campaign to save Gwaii Haanas. "Their numbers vary from day-to-day and shift-to-shift, from a few overnighters to several hundred by day. There's a donation account at the local credit union. Hot meals are prepared in community kitchens and delivered to the line, where you'll find a lot of local seafood, fresh baking and good company. At the checkpoints near Port Clements and in Queen Charlotte City, the line in the road is marked with a two-by-four wooden speed bump, flanked by flags and signs that say Enough Is Enough.

"Security is coordinated by two Haida ex-Mounties, in regular contact with the RCMP who visit several times a day. Like a rainforest version of Wal-Mart greeters, women and men in reflective vests greet every vehicle and pedestrian at the line, inquiring cheerfully what they're looking for today. They seem to know from a hundred metres

who's in most of the approaching vehicles, many of them locals coming to visit, bring food or grab a truckload of gravel down the road,
and they get through. Weyerhaeuser's main contractor drives out
from Port Clements to the line at the Yakoun River every morning,
then returns to town to report to the crew there'll be no logging
today. Some stay at home, others visit the checkpoints to stand around
a bonfire, trade news and talk about what's going on. There are financial worries to deal with, security matters to discuss, warm food and
drink, a bit of raunchy humour, many songs and prayers."

And there was something else: a new generation of Haida warriors and, speaking for them, none other than Gwaai Edenshaw,
Guujaaw's eldest son. "This is not just a Council of the Haida Nation
thing," Gwaai told a local writer. "It's a Haida Gwaii thing. We are
not against people trying to eke out a living from the resources, we
are against corporations making a money grab. Weyerhaeuser is selling out to Brascan and they're taking everything on their way out.
We want to draw attention to the way business is being done here.
There will be nothing left for the next generation. We want to make
sure there will be work for island people for the future." Tellingly,
magnificently, Gwaai picked up the mantle from the elders. "I have
seen what the corporations have been doing here all my life. I was
born here. Things are just getting worse. This blockade is something
we've been waiting for practically all our lives." Jail us all if you wish,
they had told Allan McEachern in 1985, there are more where we
came from. Twenty years a'growing, as they say in Ireland, and there
were evidently more still a'growing on Haida Gwaii.

What brought the blockades down in the end were promises by
the province that Duu Guusd would remain untouched for at least
four years, removing the entire area from the allowable annual cut;
that culturally modified trees would be protected; that an end to bear
hunting on the islands would be sought, and that the whole basis for
land-use planning would change in favour of a made–in–Haida
Gwaii process that focussed on local sustainability. There was also a

commitment—dramatic in a place where in some years nearly three million cubic metres of wood was extracted—to find a way to reduce the annual harvest for all tenures on the islands to 900,000 cubic metres in total.

The Haida and the province thought that would take two years to figure out. It took longer, though this time it was the Haida who strung out discussions with the provincial government, including one rather comical episode in December 2006 when the provincial lands minister at the time, Pat Bell, flew up to a meeting in Skidegate to sign a land-use plan—only for the Haida to balk and send the minister back to Victoria empty-handed. The back page of the *Observer* featured a photograph of Bell sitting poker-faced over a map of the islands, staring at Guujaaw, with Arnie Bellis looking on. The paper captioned the event as a "non-signing." In an accompanying article, the *Observer* said, "When asked for the meat of the reason he was on the islands, the minister replied, 'There are a lot of vegetables.'"

IT IS DECEMBER 2007, in a downstairs ballroom of the Waterfront Hotel in Vancouver, and Robert Davidson leads the Rainbow Creek Dancers in song and dance as Premier Gordon Campbell, Guujaaw, Lands Minister Pat Bell, Arnie Bellis, Chief Skidegate, Chief Iljawass and other luminaries enter the room. There are three flags on the raised podium, representing British Columbia, Canada and the Haida Nation. Gordon Campbell introduces the dignitaries seated in a crescent beside him, including his "good friend Guujaaw." Campbell commits a faux pas when he omits Chief Sgaan ʔiwʔwaans, Allan Wilson. The premier talks about Guujaaw being "clear-sighted" and "tenacious," about the building of trust and about finding "industrial certainty and conservation" in one place. Minister Bell speaks glowingly of Guujaaw being a "leader among leaders." Then it is Guujaaw's turn, and he immediately gets a laugh when he speculates that the province "is trying to disarm me by flattering me." He warms to his enduring themes—governments are terrified to do the right thing because they fear the consequences; Haida people are adamant that the solution is to look after the things that have given them life; the struggles of the Haida Nation represent all peoples' struggles in trying to do what is right for "this poor old world of ours." To Gordon Campbell, he says, "I think you are the right person in the right place." While a standing ovation erupts, the two leaders make for a table to sign their agreement.

"Nearly half of the land base of Haida Gwaii will rest within protected areas as a result of a strategic land-use agreement announced today by Premier Gordon Campbell and Guujaaw, President of the Council of the Haida Nation," said the government press release prepared for the occasion. Duu Guusd, the tribal park the Haida had unilaterally declared protected a quarter of a century earlier: protected. The cut, which had once peaked at almost three million cubic metres annually: now 800,000 cubic metres, all under ecosystem-based management. (Western Forest Products, the largest forest licensee on Haida Gwaii with about 45 per cent of the islands' timber harvest, said later that day it would "be seeking appropriate compensation should there be any deletions from Western's tenures.") Smaller stuff, too, such as "100 per cent timber retention areas" to protect habitat for the Queen Charlotte goshawk, saw-whet owls and blue herons. This concession added up to less than 3,000 hectares, but it was enough to have held up the agreement by several months.

Amid the hubbub of self-congratulation, Chief Sg̱aan ʔiwʔwaans takes centre stage. He seems not to have taken offence about being overlooked in the premier's introductions. He does, however, have something to say. "This is cool," Chief Sg̱aan ʔiwʔwaans offers. "We've been fighting for this for two hundred years." And then he shares a story with the crowd. "My Aunty Ethel was arrested at Lyell Island," the chief says. "I was the one who arrested her." Allan Wilson, then an RCMP officer, had taken Ethel Wilson into custody on the day the elders stood their ground for Athlii Gwaii. Two decades later, no longer a Mountie, he had joined the Islands Spirit Rising blockade as a protester. He recalls for the audience that the smell of woodsmoke at Yakoun in 2005 was the same as that on the logging road on Lyell Island back in 1985, as if acknowledging that he had always been on the side of the Haida, and of the land. Haida Gwaii, he says, is his backyard, it's his front yard and, touching his heart, "it's home."

With that, Robert Davidson ends the proceedings, leading a rousing rendition of the national anthem. No, not that one, the other one. The Lyell Island song. The Haida national anthem.

TWELVE

YES,

WE CAN

ON A GORGEOUS summer's night, when the last place anyone wants to be is cooped up inside, Guujaaw and Arnie Bellis are working hard under the buzz of fluorescent lights in the Port Clements Community Hall. They are at a protocol meeting. With them are two senior leaders from the Council of the Haida Nation, Old Massett Chief Councillor Elizabeth Moore and the mayors and some councillors from Masset, Queen Charlotte City and Port Clements. There are about thirty people in the audience. These protocol meetings, open to the public, are where the Haida's new world order gets pressure-treated by local non-Haida governments, in an effort to fuse the political ambitions of all the communities on the islands. By the time of this meeting, the town of Port Clements, along with Masset and the Queen Charlotte Regional District, has already signed a protocol with the Haida in which it is agreed that "the management of land and marine resources over the past 50 years has put the islands in a precarious position. The harmonization of Haida and Crown titles need not be divisive or exclusive, and can be taken as an opportunity to make things better." Port Clements sided with the Haida during their pivotal Supreme Court of Canada challenge in

2004. But on this night in the summer of 2006, with the signing of the land-use deal with the province still eighteen months away, there is plenty of trust building left to do.

Guujaaw gives a short summary of the attempt to amalgamate some forestry tenures under Haida management. Randy O'Brien, a logging and transportation contractor, sits beside his wife, Gloria, and the more Guujaaw talks, the faster their jaws work overtime on some chewing gum. The O'Briens aren't outsiders. They live on the islands and have built a good business in a tough environment. But that also makes them tough to convince that having the Haida in charge of the forests is going to be good for them. They seem to be here tonight almost to steal a trick from Giindajin himself—to question everything.

Are the Haida negotiating to buy the biggest remaining forest tenure on the islands? Randy O'Brien asks. Guujaaw replies that licences are a commodity. "Let's snap them up," he says, and run them on the islands. "The continued flipping of licences by people who come and make money and leave is unacceptable to us." Guujaaw gets support from Jim Abbott, a local mill owner who has struggled for years to get enough wood supply to run his operation. "We're going to have to come up with a model that's island-built, otherwise it's not going to work," says Abbott. Randy O'Brien seems skeptical. "There has to be an open market. We don't want handouts or welfare." There ensues a lengthy debate about community forestry, and how to pay for it, until O'Brien pipes up that he's heard the Haida are negotiating to buy tenures with money from the Gwaii Trust, an all-islands fund set up as part of the negotiations to settle the Gwaii Haanas dispute two decades earlier. If the Haida are scheming to buy tenures, O'Brien says sharply, "That's not right." "Absolutely wrong," counters Guujaaw. "You hear rumours like that, you tell us." "I'm telling ya," O'Brien says. "You're accusing us," Guujaaw says. "I'm telling ya," says O'Brien. Let's form a committee, offers the mayor of Masset. Sure, says Guuj, and let's look at all the tenures on the islands. "I don't have a problem with that," says O'Brien. A motion is made to form a committee, and as soon as it is carried, Randy and Gloria O'Brien leave.

Guujaaw then fills the crowd in on developments on the mainland to build a pipeline to bring tar sands oil from Alberta to either Kitimat or Prince Rupert. That would bring tankers into the waters of Haida Gwaii, and the Haida are dead set against it. Guujaaw outlines the risks of potential oil spills, ballast getting emptied into local waters and big changes to marine traffic in the region. "We've taken the position that we are opposed because the technology is not foolproof," he says. "Anyways," he adds with a grin, "I don't wanna radicalize all the communities here, just want to get you thinking about it." By the time he has also got them thinking about protected areas, revenue sharing, the upcoming fall bear hunt (which the Haida oppose), land-use planning, court rulings, the failings of the ferry system and a few other things, it is after half past ten at night. What is fascinating to watch is how Guujaaw commands attention not just because he's Guujaaw, but because his knowledge of the issues is comprehensive and deep. While some at the meeting may disagree with him, it is clear he is trusted utterly to stand up for Haida Gwaii, no matter what the odds, no matter how powerful the foe, no matter where the next assault might come from. People listen deeply, because their future depends on knowing what Guujaaw knows about the outside world. He holds court, a puissant lord returned from battles in a foreign land, and yet he conducts himself with a quiet, almost diffident air.

A couple of years after the tense exchange with Randy O'Brien, a lead story in the *Queen Charlotte Islands Observer* reads, "Gwaii Forest may buy TFL." In the letters section of the same edition, Randy O'Brien writes that he has "practically begged" the province for input into land-use planning, and his attempts to get involved in the Haida's forestry plans have been ignored. A few months after that, amid a worldwide financial crisis, Western Forest Products announces an indefinite shutdown of its operations on Haida Gwaii. "It's a disaster for the islands," Wally Cheer, a Port Clements councillor and a logging contractor, told the *Observer*.

The Haida have said outright that they intend to build a new island economy. They might yet end up owning Western Forest Products' forest tenure. But it is inevitable, now that the Haida are coming back into their power, that many people will have questions about the direction in which the Council of the Haida Nation is taking the islands. And it's predictable that the Haida, in power, will find the legal shoe on the other foot sometimes; after years of the Haida suing for their rights, others might sue the Haida for what they believe to be theirs. In Sandspit, where some people still feel they got hornswoggled into the deal to protect Gwaii Haanas, one of the Haida's most noisy and persistent foes is Doug Gould. Born and raised on Haida Gwaii, and a logger until he realized South Moresby was going to become a park, not a tree farm, Gould and a partner established Moresby Explorers in 1988 to run ecotours into the park. Many an unsuspecting tourist has taken a trip with Gould and been given a more rasping than rapturous running commentary on the wonders of Haida Gwaii. Gould snorts at the mention of Guujaaw—"government-grant-Gary," as he calls him—and he has gone to court over what he claims is reverse racism that has affected his business. Gould's judicial target has been the Attorney-General of Canada, but his more specific complaint is with the operation of the Gwaii Haanas Archipelago Management Board, which sets a quota for using the park reserve. The AMB is jointly administered by Haida and non-Haida national parks delegates, and it divides available "user days" equally between Haida and non-Haida under a Haida Allocation Policy. In a nutshell, Gould claims that he has been discriminated against because the Haida don't use their full quota, but he cannot get access to it because he's not native. Gould lost his case in the Federal Court of Canada, and the Supreme Court of Canada refused to hear an appeal. "Sad news for racial equality on the Queen Charlotte Islands," said the Canadian Constitution Foundation in early

2008. (The foundation, which champions "liberticidal" views from
its base in Calgary, provided funds to support Gould's journey
through the courts.) The ruling seemed to take some of the wind out
of Doug Gould, who stepped back from day-to-day management of
his company and eventually sold it to his employees.

Up in Tlell, another family is on a collision course with the Council of the Haida Nation. "Stop the Bear Hunt" posters and buttons
abound on Haida Gwaii, and since Kevin and Victoria Olmstead
started hunting bears on the islands when they bought two big-game
licences in 1999 and 2002, the posters are directed squarely at stopping them. The Olmsteads, who gave the dilapidated Tlell River
House a kind of faux Davy Crockett makeover and threw in a spa
option as a concession to the times, use the place as a base for enter-
taining bear hunters, who pay upwards of $7,500 to get a crack at an
Ursus americanus carlottae—the biggest black bear in the world. The
agreement the Haida signed with the B.C. government in 2007, which
contemplated an end to the bear hunt, depends on the licensees being
bought out, and that hasn't yet happened. When the Haida offered
the Olmsteads money to shut down the hunt in the fall of 2008, they
said it wasn't enough. Nonetheless, Guujaaw growls that the Haida
will stop the hunt, "one way or another." In response to those who
worry that the Haida, by buying out money-making enterprises and
closing down access to resources, could beggar the ability of islanders to build an economy, he says bluntly, "We're investing in life."

But what of hereditary Chief Thasi, Ken Edgars, with investors
lined up to back his proposed fishing lodge in Naden Harbour, which
happens also to be in the Duu Guusd protected area and the traditional territory of Chief ʔIdansuu? Back in 2006, Arnie Bellis told a
public meeting in Masset that the argument between Chief Thasi
and the Council of the Haida Nation was "internal Haida Nation
business" that would not be debated in public. "We're not against
Haida economics," he said, "but there is a process going on." However, the rezoning that Edgars seeks needs the approval of the

regional district, a body that seats not a single Haida representative, so there are in effect *two* processes going on. In Guujaaw's view, Chief Thasi erred when he "went and asked the province, not us" for permission to build his lodge. Until people begin to respect the authority of the Haida in every aspect of life on the islands, he says, there will continue to be what he has earlier described as "the squabbles within"—to the point that "we could end up with a lot of little kingdoms on Haida Gwaii."

Yet couldn't the Haida end up with one little kingdom *of* Haida Gwaii? One day at a coffee shop near Skidegate, a non-aboriginal woman who claims to be supportive of the Council of the Haida Nation worries that their governance model seems to be too much about Haida internal process. "They've got committees and committees and committees," she says. "What they don't have is investors."

That's not strictly true. The Haida and NaiKun Wind Energy Group announced in January 2009 a fifty-fifty partnership in a company that will operate and maintain a massive offshore wind farm proposed for Hecate Strait, which at 1,750 megawatts when fully operational would be an energy source sufficient to power 600,000 B.C. homes. NaiKun is potentially a big deal—its estimated capital costs are between $500 million and $1 billion—although it is far from a done deal; even if it survives the Canadian and B.C. environmental assessment process, there's no guarantee it will survive the Haida's. Guujaaw recalls that when the wind developers first turned up on the islands, "We told them, 'Bugger off. Don't come flashing federal and provincial permits at us.'" But now they are partners, with Haida environmental standards that are higher than federal and provincial standards. If the project proceeds, there will be a lot of construction jobs, with fifty full-time jobs beyond that. Music to Guujaaw's ears, NaiKun's vice-president of commercial operations, Matt Burns, is unafraid to say in public what few industry leaders ever have: "We assume that it is Haida traditional territory, full stop." With that out of the way, it is easy to see how wind power fits logically

within the Haida's overarching goal of achieving economic indepen-
dence and self-reliance without having to concede an inch on title.

To that end, the Haida have also considered the findings of a Harvard University study that assesses successful economic development
in what it calls "Indian country" across North America. The Harvard
study urges indigenous nations to separate politics and business and
to ensure that their governing institutions are culturally appropriate
and transparent. On Haida Gwaii, Guujaaw says the nation's business
will be conducted through an organization that is "arm's length from
all the councils." Until that is in place, however, there is little that
would guide a potential investor to any place in the CHN structure
other than Guujaaw himself. People routinely pitch up on Haida Gwaii
with business or investment ideas, and inevitably they are steered to
the CHN president. Yet a common criticism of Guujaaw from off-
islands is that it's almost impossible to do a deal with him. Doug
Caul, a senior provincial bureaucrat who tangled with Guujaaw on
the 20 per cent land offer, says, "There's always a formula with Guujaaw. His simple formula is he'll negotiate with you, get what he wants,
but he won't sign anything. Then he'll use *that* as a starting point to do
it all over again. I think people become wary of him and his ability to
close a deal, or even if he intended to do a deal in the first place."

It's not just non-Haida who question Guujaaw's leadership on the
economy. Elizabeth Moore is the first woman chief in Old Massett, a
former legal aid and restorative justice worker, and she attributes her
electoral win at least in part to the fact that people are tired of a male-
dominated political elite in this matriarchal culture where "women
used to run the show." According to Moore, "Not everybody gets to
eat three meals a day in Old Massett. Some people don't even have a
place to live. People are in denial about it. People are feeling frustrated.
We are poor, we don't seem to be getting anywhere, it's just tough,
long—people want something to happen." Does she support Guujaaw? "I guess I'd have to say no." She is critical of the Haida House of

Assembly, from which, she says, issues of housing, education, health care and poverty get short shrift. "They always say, 'That's not our mandate, that's not what we do. We're here for forestry and fisheries.' But if you don't have healthy, educated people, who's gonna look after whatever is left? Who's gonna take over the positions of the ministry of forests, or ministry of oceans, water?" Moore supports Haida rights and title, but not the court case. She is offended that the Haida would stoop to argue their case in Canada's courts, a "crappy system" that she doubts will deliver what the Haida want. "We shouldn't be spending our energy, time and money proving that we've been here." If anything, Moore believes, the Haida should become even more radical. "I've always had this fantasy that all the First Nations people across Canada should just shut it down. You know, shut down whatever access there is for a road to a mine, a logging road or whatever, just shut everything down for a day and see how quickly the government will quit stalling and be realistic." She thinks title is important, but not if it means spending millions in court when the communities are mired in poverty. "I don't have the ['I Support Haida Title'] sticker everyone else has on their car," she says. What she wants is better health care, tangible support for the women struggling against domestic abuse and the kids falling prey to drug dealers.

And like any politician, Moore wants jobs. A 2006 labour market survey by the Skeena Native Development Society put the unemployment rate in Old Massett at 64.6 per cent; in Skidegate it was 36.9 per cent. The Skidegate rate was the lowest of all twenty-five communities in the SNDS service area; the rate in Old Massett was fairly typical of First Nations communities in the region, though the national unemployment rate was about 6 per cent at the time. Between 1994 and 2006, Old Massett's unemployment rate never fell below 53 per cent—a number that, in non-native Canada, would be a social and political calamity. In the labour market survey, subjective responses to this level of unemployment list the number-one reason as the availability of "seasonal opportunities only." Other reasons include "dependency on social assistance / no incentive," "lack of education / training / skills" and "low self-esteem."

Raven, a force of nature in her late twenties and veteran of three Rediscovery camps, gravitates between Old Massett and Vancouver in an attempt to put together a life and a livelihood. She remembers that when Guujaaw was asked to speak to a group of aboriginal kids in Vancouver about Haida rites of passage, all he talked about was rights and title. She admires Guujaaw, and she supports the title case, but "maybe I'm just young and impatient... People need to work, and people need to live and people need to feed their kids, and if people can't fulfill their basic needs, they're not going to give shit about the trees." In many ways, she lives in the tension that characterizes the distance between how far the Haida have come and how far they have to go. "Who's going to be in charge? If we're logging, is that money going to be going back to the community? Is there going to be private ownership? How is that all going to pan out?"

Miles Richardson says that Guujaaw seems "reluctant" to build a team with demonstrated expertise in economic development. "Sure, protecting the land is a priority, it's very important...but Haida people live in the twenty-first century, and having a strong economy is very important. The opportunities are expanding. We're not expanding to take advantage of those opportunities, and we must." Wanagan, the Skidegate elder with whom Guujaaw once roamed the woods looking for culturally modified trees, and one of the key figures in the defence of Gwaii Haanas, says Guujaaw almost can't help coming off as an environmentalist: "In a lot of ways you have to be, because the province and the feds push you into that. What they do is keep stalling you and stalling you, and meanwhile all the fish are gone and the land has been logged. Without these resources for generating wealth inside the community, we can't *have* social programs." Arnie Bellis also defends Guujaaw. "What Guuj has said is the Haida won't sign a bad deal." Guujaaw elaborates: "We're not going to sign deals just for the sake of signing deals. You know, a 20 per cent deal, we're not going to sign something like that." That is, the new Haida way won't be the same as the old, non-Haida way. Terri-Lynn Williams-Davidson, speaking at Simon Fraser University's downtown campus during a 2007 seminar staged by the Interfaith Summer Institute for Justice, Peace and Social Movements, put it another way. "We cannot achieve peace within ourselves unless we achieve peace with the land, unless we find a new way."

This search for a new way is the battle of our age the world over. Capitalism is hardly on its last legs, but global commodity markets might well be, and global financial markets are in utter disarray. In his book *Blessed Unrest,* environmentalist and entrepreneur Paul Hawken estimates there are at least one million organizations around the world working towards ecological sustainability and social justice. They are populated, he writes, by "coherent, organic, self-organized congregations involving tens of millions of people dedicated to change...a current of humanity...[whose] lineage can be traced back to healers, priestesses, philosophers, monks, rabbis, poets and artists 'who speak for the planet, for other species, for interdependence, a life that courses under and through and around empires.'" Guujaaw, asked if he is advocating a socialist or communist approach on Haida Gwaii, replies, "Well, it is communistic in the fact that the property is owned by everyone, so where an individual wants to be a beneficiary, there can be trouble... The majority would say if you want to get rich, go and do it, but if you want to use the common property there's something wrong with that. If you want to take the property of the collective and get rich off it, you can't do that and leave the people behind." The Haida intend to build an economy consistent with their own Yah'guudang. Since 1999, the Council of the Haida Nation has operated the *Haida Provider,* a seventeen-metre aluminum seine boat that fishes the halibut, salmon and herring licences held by the CHN. The fish that are caught are distributed to elders in Old Massett and Skidegate. Yet while sports fishing lodges crow about their "prime sites" on Haida Gwaii, in 2008 the *Provider* caught barely 1,300 salmon in forty sets of the net along the west coast. You can almost hear the clock ticking down on the Haida's uneasy truce with the lodges.

Asked if there are economic models around the globe that appeal to him, Guujaaw answers, "It's like carving, eh? Learn a bit off one, and then the other." He cites elements of the Chinese agrarian economy as worth a look, and aspects of Gorbachev-era Soviet Communism. He seems to be arguing for the space to pursue what Naomi Klein, in her book *The Shock Doctrine,* has called "unscripted self-determination," the development of economic ideas "outside the free-market lock box"—maybe the sort of "third way" that Lech Wałęsa fought for in Poland, or something along the lines of South Africa's Freedom Charter, or perhaps something analogous to the cooperative economy of the Emilia-Romagna region in northern Italy. "A lot of people are farther ahead [than the Haida] in many ways," says Guujaaw. "The difference is that we start with the environment, the well-being of the environment, and we'll build an economy from that."

BACK BEFORE U.S. president Barack Obama popularized the phrase, Vice-President Arnie Bellis, sitting in Pearl's Dining Room in Masset, used it in replying to the question of whether the Haida can build a modern economy on their islands—become, in all ways, a nation. "Yes, we can," Bellis said. "Yes, we can." The Haida's hope is audacious. They want to construct a finely crafted contemporary society in their homeland, which they believe is as well-made as any place on Earth. After a kind of "service interruption" brought about by the coming of the white man, the Haida are determined to build a society and an economy that is a fitting match for the land and the sky and the waters and the spirit world they were lucky enough to inherit. It is hardly an overstatement to suggest that the Haida have set out to articulate a new code of human conduct for our planet, and they might just possess a genius for community that seems to have eluded modern, or at least Western, society.

Their experiment is taking place on a land mass that amounts to just 0.0068 per cent of the Earth's surface, or 0.1 per cent of Canada's land mass; the total population of the islands, fewer than 6,000 souls, is 0.00009 of the world population, or 0.02 per cent of Canada's. Statistically, it could be said that what happens on Haida Gwaii is irrelevant to the future of the world. But if the world—with its diminishing resources and its exploding populations—is to succeed at building what Jane Jacobs famously labelled "reliably prosperous" communities, why not start here, with a warrior people in a peace-loving country for whom their land is all the world they want?

In September 2002, John Ralston Saul—philosopher, author, provocateur and consort to then Governor General Adrienne Clarkson—visited Haida Gwaii. Ralston Saul is, among other things, a careful student of government. So his words had special resonance when, speaking to islanders at a public forum on leadership and the environment, he told the audience, "Haida Gwaii is in a process of becoming one of the most exciting places in Canada in terms of the way in which Canadians are rethinking how we are going to run the country, how we are going to live together, how we are going to make sense of who we are, who we were and who we will be in the future, both as communities and as societies and as economies." What is afoot, he said, is the fusing of ancient and modern ways of organizing cultural and economic life, and of native and non-native world views. "Aboriginal peoples are finding their way back into the centre of the Canadian debate and the Canadian experience. All across what might be called the near north, new relationships are being forged with local communities. Non-aboriginals are looking around and saying, 'We're not leaving. Who else [who] lives here is not leaving?' The natural answer to this is the aboriginal peoples. From this simple observation of reality, these new alliances are being formed."

The search for a new kind of balance is occurring around the world, in part because in almost every place where there are natural resources there are also natural communities of indigenous people, whose voices are not as easily suppressed as they were a century ago. There is increasing global awareness, too, that nature states are just as important as nation states, and that what builds real communities isn't commerce but culture. Ralston Saul's speech continued, "Guujaaw wrote a little while ago that culture was 'something to do with bearing witness.' When people say that society is driven by self-interest or technology or whatever they sell, they are completely missing the point that civilizations are about people and the circumstances in which they live and that civilization is about people bearing witness about themselves and about where they live. And that means bearing witness about who came forth and who will follow them...Leadership is dependent on the sense that you, the citizens, can shape your society; that you are not afraid of great global forces; that you do not believe they are inevitable or capable of preventing you from shaping your society...Leadership is an integrated view of society, culture and economics."

Terri-Lynn Williams-Davidson says her "first passion is culture... I've heard kids say when they see the bringing together of art and culture and ceremony, asking their parents, 'What kind of magic was that?' And I think we are creating magic when we do that. Everything I have done has been motivated by a desire to protect and keep culture alive." At an interfaith seminar at Simon Fraser University in 2007, Williams-Davidson told the audience that the title and rights case the Haida are pursuing is about more than simply proving who owns Haida Gwaii: "We want to also use the litigation to develop a model for sustainable coexistence with Canada." She conceded that litigation is an adversarial tool. "But we can use those tools in combination with peacemaking tools," she said, "like building community relationships, like visioning what our collective future might look like. So I think it is possible to use the master's tools, not to take down the master's house, but to build a new house that we would live in collectively in the future."

It demands such a fine balance, this nuanced approach. While an underlay of menace threads through everything the Haida do, it is relieved by a rich and buoyant vision of the future. It speaks to the sort of leadership that won Guujaaw the Buffett Award for Indigenous Leadership in 2006. "Guujaaw is a warrior. We like that," said Spencer B. Beebe, president of Ecotrust, which administered the award. In support of Guujaaw's nomination, Wade Davis wrote to the jury that "[Guujaaw] is the most thoroughly authentic man I know." Michael Nicoll Yahgulanaas wrote, "His name translates as 'drum' and he truly has set the beat for many young people. His presence is so striking that youngsters have named rubber boots Air Guujaaws." Nicoll Yahgulanaas cautioned the jury, however, that it was as a member of the "cultural family" of the Haida that Guujaaw should be recognized. "It would do him a disservice to take him out of that context of family and to paint him as a lone hero saving his community." Indeed, after collecting the US$25,000 prize money attached to the Buffett Award, Guujaaw gave the money to the Council of the Haida Nation, specifying that it be used to develop the CHN website and for travel expenses, bursaries and developing and equipping an outdoor youth program.

In 2008, interviewed upon the release of his new book *A Fair Country*, John Ralston Saul told the *Globe and Mail* that his view of Canada had been dramatically changed by his contact with emergent leaders, especially in aboriginal communities, during his travels with the former Governor General. "I think it was those six years travelling around the country and suddenly seeing thousands and thousands and thousands of people…hearing what they had to say; you know, sitting down with [Nisga'a leader] Joe Gosnell, and Guujaaw. These are remarkable people, these are some of the most remarkable people in the country. When you meet them, you think, 'So that's what a leader is supposed to look like.'" Guujaaw shrugs off the accolades. "It's not as if I'm a guru or anything," he says. Then he adds with a laugh, "Wait a couple of years for that." In the context of the Haida Nation, he considers himself "fairly normal. Everybody should be fighting for the land, everybody should have a relationship with the land, everybody should be doing something cultural."

This idea of leadership being rooted in culture is an ancient one, and on Haida Gwaii another way it has found modern expression is in the Rediscovery program. A visitor today can climb a rise behind the old cabin that Thom Henley built at Daalung Stl'ang, on the beach that has everything, and look down on four bunkhouses and a cookhouse, all built in the Haida style. Seeing the buildings snugged together and looking past them to the sea, it is possible to imagine what an ancient Haida village might have looked like—a curved, protected bay, a beach and a string of cedar buildings squat against the forest fringe, woodsmoke and voices rising from them. Native and non-native kids come here in groups of twenty or so each summer for camps that last ten days. Some are escaping the addictions of reserve or village life; many have not spent much time in the wild. Always, there is an elder who will tell them stories around the campfire, show them how to clean fish, explain the use of plants in cooking or as medicines, teach a few words of the language. The kids pass the *tangee* (salt) or *paapagee* (pepper), drink xaw (tea or coffee), *Gan xwa* (juice), or feast on *xagu* (halibut) or *kuustan* (crab). Among the young staff leaders are some who have come to Rediscovery in the past, who remember what it's like to sit around the sacred circle fire for the first time, passing the feather and sharing the day's adventures. At every camp, there is Waanagan time, in which kids as young as nine years old spend a night doing a solo in the wilderness.

The program Huck and Guujaaw launched in 1978 has, over the years, served to provide basic training for environmental warriors— a kind of boot camp, except in sandals. Importantly, too, Rediscovery has spread to other homelands. The Kitlope Valley, on British Columbia's mainland, might not be protected today but for the awakening that a Rediscovery program created there among the Haisla people; so too the Stein Valley, near Vancouver. David Suzuki extols Rediscovery's ability to provide "access to ancient wisdom...[a] sense of sanctity of the land…a belief and value system which is radically different, and which we must all rediscover to help deflect us from our headlong rush to destruction." Bill Reid loved the idea of Rediscovery because it allows for myth to take its place alongside science. "The wonderful thing about Rediscovery is that it has enabled all these different truths to exist side by side. It provides for a few more trips up and down the beach where traditional teaching can still take place, and helps young people whose private universes seem empty and chaotic to discover there is some order in their lives and their world. And even if there isn't, some may be inspired to turn the raw material of chaos into a structured hope for the future."

THIS STRUCTURED HOPE for the future, these attempts to build a new house, are integral parts of the nation that Arnie Bellis sees when he ponders a serving of pie and ice cream at Pearl's Dining Room, the Chinese restaurant in Masset. It's a magnificent idea the Haida have. But as a wise man once said, eventually all good ideas degenerate into work. To that end, in Canadian First Nations terms, the Haida are much further ahead than most. In 1995, the federal government honoured a commitment made as part of negotiations to protect Gwaii Haanas and donated $38.2 million to the Gwaii Trust, which had been established one year earlier. The Gwaii Trust funds native and non-native projects alike. A Haida chairs the fund's board, and four of its eight directors are appointed by the Council of the Haida Nation. The trust is a tangible benefit to the Haida, and a significant economic bridge between Haida and non-Haida communities. Despite being battered in world market woes, in late 2008 the fund stood at $66 million or so. In addition, the trust manages a $24 million endowment, Gwaii Forest, that the provincial and federal governments funded in the late 1980s to help buffer island forest workers from the effects of reductions to the timber harvesting land base. Added to that, the Haida negotiated about $20 million in allocations from the $120-million conservation finance deal struck in

2007 to protect the so-called Great Bear Rainforest. That's more than a $100-million nest egg for Haida Gwaii on top of regular transfer payments and ongoing economic activity, all without the Haida having signed a treaty. Winning recognition of their rights and title could put them in line for many more millions in compensation. More than 50 per cent of the land base on the islands is now under some form of protection, and other than fee-simple land, the Haida have not ceded a single square inch of Haida Gwaii to anyone. Their natural capital, in other words, is in remarkably good shape. No wonder Guujaaw sees little merit in negotiating a treaty unless it is based on recognizing Haida title, not extinguishing it. No wonder he has fought so hard to build an economy based on natural capital. Former Attorney-General Geoff Plant is sympathetic but unconvinced. "I am not sure the Haida can articulate a vision [of an economy] that is comprehensive and that can be sustained," Plant says. But as Paul Hawken writes in *Blessed Unrest*, "living within the biological constraints of the Earth may be the most civilized activity a person can pursue...There is no reason we cannot build an exquisitely designed economy that matches biology in its diversity, and integrates complexity rather than extinguishing it. In accomplishing this, there is much to be gained from those who have not forgotten the land."

In Canada, the settling of the land question—be it in Nunavut, the Yukon, northern Quebec or British Columbia—has yet to generate a comprehensive model of what distinct nationhood looks like for First Nations. "Nothing better illustrates the marginal position of Indians in the New World even today," writes Tony Penikett in his book *Reconciliation,* "than the fact that no Aboriginal American people are recognized as a nation state; therefore none is a member of the United Nations." In 2006, Prime Minister Stephen Harper surprised people across the political spectrum when he proposed to recognize Quebec as a "nation" within a united Canada. Phil Fontaine, national chief of the Assembly of First Nations, jumped on

Harper's move, insisting that aboriginal people were "not of a lesser status [than] the Quebecois...or any people in this country" and should be similarly recognized. B.C. premier Gordon Campbell supported Harper's stance and went further: "It is high time we acknowledged Canada's 'third solitude'—the Aboriginal peoples of Canada. We should do that formally, proudly and emphatically in a similar resolution that embraces our heritage as a nation of nations." That sounds good, until you remember that Campbell (like Harper) heads up a government that, for legal reasons, has denied the existence of the Haida as a nation. "Governments are still getting their way," Guujaaw said once, still moving the bull's eye. "Resources are still being depleted, lands are still being spoiled. It's not going to get easy all of a sudden. It's going to be hard to retrain them."

Although Guujaaw has said publicly that the Haida Nation will remain part of Canada, unless something goes dramatically wrong in future negotiations, one legal analysis suggests that the Haida already come close to qualifying as an independent state under international law. "It appears that the Haida Nation of Haida Gwaii have satisfied three of the four criteria set out by the *Montevideo Convention*," writes lawyer Tony Fogarassy in a briefing for the Vancouver law firm Clark Wilson. The Haida occupy a defined territory; they have a permanent population; they have a "coherent" government. What they lack is recognition by other states "as an independent entity for the purpose of engaging in international relations." But who is to say that won't happen? What is to prevent Hugo Chavez or Muammar Gaddafi pitching up on Second Beach one day and giving a speech that roughly translates as "*Vivent les Haidas libres*"? As indigenous communities around the world step into the global limelight, how they are recognized and by whom will have tremendous implications for countries with significant indigenous populations inside their borders. Guujaaw once floated the notion, for instance, that aboriginal leaders in the Pacific Northwest could unilaterally sign onto the Kyoto Accord. It is possible to envision an international body, something akin to la Francophonie, through which indigenous nations transact significant business with each other—not just cultural exchanges—and which begins to supplant many of the functions of centralized governments.

John Ralston Saul argues in *A Fair Country* that Canada is an innately aboriginal country. The country began not with the English and the French trying to learn how to live together, but "with illiterate, impoverished Europeans coming into contact with superior Aboriginal societies and being accepted by them," wrote Michael Valpy about Ralston Saul's ideas in the the *Globe and Mail*. Whether non-aboriginals will ever *accept* aboriginal societies, let alone recognize anything superior in them, is a question that confronts settler societies the world over. It is, to be sure, partly a land question. But it also goes fundamentally to whether or not countries like Canada and Australia, which seem to have achieved relative comfort with multiculturalism, will ever be able to tolerate a kind of multinationalism *within*. Like the land question, that won't be answered any time soon. Debra Hanuse, a member of the 'Namgis Nation and a former treaty commissioner in British Columbia, once said at a conference on native governance that it took 150 years to dismantle First Nations, and it will take another 150 years to reconstitute them. But that is the work that lies ahead for all Canadians. As a country, in deciding how to do so, Canada will surely reconstitute itself.

THIRTEEN

WHAT IS

TO COME

IN DOWNTOWN VANCOUVER one fine day in June, one fine National Aboriginal Day, to be precise, half of a major thorough-fare, Burrard Street, is closed off to traffic to allow a few hundred people to journey on foot from Vanier Park, over the Burrard Street Bridge and through the middle of the city to Library Square for a peaceful rally. The police look on while vehicle traffic moves slowly but freely in two directions on the other side of the street. A middle-aged white man in a dark-coloured suv, driving in the opposite direction to the marchers, is squirming in his seat, swearing loudly, white-knuckled hands gripping the steering wheel except when he gives the small crowd the finger to express his disgust. His disgust at what? Why is he so angry? What is it about aboriginal people that so outrages the man in the suv and so many others like him? Are they afraid the natives are going to somehow get it all? Can they not sleep at night in their comfortable beds, because of what novelist Janette Turner Hospital once masterfully described as the "soft thump thump of their fears"? Do they worry that through efforts to resolve the tension between "them" and "us" they'll somehow lose what they've gained or inherited? Canada, the country, has apologized to its indigenous peoples. Canada, this white man in an SUV, has not, and isn't about to anytime soon.

On a chill February night in 2008, composer Bruce Ruddell stands before almost 300 people in Vancouver's stately Christ Church Cathedral. The cathedral is built in Gothic revival style, and its ceiling and beams form a remarkable canopy of local cedar and Douglas fir timbers, arched over a chancel that is home to one of Canada's most celebrated church choirs. The reserved seats are filled almost entirely with First Nations dignitaries, who warm to a Coast Salish welcome from Chief Leah George-Wilson of the Tsleil-Waututh Nation. Tucked along the back of each pew are copies of the *Anglican Book of Common Praise,* along with the *Book of Alternative Services.* While people are not congregated this evening for a religious service, it is safe to say that the performance they are about to see is about as alternative as it gets in a cathedral.

It is almost ten years since the death of Haida artist Bill Reid, who was buried at Tanu in his beloved Gwaii Haanas to the sound of Guujaaw's drum. Tonight, Reid's spirit lives on. *The Spirit of Haida Gwaii Oratorio* is a piece inspired by a poem Reid composed to mark the unveiling of *The Spirit of Haida Gwaii: The Black Canoe,* that powerfully energetic and enigmatic landmark in the courtyard of the Canadian embassy in Washington.

"Here we are at last," the poem goes, "a long way from Haida Gwaii, not too sure where we are or where we're going, still squabbling and vying for position in the boat, but somehow managing to appear to be heading in some direction; at least the paddles are together, and the man in the middle seems to have some vision of what is to come." The poem comprises the lyrics of the oratorio, and as the music swells and the words rise through the nave of the cathedral, the man in the middle tonight is Guujaaw. Before the oratorio began, he and Terri-Lynn Williams-Davidson performed a short repertoire of Haida songs, fittingly starting with a prayer song. When Williams-Davidson completed a gorgeous solo to the accompaniment of a wooden rattle,

Guujaaw let out a long, satisfied "mmmm." He himself sang a song he explained had been composed by a Haida condemned to the gallows. "And you know, I could easily see myself in that position," he said with a laugh. Williams-Davidson is resplendent this evening in a woven hat, knee-length black skirt, a tassled pouch and moccasins, with the lights of the cathedral reflecting off buttons made of abalone shells. Guujaaw wears work shoes, grey pants, a short-sleeved shirt and a Mountain Equipment Co-op fleece vest. When the two of them combine on the "Spirit Song," several Haida in the audience hum along quietly. The song has a hymnal quality, and its sound drapes over the congregation.

Once the oratorio is enjoined, in the whorl of music radiating out from the two soloists—both of them First Nations singers, baritone Clarence Logan and soprano Melody Mercredi—and in the colourful rustle of Haida vests worn by the two dozen or so members of the Christ Church Cathedral Choir, it is possible to be lulled into thinking that salvation is at hand. That we are all paddlers in the Haida canoe.

ON HAIDA GWAII, the mist in Skidegate, Sea Lion Town, lifts to reveal people gathered on the beach around an almost completed canoe, a real one this time. Somehow—in between court cases and protocol meetings and land-use plans and potlatches and performances— Guujaaw has found time to carve a twelve-metre canoe with the assistance of his son Jaalen Edenshaw. Canoe design isn't something that evolved on the islands, Guujaaw says, but rather was a gift to Haida ancestors from the supernaturals. Their design features flared prows, which Europeans hadn't seen until they encountered the Haida. The process of steaming the canoe, carved from a single cedar log, takes several hours. The hollowed bottom is first lined with cedar boughs. Rocks heated on a nearby fire are placed on the boughs in a few inches of sea water, and then the whole canoe is covered in cloth to retain the steam. When the cedar is sufficiently softened, the cloth is removed. Precut spreaders are installed to stretch the gunwales and ensure the canoe takes on a swooping shape that gives the bottom a rockable curve, allowing it to pivot and turn. This canoe, the third of three carved to mark the opening of the Haida Heritage Centre at Ḵaay Llnagaay, marks the first time Guujaaw has been lead carver on a canoe project. Technically, carving a canoe is a far more complex, unforgiving undertaking even than carving a totem pole. There's a risk the cedar will crack, so Guujaaw isn't all that pleased a crowd has gathered to witness the steaming. "It's not really a thing where you want a bunch of people around," he says. "It's probably the biggest test you put yourself through when you do these things." The canoe steaming lasts almost till midnight, and in the end it all works out fine, another well-made object available for use not just as a showpiece but for community events and for families wanting to get out on the land.

A canoe, Guujaaw says, is carved into one shape in the full knowledge that it will take on another. Seemingly, that is true with almost everything the Haida put their hands to. The title and rights claim, for example, may itself change shape, if the Haida keep winning back their lands and their rights without having to pursue the case in court. "If we don't need to, we won't do it. If we can resolve these things without it [arguing the case], all the better," Guujaaw says. Other court cases have done little to clarify the issue of title and rights for aboriginal people in British Columbia. Most notably, in a case involving the Xeni Gwet'in, or Tsilhqot'in, B.C. Supreme Court justice David Vickers made no one happy with his ruling in late 2007 in *William*. Like the Haida, the Xeni Gwet'in had beaten back logging from a large part of their traditional territory in the 1980s and then launched a comprehensive title and rights case. After testimony that spanned 339 days in court, Justice Vickers said Tsilhqot'in rights and title may exist in wide swaths of territory both inside and beyond the area claimed, but he frustrated First Nations by declaring his ruling non-binding, saying they should go back to negotiating with the government that had denied their rights in the first place.

Certainly, the *William* ruling did nothing to resolve the overarching questions the Haida claim seeks to settle.

Nor has relief come in the form of legislative action. "We are all here to stay," said the declaration in 2005 that heralded what Gordon Campbell's government called a "New Relationship" with B.C. First Nations. "We agree to a new government-to-government relationship based on respect, recognition and accommodation of aboriginal title and rights." In 2006, the B.C. government backed that up with a $100 million trust fund to build capacity in First Nations communities. But very little changed on the ground with regard to title and rights. It wasn't until late in 2008 that Campbell—threatened with a new round of road blockades and the spectre of ugly scenes at the 2010 Winter Olympics—agreed to open high-level political discussions about legislation that might, once and for all, recognize aboriginal title and rights. "I would like my government to be the first in this country to take such an historic step," the premier said in a letter to native leaders. Without it, those leaders subsequently warned, they won't believe the government is serious. "We've been talking about this for years," said First Nations Summit Grand Chief Doug Kelly. "It's time for action." A proposed Recognition and Reconciliation Act—legislation that would enshrine Aboriginal title in British Columbia and, in doing so, turn 150 years of history on its head—came within a whisper of being brought before the Legislature in April 2009, only to be scuttled by, predictably, the business community. "I think we achieved the goal we set out to do, which is to slow down the process," said B.C. Chamber of Commerce president John Winter at the time.

But such obduracy has an increasing air of futility about it; such tactical "victories" seem more and more pyrrhic. In the continued absence of legislation that recognizes First Nations title and reconciles their rights, First Nations have continued to rely heavily on the Haida's 2004 win in the Supreme Court of Canada, the TFL 39 case, to get beneficial judgements of their own. In late 2008, for instance,

the Haida case was cited in a ruling that rebuked the B.C. government for failing to consult seriously with the Hupacasath First Nation
on Vancouver Island when it allowed 70,000 hectares of forest land
to be removed from a tree farm licence. Hupacasath chief Judith
Sayers told the press the lands comprised almost one-third of her
nation's traditional territory; by clearing the way for some of that
territory to be sold to property developers, the government was giving away the community's right to access wild lands. The ruling
ordered the government to resume negotiations with the Hupacasath,
and Judith Sayers said compensation ranging from $25 million to
$40 million would be a key issue when talks resumed.

Although the Haida don't explicitly take credit for all that has
flowed from the cases they have won in court or the precedents they
have secured at negotiating tables, they are obviously pleased to highlight the gains for aboriginal people around the world on the Council
of the Haida Nation's website. The Australian High Court has ruled
that "Aborigines control more than 80 per cent of the Northern Territory coast, ending a 30-year battle for indigenous rights to the sea.
Prime Minister Kevin Rudd called for calm following the landmark
ruling." The Ainu, whose cause Guujaaw championed during his several visits to Japan, have since unexpectedly won recognition as
indigenous peoples. Ecuador is billed as the first nation in the world
to grant constitutional rights to the natural environment (though,
strictly speaking, the Haida did that long before Ecuador). Closer to
home, the Tahltan have succeeded in turning away Shell Canada's bid
to drill for coal-bed methane up by Robert Quock's beloved Beauty
Camp—at least for now.

The CHN website chronicles the litany of threats to Haida Gwaii:
offshore oil and gas drilling, tanker traffic, climate change, ocean
pollution, fish farms. It is a place, too, where locals and outsiders can
keep track of the workings of the Haida government. The CHN's once
sporadic newsletter, *Haida Laas,* is now a frequent, handsome, richly
illustrated publication in which the workings of the Haida House of

Assembly are chronicled and an entirely Haida world view is expressed, in a way that depends neither on the pretence of journalistic objectivity nor on revenues from advertising. It is here that people can learn who has been elected to various committees, see photos from potlatches, find out who has been awarded "cultural wood" for totem poles, bentwood boxes or a longhouse. Votes are recorded and committee reports are presented. The president of the CHN reports to the constituents in a regular column. "The big [Prime Minister Stephen Harper's] apology from Canada for its deliberate efforts to break our people and destroy our culture has got to be taken," Guujaaw writes in the November 2008 edition, "and we have to move on."

Moving on means rebuilding almost everything. Most critically, in Canadian First Nations communities, it has meant rebuilding populations. In less than a century, aboriginal populations have increased to the point that in 2007 there were more than 1.2 million aboriginal people in the country, more than twelve times the lowest point in their numbers. In British Columbia, there are now more First Nations people than there were at the time of contact. The Haida population has rebounded to perhaps one-third of its original size, a five-fold increase from its lowest point. That's a lot of new voices on the land, and for the land, and inevitably that will mean a wider diversity of opinions. Whether the Council of the Haida Nation will always be the natural governing party of Haida Gwaii is debatable, though it's fairly certain that if there ever emerges a Loyal Opposition, it won't be Her Majesty's. Guujaaw concedes that the CHN's success at protecting lands, stopping oil tankers and the like is not a sufficient remedy to all the Haida's needs. Such actions don't change things at the village level, he acknowledges, but they "are essential to ensure there isn't a loss."

Some things are also beyond the CHN's control. The effects of climate change are already showing up on the islands. On the east coast of Graham Island, Highway 16 seems perilously close to tumbling into Hecate Strait, as storms batter the shoreline with increasing severity. If Al Gore's prophecy of rising sea levels does come true, it is island nations like Haida Gwaii that will feel the direct effects most acutely. The waters have risen before in Haida Gwaii, though. If they rise again, there will be room for a lot of people, just as there was back then, in the mountains of Duu Guusd.

"THANK GOODNESS," SAYS Nika Collison. "It's about time we had one in Skidegate." She is gesturing towards one of six totem poles outside the Haida Heritage Centre at Ḵaay Llnagaay. It is a pole carved by Guujaaw, whose poles stand in Japan and Indonesia and the B.C. ski resort of Whistler but only now in Haida Gwaii. Nika Collison, a curator of the magnificent new museum building facing the beach where the *Loo Taas* once made its triumphal return to Haida Gwaii, finds it enormously important that Guujaaw's Cumshewa pole stands alongside the works of Jim Hart and others outside the Ḵaay Centre, as it is known locally. "I think he's right up there with the best we have of the Haida artists," she says of Guujaaw. "He's well-studied, he understands what three-dimensional formline is, and he's got one of those odd eyes that catches things other people wouldn't. He's got a quirky head."

As the Haida set out to reconstitute themselves, their focus has been on raising totem poles, relearning the Haida language, repatriating human remains from places like the Smithsonian Institution and Chicago's Field Museum, holding potlatches and protecting the land—multiple ways of "creating magic," in the words of Terri-Lynn Williams-Davidson. As artist Robert Davidson phrases it, "We're just now coming into a renaissance. I don't know of a Haida word that would describe what's happening now. It's almost like a reawakening." How better to explain *Sin Xiigangu,* or *Sounding Gambling Sticks,* the first full-length play in the Haida language, written by Guujaaw's sons Jaalen and Gwaai Edenshaw and based on a story recorded by John Swanton a hundred years earlier. "I wanted to explore new ways of getting Haida language into the community,"

Jaalen says, "and it was a good way to force myself and others to learn some more." Jaalen and Gwaai developed a treatment for the play, wrote the script and revised it, translating it back and forth between English and Haida with the help of Old Massett Haida speakers. It was a long, complicated process, and they almost threw in the towel before their mother, Jenny Nelson, stepped into the role of impresario. Aided by a cast and crew of more than fifty people, *Sin Xiigangu* opened in early 2008 to packed houses in Masset and Skidegate.

In Skidegate, the elders who turned out for the play—and there were many of them—wept at the sound of the Haida language filling the hall in the Performing House at the Ḵaay Centre. The $26 million centre is perhaps the most stunning embodiment physically of what the Haida have worked so hard to achieve. Its five linked cedar longhouses cover more than 50,000 square feet, comprising a Greeting House, Trading House, Eating House, Bill Reid Teaching House, Canoe House (in which the *Loo Taas* is stored), Saving Things House (new home of the Haida Gwaii Museum) and an open-walled Carving House. It takes up almost the entire shoreline of Sea Lion Town. Listening to Nika Collison talk about it, it becomes clear that the Ḵaay Centre is a place of flux, of flow, where each day the tides of Skidegate Inlet seem to bring with them more and more of the Haida's past and their future. Collison knows there are tens of thousands of Haida artifacts scattered in museums all around the world, and the Haida are patiently bringing as many as they can home to Haida Gwaii. What's less obvious to the outsider about the function of the Ḵaay Centre is that it is a place where shards of stories and traditional knowledge are pieced back together. "So we're looking at a halibut hook," Collison says, "and it's made of yew, and Ernie Wilson, Chief Niis Wes, is talking and he says, 'That's an iron,' the hook part, like the sharp part that would get stuck in the halibut. 'That's an iron piece, but before iron was plentiful, they used to use the bone of a bear penis, because it's sharp and it's strong and it doesn't break.' And then James Young, he talked about how they used to fish halibut before there were canoes, and lay the long line, and it's so cool. You don't get that information necessarily without the pieces coming forward. Those little pieces are so important...It's the little things, we need them. We're not just masks and totems." Or, as Guujaaw once wrote, "And know that Haida culture is not simply song and dance, graven images, stories, language, even blood. It's all of these things and then..."

AND THEN.

And then...what?

In the case of Guujaaw, the Raven and trickster has important work still to do. He points out that "the Haida Nation has gone from having practically no say over the use of resources to protecting half the land mass of Haida Gwaii, cutting logging back to one-third of what it had been, and the establishment of a more responsible forest management regime that considers fish, wildlife and culture, as well as communities. We are poised to control most of the forest industry. In protecting our lands, we have not acquiesced to the authority of the Crown." Now, the Haida have an economy to build based on their own authority. In other words, Guujaaw has more songs to bring back to the land. Soon after the performance of the oratorio in Vancouver's Christ Church Cathedral, a boxed set of five CDs, *Songs of Haida Gwaii,* was released under the auspices of the Haida Gwaii Singers Society. What began almost a half-century ago, with Guujaaw and others retrieving lost songs from the elders and through sheer persistence and willpower enabling the Haida to come out of the silence, is now an annotated collection of more than 100 songs you can download onto an iPod. Guujaaw writes in the liner notes,

> We are the song
> our grandmothers within
> of the earth...the sea   the forest   the sky people
> Kaayxil and Kuustayk
> is who we are

The Haida are the song, and they are their name. The Council of the Haida Nation decided in the fall of 2008 that it was time to return the name "Queen Charlotte Islands" to its original owners. The name might be precious to the Crown, Guujaaw said after the annual House of Assembly meeting in Old Massett, "but it doesn't mean anything to this place. We'll figure out how to do it properly, how to return the name, how to package it up somehow." Names are one of the most important properties in Haida culture, Guujaaw said. He has strived for decades to make his own name, not live with an adopted one, and he believes it is time for his nation to do the same thing. Guujaaw has earned his name, Miles Richardson says. "He has made it a very good name. That's all of our challenges when we get a name, is to make our name good." The Haida want no less for all of Haida Gwaii.

DAVID PHILLIPS ONCE said that Guujaaw always likes to get the last word. So it seems appropriate that the last words here are his, spoken at a symposium in 1999 entitled "The Legacy of Bill Reid." His comments about the great master might also be seen as fitting commentary on the Haida's own fight to be respected for their way of being in the world.

"Good people: I think that Bill Reid must be the most dissected thing outside of a laboratory—and when you start chopping things up, the more pieces you put in it, the smaller it gets, the harder it is to recognize what it originally was. I knew Bill pretty good from working with him... He figured that the real problem with the earth is that everyone got so civilized that they are losing their humanity... he wanted me to give them a course in de-civilization... We don't need to dissect Bill. We don't even need to try to understand him. We should just be happy he came amongst us.

"What I'd like to do is sing a song to finalize this part of it. I want to get Bill's granddaughter, Nika Collison, to sing a song with me. Bill always enjoyed the song, enjoyed the dance, and tried to integrate our culture into his life as much as he could.

"This song is about the moon as you can see it from Skidegate—the way it looks when it's shimmering across the water. The song first dismisses the singer as being of little importance and turns attention to the moon: the moon has shattered. This song would be sung by Ravens, who are teasing the Eagle ladies to pick up the pieces. The concept is too high to be considered an insult.

> *ha way ee ya, ah wa ee ya, hay hay ho, oh*
> *ha wa he yay, ha wa ee ya, hay hay ho*
> *oh ho ah ho*
> *gam giinaaguu, dii ?isgangaa*
> *hay hay ho, oh*
> *kungaay ?uu xuusdaayaagaanii*
> *hay hay ho, oh*
> *giid?in jaads ?uu 'll gugwaaykinst'aagaa*
> *hay hay ho*
> *?o ho, ah ho.*

"I was going to say just one more thing about the buzz over whether Bill was Haida. Like me, that was what he was—Haida—and there was nothing he could do about it."

CHRONOLOGY OF EVENTS

Over 10,000 years ago   The first Haida emerges from a cockle shell at Rose Spit, Haida Gwaii

1774   Spaniard Juan Pérez sails close to Haida Gwaii but doesn't land

1787   English Captain George Dixon meets Haida people offshore and names the Queen Charlotte Islands after his ship

1849   Colony of Vancouver Island formed

1858   Colony of British Columbia formed; James Douglas becomes governor of British Columbia

1864   Chilcotin uprising

1866   Union of Vancouver Island and B.C. colonies

1867   Canada formed by the British North American Act

1871   British Columbia enters Confederation

1884 (to 1951)   Indian Act prohibition against the potlatch

September 1913 McKenna-McBride Commission hears evidence at the
Queen Charlotte Agency

Haida population estimate: 597

April 1953 Gary Edenshaw born

1969 Robert Davidson raises the first totem pole in Old Massett
in more than a hundred years

1973 In *Calder v. Attorney General of B.C.*, the Supreme
Court of Canada confirms that aboriginal title exists,
but does not conclude whether title had been extinguished
in British Columbia

Fall 1974 Skidegate Band Council, with Guujaaw and Thom Henley,
opposes Rayonier's plans to log Burnaby Island

Islands Protection Committee formed. South Moresby
Wilderness Proposal sent to the Province of British
Columbia. More than 500 people sign a petition calling
for a moratorium on logging in the South Moresby area

December 1974 Founding meeting of the Council of the Haida Nation
(CHN)

Spring 1975 Rayonier starts logging Lyell Island

June 3, 1978 Protest in Masset against freedom of the village for
Canadian military

1979 In *Haida v. British Columbia (Minister of Forests)*,
a petition to the B.C. Supreme Court, Chief Tanu and
Gary Edenshaw claim the minister of forests acted
unfairly in renewing TFL 24. They lose, and lose their
appeal in 1981

1980 CHN governance reconstituted; Haida make formal land
claim to the federal government entitled
Declaration and Claim to the Haida Gwaii

1981   Elders give Guujaaw his name

Haida formally register boundaries of Haida Gwaii with United Nations

CHN designates Duu Guusd Tribal Park

April 1982   Constitution Act, 1982, s. 35 entrenches existing aboriginal and treaty rights

1984   *Islands at the Edge* published by the Islands Protection Society

1985   Haida Nation designates Gwaii Haanas as Haida Heritage Site

October 1985   Haida blockades set up at Lyell Island; seventy-two Haida arrested

November 1985   Ten Haida, including Guujaaw, convicted of contempt of court by Justice McEachern

March 1986   Western Canada Wilderness Committee Save South Moresby Caravan travels across Canada

July 1986   Miles Richardson, Guujaaw and others renounce Canadian citizenship

July 1987   Canada and British Columbia sign South Moresby Memorandum of Understanding to protect Gwaii Haanas National Park (deal finally concluded in 1993)

January 1989   Haida issue their own passports; withdraw from federal comprehensive claims

1990   In *R. v. Sparrow*, the Supreme Court of Canada confirms aboriginal rights that existed in 1982 are protected under the constitution and cannot be infringed upon without justification

July to September 1990   Oka standoff in Quebec

1991   Justice McEachern's B.C. Supreme Court decides
Delgamuukw v. British Columbia

January 1993   Gwaii Haanas Agreement signed

1995   In CHN *and Richardson v. Minister of Forests and
MacMillan Bloedel,* Justice Cohen dismisses the Haida
claim that aboriginal title is an encumbrance under the
Forest Act

1996   Islands Community Stability Initiative consensus
reached

1997   In *Delgamuukw v. British Columbia,* the Supreme Court
of Canada confirms the existence of aboriginal title

1999   Guujaaw becomes president of the CHN

2000   Nisga'a treaty becomes law

June 2000   Turning Point Declaration signed

August 2000   In CHN *and Guujaaw v. British Columbia (Minister of
Forests) and Weyerhaeuser Company,* Justice Halfyard
dismisses the Haida Nation's petition

2001   Annual House of Assembly resolution to develop a
thousand-year plan for cedar

February 2002   In CHN *and Guujaaw v. British Columbia and
Weyerhaeuser Company,* the B.C. Court of Appeal
overturns the decision of August 2000

March 6, 2002   CHN and Guujaaw file writ in B.C. Supreme Court

August 2002   In CHN *and Guujaaw v. British Columbia and
Weyerhaeuser Company,* the B.C. Court of Appeal
confirms its earlier ruling

November 2002   Haida Statement of Claim filed

September 2003   British Columbia offers 20 per cent of Haida Gwaii. Haida reject the offer

March 2004   Protocol Agreement between CHN, Port Clements and Masset; Protocol Agreements between CHN and other communities have followed

November 18, 2004   In *CHN and Guujaaw v. British Columbia and Weyerhaeuser Company,* the Supreme Court of Canada confirms that British Columbia has a duty to consult and accommodate with the Haida on how exploitation of the land should proceed

March 2005   Islands Spirit Rising blockades protest sale of Weyerhaeuser's TFL to Brascan

Province of British Columbia announces a New Relationship with Aboriginal People

April 22, 2005   Haida and Province of British Columbia sign a letter of understanding regarding the blockade issues

April 2005   *Haida Land Use Vision* finalized

August 2006   Jim Hart and Christian White potlatches in Old Massett

November 2007   *Tsilhqot'in Nation v. British Columbia,* also known as the *William* case, decided

December 2007   The Province of British Columbia and Haida sign Haida Land Use Agreement

May 2008   First Haida-language play debuts in Haida Gwaii

Fall 2008   Haida vow to return the name "Queen Charlotte Islands"

NOTES

A book of this nature is an amalgam of myriad sources. Some are archival, others are first- or second-hand accounts gleaned from interviews and yet others are my own observations based on my own readings and recollections from more than a quarter of a century of interest in and visits to Haida Gwaii. Piecing together many of the events in this book has been as much forensic science as historical research, because a great deal of the narrative of Haida Gwaii isn't written down. When it is, there are sometimes contradictory accounts, conflicting spellings, jumbled dates and mixed messages. I have tried to resolve these through multiple cross-referencing and fact-checking, but I have not presumed to write a definitive historical account, since I have neither the qualifications nor all the data to do so.

Where there are language variations between different dialects and old and new forms, I have relied on linguist Robert Bringhurst to provide most current usage.

A great deal of the book relies on interviews conducted over a three-year period beginning in 2006. Some of the scenes I describe are further reconstructed from documentary film accounts, especially the events in Gwaii Haanas. In the notes that follow, I have attempted to give a comprehensive although not exhaustive summary of the sources that have informed this work.

Readers will also note that I refer to Guujaaw even when, chronologically, he had not yet abandoned the name Gary Edenshaw. Guujaaw has on occasion expressed a wish that the issue of his name not be assigned any great importance. I have attempted to honour that wish, limiting references to Gary Edenshaw to instances where I feel it is required to make sense of his story.

Quotes in the text: Unless stated otherwise, quotes from Guujaaw or other members of the Haida Nation, along with others on and off the islands, are from interviews I conducted, from numerous emails, or from notes I took at public events over a period of several years. Quotes taken from documented sources are noted in the text or in these notes.

ONE: THEN AND NOW

page 2 *Robert Davidson's totem pole:* Prior to Robert Davidson's pole raising in 1969, there hadn't been a totem pole raised in Old Massett in more than a hundred years, and there was only one ancient pole still standing at the time in the other principal Haida village, Skidegate. Davidson's pole raising was an important turning point in what the Haida call the "taking out of concealment" of their songs and ceremonies. A short account of the importance of the pole raising can be found in a companion booklet in the compact disk anthology: Reg Davidson, Robert Davidson, Guujaaw, Marianne Jones, Terri-Lynn Williams-Davidson, *Songs of Haida Gwaii: Haida Gwaii Singers Anthology* (Surrey: Haida Gwaii Singers Society and Haida Nation, 2008), 5–6. A more detailed account of the carving and raising of the pole is in Ulli Steltzer and Robert Davidson, *Eagle Transforming: The Art of Robert Davidson* (Vancouver and Seattle: Douglas & McIntyre and University of Washington, 1994), 21–25.

page 2 *Chief ʔIdansuu's potlatch:* Chief ʔIdansuu's house-front raising and potlatch, along with Christian White's totem pole raising and potlatch, took place on the weekend of August 19–20, 2006.

page 6 *Painted house fronts were rare among the Haida:* George F. MacDonald, *Haida Art* (Vancouver: Douglas & McIntyre, 1996), 105.

page 7 *The potlatch law:* In 1884, federal legislation made it a misdemeanour, punishable by imprisonment, to engage or assist in a potlatch: Canada, *An Act to Further Amend the Indian Act, 1880,* S.C. 1884, 47 Vict., c. 27, s. 3. See also Jean Barman, *The West Beyond the West: A History of British Columbia* (Toronto: University of Toronto Press, 1991), 160.

page 7 *Performances throughout the evening:* Although the author was present and witnessed the songs and dances at Chief ʔIdansuu's potlatch, a further explanation of their importance and their meaning was provided by Nika Collison. The Haida take songs—their creation, their ownership and their performance—very seriously. The use of songs is governed by an evolving Song Protocol, according to the companion booklet to *Songs of Haida Gwaii.* It says the Protocol "is the set of rules about when certain kinds of songs may be used and what kind of dance or ceremony accompanies a song. It also encompasses who may use certain songs and the need to obtain permission to sing songs and to acknowledge song owners and teachers. It even embraces new rules such as what kinds of songs—based on the essence of the song—may be used in present day ceremonies": Davidson et al., *Songs of Haida Gwaii*, 9.

page 9 *The legendary candlefish:* Oolichans, or eulachons (*Thaleichthys pacificus*) are small, short-lived, anadromous smelts (like sardines) that can be found from the southern Bering Sea to northern California. Within British Columbia, they have been documented spawning in thirty-three rivers, but in only fourteen or fif-teen rivers on a sustained basis. Oolichans are so high in oil content that they can be dried, fitted with a wick through the mouth and used as a candle. The oil is unique among fish oils in that it is a solid at room temperatures, with the consistency of soft butter and with a golden hue. It can also be rendered as a grease. In whatever form, the oolichan is an important part of a traditional First Nations diet—but it is an acquired taste, to say the least.

TWO: LAND TROUBLES

page 18 *A compromise with Canada:* The reference to a "compromise" with Canada, as opposed to the United States, Russia or Japan, comes from an interview conducted by Ian Lordon in *SpruceRoots,* a magazine that for several years chronicled events on Haida Gwaii but is now defunct: "Reconciling Differences and Inspiring Change," *SpruceRoots,* Queen Charlotte, Haida Gwaii: Gowgaia Institute, February 2000.

page 20 *The Haida describe their homeland:* Council of the Haida Nation, *Haida Land Use Vision: Haida Gwaii Yah'guudang [respecting Haida Gwaii],* April 2005.

page 22 *Immune from attack:* Christie Harris, *Raven's Cry* (Vancouver: Douglas & McIntyre, 1966), 92.

page 23 *A language isolate:* Nancy J. Turner says in *Plants of Haida Gwaii* (Winlaw, B.C.: Sono Nis Press, 2004), 37, that "Haida has no demonstrable relationship with any other language, and is thus considered a Language Isolate." The Haida have their own oral histories of their islands, cultures and traditions. For a sum-mary of Haida oral traditions see Kiiʔiljuus (Barbara J. Wilson) and Heather Harris, "Tllsda Xaaydas Kʼaaygang.nga: Long, Long Ago Haida Ancient Stories," chapter 7 in Daryl W. Fedje and Rolf W. Mathewes, eds., *Haida Gwaii: Human History and Environment from the Time of Loon to the Time of the Iron People* (Vancouver: University of British Columbia Press, 2005), 121–139. Robert Bringhurst, in *A Story as Sharp as a Knife: The Classical Mythtellers and Their World* (Vancou-ver: Douglas & McIntyre, 1999), 13, notes that Haida is "one of the world's richer classical literatures, embodying one of the world's great mythologies."

page 23 *Calder, Sparrow, Van der peet, N.T.C. Smokehouse, Gladstone, Delgamuukw, Haida:*

> *Calder v. British Columbia (Attorney General),* [1973] S.C.R. 313, http://scc.lexum
> .umontreal.ca/en/1973/1973rcs0-313/1973rcs0-313.html (accessed February 24,
> 2009).
>
> *Delgamuukw v. British Columbia,* [1997] 3 S.C.R. 1010, http://csc.lexum
> .umontreal.ca/en/1997/1997rcs3-1010/1997rcs3-1010.html (accessed
> February 24, 2009).
>
> *Haida Nation v. British Columbia (Minister of Forests),* 2004 SCC 73,
> http://scc.lexum.umontreal.ca/en/2004/2004scc73/2004scc73.html
> (accessed February 24, 2009).
>
> *R. v. Gladstone,* [1996] 2 S.C.R. 723, http://scc.lexum.umontreal.ca/
> en/1996/1996rcs2-723/1996rcs2-723.html (accessed February 24, 2009).
>
> *R. v. N.T.C. Smokehouse Ltd.,* [1996] 2 S.C.R. 672, http://scc.lexum.umontreal.ca/
> en/1996/1996rcs2-672/1996rcs2-672.html (accessed February 24, 2009).
>
> *R. v. Sparrow,* [1990] 1 S.C.R. 1075, http://scc.lexum.umontreal.ca/en/
> 1990/1990rcs1-1075/1990rcs1-1075.html (accessed February 24, 2009).
>
> *R. v. Van der Peet,* [1996] 2 S.C.R. 507, http://scc.lexum.umontreal.ca/en/
> 1996/1996rcs2-507/1996rcs2-507.html (accessed February 24, 2009).

page 24 *Cut and dried:* Lordon, "Reconciling Differences and Inspiring Change."

page 24 *Indigenous peoples around the world:* The estimate of the amount of land occupied by indigenous peoples, and their stewardship responsibility for so much of the world's biodiversity and cultural diversity, is by Dennis Martinez, "Land Grab on a Global Scale," *Seattle Post-Intelligencer,* April 2, 2008. Dennis Martinez is founder and co-chairman of the Indigenous Peoples' Restoration Network of the Society for Ecological Restoration International.

page 25 *A beehive of people:* Bartolemé de las Casas, *The Devastation of the Indies: A Brief Account,* trans. Herma Briffault (reprinted Baltimore: Johns Hopkins University Press, 1992), 28, cited in Charles C. Mann, *1491: New Revelations of the Americas Before Columbus* (New York: Alfred A. Knopf, 2005), 132. Bartolemé de las Casas was a priest who argued in Valladolid, Spain, for the notion that America's "Indians" were civilized, social beings who should not be enslaved. This debate was held a few years after 1492, and was among the earliest discussions of aboriginal title.

page 25 *Entire ways of life hiss away like steam:* Mann, *1491,* 111.

page 25 *An observed number of Haida warriors:* The estimate by Captain William Sturgis and the Hudson's Bay Company census, and other estimates, are discussed in Robert Boyd, *The Coming of the Spirit of Pestilence: Introduced Infectious Diseases and Population Decline among Northwest Coast Indians, 1774–1874* (Seattle: University of Washington Press, 1999), 208–209.

page 26 *Just 597 souls:* That number is comparable to the cities of London or New York being reduced to less than half a million people; Toronto shrinking to 150,000, or modern-day Vancouver ending up about the size of Moose Jaw, Saskatchewan. Royal Commission on Indian Affairs for the Province of British Columbia, *Report,* vol. 3 (1916), 726. The Royal Commission is commonly known as the McKenna-McBride Commission. The final report was printed and bound in four volumes.

page 26 *Victims of germ warfare:* Ken MacQueen, "West Coast Renaissance," *Maclean's,* October 20, 2003, 52.

page 27 *We are the nomads and They are the settlers:* J. Edward Chamberlin's *If This Is Your Land, Where Are Your Stories? Finding Common Ground* (Toronto: Alfred A. Knopf Canada, 2003), 29–30.

page 27 *When they see white people suddenly appear:* Chamberlin, *If This Is Your Land,* 31–32.

page 27 *Societies of genuine antiquity:* Bringhurst, *A Story as Sharp as a Knife,* 16.

page 28 *The Crown Colony of Vancouver Island:* The conveyance of Vancouver Island to the Hudson's Bay Company, the ascension of Governor James Douglas and Richard Blanshard's pale and short-lived contributions to the colony are documented in Barman, *The West Beyond the West,* 53–61.

page 28 *He wore two hats:* Thomas R. Berger describes the role of James Douglas in his book *One Man's Justice: A Life in the Law* (Vancouver: Douglas & McIntyre, 2002), 89–90.

page 28 *Douglas's transactions:* Ibid., 95.

page 28 *Utter savages living along the coast:* The letter from Lieutenant-Governor Joseph Trutch to Prime Minister John A. Macdonald in 1872 is cited in J. Bruce McKinnon, "Aboriginal Title: After Marshall and Bernard, Part II," *Advocate,* 65, Part 5 (September 2007), 623.

page 29 *A mighty pulverizing engine:* The *U.S. General Allotment Act of 1887* is described in Chamberlin, *If This Is Your Land,* 40. President Theodore Roosevelt spoke out against it on December 3, 1901, in his First Annual Message, http://miller center.org/scripps/archive/speeches/detail/3773 (accessed February 27, 2009).

page 29 *This gaping hole in the colonizers' paperwork:* Christopher Fritz Roth, "Without Treaty, Without Conquest: Indigenous Sovereignty in Post-*Delgamuukw* British Columbia," *Wicazo Sa Review,* 17, no. 2 (Fall 2002), 144.

page 30 *Indians must accept the inevitable:* Commissioner James McKenna's views are summarized by Barman in *The West Beyond the West,* 159.

page 30 *The Indian land question...did not disappear:* The analysis about the differing approaches to the native title by the provincial and federal governments, which led to the McKenna-McBride Commission, is from Douglas C. Harris, *Landing Native Fisheries: Indian Reserves and Fishing Rights in British Columbia, 1849–1925* (Vancouver: University of British Columbia Press, 2008), 165–166.

page 31 *We are the natives of this Country:* Bob Anderson addressed the McKenna-McBride Commission on August 25, 1913, at Bella Bella, British Columbia: Royal Commission on Indian Affairs for the Province of British Columbia Bella Coola Agency Transcript, 60, http://www.ubcic.bc.ca/gsdl/collect/royalcom/import/Bella %20Coola%20.html (accessed February 15, 2009). The author was unable to find a version in published book form of the exhibits, transcripts and proceedings of the commission so has relied on various secondary sources, including the website of the Union of British Columbia Indian Chiefs, cited here.

page 31 *We haven't got any ill feelings:* Gideon Minesque's statement to the McKenna-McBride Commission given in the Nass Valley in 1915 is cited in Berger, *One Man's Justice,* 111–112.

page 32 *The commission visited the "Queen Charlotte Agency":* A complete account of the proceedings at the McKenna-McBride Commission's visit to The Queen Charlotte Agency (Masset and Skidegate) is reproduced in the September 2001 edition of *Haida Laas, Journal* [or sometimes *Newsletter*] *of the Haida Nation.*

page 36 *Take 47,000 acres of good land:* A discussion about land being taken in and out of reserves as a result of the McKenna-McBride Commission appears in Barman, *The West Beyond the West,* 159.

page 36 *"I want to get rid of the Indian problem":* Duncan Campbell Scott's quote is from E. Brian Titley, *A Narrow Vision: Duncan Campbell Scott and the Administra-*

tion of Indian Affairs in Canada (Vancouver: University of British Columbia Press, 1986), 50, cited in Paul Tennant, *Aboriginal Peoples and Politics: The Indian Land Question in British Columbia, 1849–1989* (Vancouver: University of British Columbia Press, 1990), 92.

page 37 *Section 141 of the Indian Act:* Tennant, *Aboriginal Peoples and Politics,* 112.

page 37 *The Allied Indian Tribes:* Discussion of the Allied Indian Tribes and the Native Brotherhood in Tennant, *Aboriginal Peoples and Politics,* 94 and 116.

page 37 *"Historical might-have-beens":* Berger, *One Man's Justice,* 114. According to Berger, Prime Minister Pierre Trudeau said in Vancouver on August 8, 1969: "Our answer is no. We can't recognize Aboriginal rights because no society can be built on historical 'might have beens.'"

page 37 *Extermination through assimilation:* Harold Cardinal, *The Unjust Society: The Tragedy of Canada's Indians* (Edmonton: Hurtig, 1969), 1.

page 38 *The vocal support of Thomas Berger:* Justice Thomas Berger resigned from the bench over controversy arising from his public criticism of Trudeau and the premiers dropping reference to aboriginal rights from the Charter. The reference was later restored as section 35. See Berger, *One Man's Justice,* 146–164.

page 38 *Section 35: Constitution Act, 1982,* being Schedule B to the *Canada Act, 1982* (U.K.), 1982, c. 11.

page 38 *Sometimes a loss is almost as good as a win:* An account of the *Calder* case, "The Nisga'a Odyssey," composes Chapter 5 in Berger, *One Man's Justice.* The specific quote is from page 123. On page 124, he cites Justice Judson's "this is what Indian title means." His discussion of the outcome of the 1972 federal election and the treaties that eventually flowed as a result of *Calder* is on page 126.

page 40 *Item of concern to the Haida:* The resolution that the Old Massett Haida sent to Premier Dave Barrett in 1974 is reported in Pansy White, "Haida's Ask For Greater Say in Queen Charlotte Island Government," *Queen Charlotte Islands Observer,* August 8, 1974, 1.

page 40: *An ebullient Dave Barrett:* Premier Barrett's visit to the islands is recounted in "Premier of the Province and the Islands," *Queen Charlotte Islands Observer,* October 17, 1974, 2.

page 41 *Haida Nation executive elected:* "The Haida Nation Executive Elected at Founding Convention," *Queen Charlotte Islands Observer,* December 12, 1974, 1.

THREE: THE SPIRIT RUSHES IN THE BLOOD

page 45 *There was no road:* The road from Port Clements to Masset officially opened on June 20, 1958: Kathleen E. Dalzell, *The Queen Charlotte Islands, 1774–1966* (Madeira Park, B.C.: Harbour Publishing, 1968), 292.

page 45 *She was pretty old:* Guujaaw believes Susan Williams was 114 when she died. According to notes compiled by the Haida Gwaii Singers Society, she died in 1971, aged 109: companion booklet to Davidson et al., *Songs of Haida Gwaii,* 3.

page 46 *"Fewer than five hundred Britons":* In Tennant, *Aboriginal Peoples and Politics,* 20, citing Robin Fisher, *Contact and Conflict: Indian-European Relations in British Columbia, 1774–1890* (Vancouver: University of British Columbia Press, 1977), 42.

page 46 *There was no armed conquest:* In Tennant, *Aboriginal Peoples and Politics,* 3.

page 47 *One of the most favored regions in the world:* Newton H. Chittenden, *Official Report of the Exploration of the Queen Charlotte Islands for the Government of British Columbia* (Victoria: Queen's Printer, 1884), 64.

page 47 *Grizzly-Bear Town or K̲'uuna (Koona):* John Smyly and Carolyn Smyly, *Those Born at Koona* (Saanichton: Hancock House, 1973), 18, 20.

page 47 *Almost unnaturally perfect in shape:* Ibid., 18.

page 47 *Skedans was one of fourteen villages:* John Swanton's record of the villages on Haida Gwaii in 1900 is cited in Bringhurst, *A Story as Sharp as a Knife,* 434.

page 47 *In its statement of defence:* Statement of Defence of the Defendant Her Majesty the Queen in Right of the Province of British Columbia re: Haida Nation v. British Columbia (Attorney General) (6 June 2003), Vancouver L020662 (B.C.S.C.), para. 12.

page 48 *Consolidated at two sites, Skidegate and Masset:* Ibid., para. 13.

page 48 *Does not admit the existence of the 'Haida Nation':* Ibid., para. 2.

page 48 *An organization styled the Haida Nation: Statement of Defence of the Attorney General of Canada re: Haida Nation v. British Columbia (Attorney General)* (6 June 2003), Vancouver L020662 (B.C.S.C.), para. 3.

page 49 *Trade and potlatches took place:* MacDonald, *Haida Art,* 148. See also "Haida Excursions," *Haida Laas,* October 2005, 41.

page 49 *On a regular trading expedition:* Douglas Cole and Bradley Lockner, *To the Charlottes: George Dawson's 1878 Survey of the Queen Charlotte Islands* (Vancouver: University of British Columbia Press, 1993), 42.

page 49 *In memory of the dead:* Ibid., 41.

page 50 *Clans were made extinct:* Terri-Lynn Williams-Davidson, "Protecting and Respecting the Earth's Soul and Aboriginal Cultural Traditions." The author attended this lecture presented at the Interfaith Summer Institute for Justice, Peace and Social Movements, Vancouver, April 19, 2007.

page 51 *A favourite "hangout":* Mary Lee Stearns, *Haida Culture in Custody: The Masset Band* (Seattle: University of Washington Press, 1981), 47.

page 52 *Guujaaw also carved:* In a published, though incomplete, biography, Guujaaw's enrolment in Rufus Moody's carving class is the sole entry under "education." Informal carving instruction was always available, but formal carving lessons became available to young Haida carvers in the late 1950s and early 1960s when Rufus Moody and Claude Davidson gave carving classes in Skidegate and Masset respectively: Leslie Drew and Douglas Wilson, *Argillite: Art of the Haida* (North Vancouver: Hancock House, 1980), 109.

page 52 *Carpentry in Rupert:* Jack Knox, "Carving a Future for Haida Gwaii," *Times Colonist,* November 9, 2003, D5.

page 53 *Avocado pit faces:* Jenny Nelson, interview with Jennifer Jordan, Masset, August 2006.

page 56 *Kaa.aads nee Dancers:* Florence Davidson talks about this dance group in Margaret B. Blackman, *Florence Edenshaw Davidson: During My Time, a Haida Woman,* revised edition (Seattle: University of Washington Press, 1992), 168–170.

page 59 *The base began:* See Jerry Proc's website, http://www.jproc.ca/rrp/masset.html (accessed February 15, 2009).

page 60 *The events of June 3, 1978:* The ceremony of the awarding of the freedom of the village was advertised in the *Queen Charlotte Island Observer* on June 1, 1978, page 3, as a "Public Notice: The Residents of the Queen Charlotte Islands are Cordially Invited to Attend the Ceremony of Granting Freedom of the Village to Canadian Forces Station Masset, this event to take place on June 3, 1978, at the Masset Municipal Hall on Main Street commencing at 12:30 p.m."

page 61 *Most Canadians remember the Oka Crisis:* Geoffrey York and Loreen Pindera, *People of the Pines: The Warriors and the Legacy of Oka* (Toronto: McArthur & Company, 1991), 435.

page 62 *"Freedoms Don't Come Easily":* Queen Charlotte Islands Observer, June 8, 1978, 1.

page 63 *It could have gotten nasty:* Peter Stewart-Burton, email to the author, May 2, 2007.

page 63 *Letters to the editor of the* Observer: "Seniors Set Matters Straight" and "Re: 'Freedom of the Village'" by Michael Nicoll and "QC Resident Joins the Act" by B. Stanley Harris, all published in the *Queen Charlotte Islands Observer,* June 8, 1978, 5–7. Frank Collison, "A Gross Injustice," *Queen Charlotte Islands Observer,* June 15, 1978, 7–8.

FOUR: OUT OF HAND

page 66 *So utterly, unforgivably, unprotected:* The history of wilderness campaigning in British Columbia that is recounted here, and Paul George's account of his experiences on Haida Gwaii, draw heavily on his book, *Big Trees Not Big Stumps: 25 Years of Campaigning to Save Wilderness with the Wilderness Committee* (Vancouver: Paul George and Western Canada Wilderness Committee, 2006). The list of protected area accomplishments appears on page 465.

page 66 *A picture of unspeakable ruin:* John Broadhead, ed., *Islands at the Edge: Preserving the Queen Charlotte Islands Wilderness* (Vancouver: Douglas & McIntyre, 1984), 130.

page 67 *Enough wood to circle the Earth:* Estimates by the Gowgaia Institute of the amount of timber taken off Haida Gwaii appear in several places. The amount quoted here is drawn from Gowgaia Institute, "People Making Change: An Overview of People Working in the Forest—Haida Heritage and Forest Guardians, Research Group on Introduced Species, Gowgaia Institute," *Haida Laas,* October 2005, 36.

page 67 *They fed provincial coffers:* Gowgaia Institute, *Forest Economy Trends and Economic Conditions on Haida Gwaii,* 2007, 11. This report can be downloaded from http://www.spruceroots.org/Booklets/ForTrends.pdf (accessed February 15, 2009).

pages 67–68 *The worst environmental horror show in British Columbia:* Broadhead, *Islands at the Edge,* 130.

page 68 *Plenty of Talunkwans in the making:* The (selective) list of various places on Haida Gwaii that were under assault in the 1970s is taken from "Environmental News Briefs," *About Time for an Island,* Islands Protection Committee, Winter 1975, 32–33. The periodical was edited by, among others, Guujaaw and Thom Henley.

page 68 *A voice on behalf of all island residents:* In "By Way of Introduction," *About Time for an Island,* Winter 1975, 2.

page 70 *The benefit dance was held:* Ibid.

page 75 *A formative trip to the mainland:* Jenny Nelson's written account of the trip appears as "Coming Together: The Northwest Development Conference," *All Alone Stone,* 3 (1976), 16–17.

pages 76–77 *Kinship between bear and man:* Ghin and Jennie, "Brother Taan," *All Alone Stone,* 3 (1976), 17.

page 77 *Man embraced the tree:* Ghigndiging, "Out of Hand," *All Alone Stone,* 3 (1976), 21.

page 78 *You are what you eat:* Gary Edenshaw, "You Are What You Eat," *All Alone Stone,* [2] (1975), 33.

page 79 *We passed through a kelp field:* Gary Edenshaw, "A While Back on Rowing to Wiah Point," *About Time for an Island,* 35.

page 79 *Silence means political consent:* Bob Dalgleish, Gary Edenshaw and Vic Bell, *Queen Charlotte Islands Observer,* February 20, 1975, 6. Guujaaw's warning that the Islands Protection Committee would "die a quick death" if it didn't speak truth to power appears in the same letter.

page 80 *More than 500 people signed onto a petition:* In "South Moresby Revisited," *All Alone Stone,* 3 (1976) 2; also "Environmental News Briefs," *About Time for an Island,* 33.

page 80 *"Guujaaw did not refuse to shake my hand"*: In George, *Big Trees Not Big Stumps,* 2. Paul George devotes several early passages in his book to his first encounter with Guujaaw and the Islands Protection Committee, his attempt to produce a coffee table book, his trip to Talunkwan Island, the slide shows and public meetings and Guujaaw's first public speech. He also writes of his growing conviction that the Haida would protect South Moresby. The several quotes from *Big Trees Not Big Stumps* are from pages 1–9.

FIVE: DRUM

page 84 *To begin to know Haida Gwaii:* Robert Davidson, in conversation with the author, June 2007.

page 85 *The Indians were all very much afraid:* George M. Dawson, *Report on the Queen Charlotte Islands 1878* (Ottawa: Geological Survey of Canada, 1880), 161.

page 85 *In association with Kiusta:* MacDonald, *Haida Art,* 171.

page 86 *An online biography:* Covering the years 1968 to 1997, this online biography also links to a number of articles in *SpruceRoots,* including photo galleries featuring some of Guujaaw's work, http://www.qcislands.net/guujaaw/Bio.html (accessed February 15, 2009).

page 87 *"Help bring the village back to life"*: Plans for the construction of the Kiusta longhouse were articulated in an undated five-page proposal, "Elders Longhouse Project," that sought funds and in-kind support (mostly cedar logs and lumber) "to add a comfortable and traditional facility to an abandoned Haida village site." The proposal seems to have been written in 1979, and appears in the University of Victoria Archives Canada Wilderness Committee founder Paul George, AR337, Acc. No. 2000-071, 2.11 First Nations.

page 87 *The Haida Gwaii Watchmen program:* The Haida Gwaii Watchmen program was begun in the 1970s to protect culturally significant sites that had been subject to looting and misuse. The program was formalized in 1981 and has been replicated in other First Nations communities on the mainland. It has also prompted visits from indigenous people from the United States and Australia who seek to institute similar programs at home. Information about the Watchmen program can be found at http://www.pc.gc.ca/pn-np/bc/gwaiihaanas/edu/index_E.asp (accessed February 15, 2009). It focusses on the program in Gwaii Haanas, although Watchmen also operate at other sites throughout Haida Gwaii.

page 87 *The word* guujaaw *means "drum":* A short passage that describes the provenance of the name Guujaaw appears in Davidson et al., *Songs of Haida Gwaii,* 7.

page 88 *Hard to envision life without it:* Hilary Stewart, *Cedar: Tree of Life to the Northwest Indians* (Vancouver: Douglas & McIntyre, 1984), 13.

page 88 *Son of an itinerant entrepreneur:* Bill Reid describes his parents in Bill Reid, *Solitary Raven: Selected Writings of Bill Reid* (Vancouver: Douglas & McIntyre, 2000), 85.

page 89 *"The rich seahunting villages":* Robert Bringhurst writes about Bill Reid's cultural traditions and makes the comparison to Donatello, Yeats and Bartók, in his introduction to Bill Reid, *Solitary Raven,* 9.

page 89 *A "symbol of the past":* A description of Reid's difficulties in getting the community of Skidegate behind his totem pole project appears in Maria Tippett, *Bill Reid: The Making of an Indian* (Toronto: Vintage Canada, 2004), 209.

page 89 *These goddamn Indians:* Tippett, *Bill Reid,* 210.

page 89 *"Pitiful remnants":* Diane Brown, "The Legacy of Bill Reid: A Critical Inquiry," University of British Columbia conference, November 13, 1999, cited in Tippett, *Bill Reid,* 212.

page 90 *Legendary beings:* The features of the totem pole are described in Karen Duffek, *Bill Reid: Beyond the Essential Form,* Museum Note No. 19 (Vancouver: University of British Columbia Press, 1986), 20.

page 91 *Two female figures on the pole:* Guujaaw, "Man, Myth or Magic?" in Karen Duffek and Charlotte Townsend-Gault (eds.), *Bill Reid and Beyond: Expanding on Modern Native Art* (Vancouver: Museum of Anthropology at the University of British Columbia and Douglas & McIntyre, 2004), 62.

page 91 *Above the heads of the cheering crowd:* In Tippett, *Bill Reid,* 213.

page 91 *Ways to entrap the tensions:* Guujaaw, in Duffek and Townsend-Gault, *Bill Reid and Beyond,* 62.

page 92 *A program called Rediscovery:* Thom Henley, *Rediscovery: Ancient Pathways, New Directions* (Edmonton: Lone Pine Publishing, 1996), 17–18.

page 92 *The enormous sculpture had its beginnings:* Tippett, *Bill Reid*, 221–224. Maria Tippett traces the origin and describes the production of *The Raven and the First Men,* including quoting carver George Rammell about Reid's "throwing the French curve into everything."

page 93 *The Dangerous Native Activist:* George Rammell, "Goldsmith/Culture-smith," in Duffek and Townsend-Gault, *Bill Reid and Beyond,* 57.

page 95 *A duty to act fairly:* Paul George, *Big Trees Not Big Stumps,* 14–17.

SIX: THE SAME AS EVERYONE ELSE

pages 98–99 *"O Canada":* The three additional though largely unsung verses to "O Canada" appear in the "Full History of 'O Canada' " section of the Department of Canadian Heritage website at http://www.pch.gc.ca/pgm/ceem-cced/symbl/ anthem-eng.cfm#a2 (accessed February 15, 2009).

page 100 *Duty and authorities of the ancient lineage mothers:* Michael Nicoll Yahgula-naas's description of the Council of the Haida Nation is in a letter to the jury of the Buffett Award for Indigenous Leadership, in which he nominated Guujaaw for the award, May 10, 2006.

page 101 *A moral obligation to defend our resources:* Percy Williams in Evelyn Pinkerton, "Taking the Minister to Court: Changes in Public Opinion about For-est Management and Their Expression in Haida Land Claims," *B.C. Studies,* no. 57 (1983), 68.

page 102 *A tribal park called Duu Guusd:* See "Duu Guusd Tribal Park," *Haida Laas,* Special Edition, February 1986. The designation of Duu Guusd as a Haida protected area is also discussed on the website of the Council of the Haida Nation, http:// www.haidanation.ca (accessed February 15, 2009).

page 102 *At the time before people:* Guujaaw, "It Was Told," foreword to Daryl W. Fedje and Rolf W. Mathewes, eds., *Haida Gwaii: Human History and Environment from the Time of Loon to the Time of the Iron People* (Vancouver: University of British Columbia Press, 2005), xii.

pages 102–103 *Selected for protection:* Michael Nicoll Yahgulanaas's recollection of the Haida's choice of Duu Guusd for protection, and the dinner held for the loggers, is from his Buffett Award nomination letter, May 10, 2006.

page 103 *My job was to extract timber:* Wade Davis's description of logging at Dinan Bay is in a letter to the Buffett Award jury, May 14, 2006.

page 103 *The most important denizen of the Pacific slope:* Wade Davis in Wade Davis (text) and Graham Osborne (photos), *Rainforest: Ancient Realm of the Pacific Northwest* (Vancouver / Toronto: Greystone Books, 1998), 24–31.

page 104 *Logging industry directly employed up to 25,000 people:* This figure is estimated in M. Patricia Marchak, Scott L. Aycock and Deborah M. Herbert, *Falldown: Forest Policy in British Columbia* (Vancouver: David Suzuki Foundation and Ecotrust Canada, 1999), 197. In addition to logging jobs, the forest industry generated jobs in sawmills and planing mills, and in pulp and paper mills. Forest-based employment and multiplier effects are discussed in Chapter 5 of *Falldown.*

page 104 *Pine was as valuable as an oil field:* John Vaillant, *The Golden Spruce: A True Story of Myth, Madness and Greed* (Toronto: Alfred A. Knopf Canada, 2005), 82.

page 104 *Timber is why they stayed:* Ibid., 79.

page 105 *It was a one-time deal:* Davis, in Davis and Osborne, *Rainforest,* 31–33.

page 106 *Massive harvest levels continue:* Figures on contemporary logging harvest levels are from the harvest billing system operated by the revenue branch of British Columbia's Ministry of Forests and Range. They were compiled and supplied to the author by Victoria-based forest policy writer and analyst Ben Parfitt.

page 107 *Almost 50 million cubic metres of wood were cut:* Gowgaia Institute, *Forest Economy Trends and Economic Conditions on Haida Gwaii,* 2007, 7.

page 107 *94 per cent left as raw wood:* B.C. Wild, *Taking It All Away: Communities on Haida Gwaii Say Enough Is Enough,* pamphlet (1996), 1.

page 107 *Employment for local people was modest:* B.C. Wild, *Taking It All Away,* 4–13.

page 108 *I meant no harm. I most truly did not.:* Dr. Seuss, *The Lorax* (New York: Random House, 1971), 41.

page 108 *A purely quixotic gesture:* Davis, letter to the Buffett Award jury, May 14, 2006.

page 108 *We needed to shift our efforts:* George, *Big Trees Not Big Stumps,* 27.

page 109 *An array of staggeringly ineffective programs:* Assembly of First Nations, *The $9 Billion Myth Exposed: Why First Nations Poverty Endures,* information sheet (Ottawa: February 24, 2007), http://www.afn.ca/cmslib/general/M-Ex.pdf (accessed February 15, 2009).

pages 109–110 *The first that official Ottawa heard of South Moresby:* George, *Big Trees Not Big Stumps,* 27. George gives an account of Ian Waddell's sponsorship of Bill C-454 and Jim Fulton's fear of alienating loggers in his riding. "National Parks Act: Amendment to Establish Park on Moresby Island and Adjacent Islands," is recorded in House of Commons, *Debates,* April 22, 1983, 24771.

page 110 *The combative and populist Suzuki:* A complete biography of David Suzuki can be viewed at http://www.davidsuzuki.org/About_us/Dr_David_Suzuki (accessed February 15, 2009).

page 111 *Suzuki's Windy Bay show:* George, *Big Trees Not Big Stumps,* 28.

page 111 *Suzuki extols South Moresby's virtues:* David Suzuki's description of South Moresby and his interview with Guujaaw are transcribed from *The Nature of Things with David Suzuki: Windy Bay,* videocassette, Canadian Broadcasting Corporation, Television, January 27, 1982.

page 112 *A radically different way of looking at the world:* David Suzuki, "Ecological Millennium: Setting the Bottom Line," presented to the Canadian Conference on International Health, November 14–17, 1999.

page 113 *Put in the hands of a government process:* George, *Big Trees Not Big Stumps,* 471. John Broadhead of the Islands Protection Society discusses the government processes put in place to deal with South Moresby in *Islands at the Edge,* 130–140.

page 114 *Guujaaw put him down and won:* Paul George, *Big Trees Not Big Stumps,* 33.

page 114 Redneck News: R.L. "Redneck" Smith's editions of the *Redneck News* amounted to about 200,000 words about "sissy environmentalists," people's right to work, politicians and David Suzuki's broadcasts. Highlights of his colourful commentary are reprinted in Ian Lordon, "What Do You Do with Old Rednecks?" *SpruceRoots,* July 1998.

page 115 *On Easter weekend, 1984:* George, *Big Trees Not Big Stumps,* 51.

page 116 *The first logging blockade in Canadian history:* George, *Big Trees Not Big Stumps,* 55.

page 116 *Meticulous attention to detail:* Elizabeth May, *Paradise Won: The Struggle for South Moresby* (Toronto: McClelland & Stewart, 1990), 55.

page 117 *Registered the hereditary boundaries of Haida Gwaii:* May, *Paradise Won,* 59.

page 117 *Law of the Sea Convention:* The Haida Nation filed a notice of dispute with the Secretary General of the United Nations on February 11, 1983; see "The Law of the Sea," *Haida Laas,* February 1986. Details of the Convention are outlined in the United Nations Division for Ocean Affairs and the Law of the Sea at http://www.un.org/Depts/los/convention_agreements/convention_historical_perspective.htm (accessed February 15, 2009).

page 118 *Stories about the Indians of Canada:* Simon Baker and Verna J. Kirkness, *Khot-La-Cha: The Autobiography of Chief Simon Baker* (Vancouver: Douglas & McIntyre, 1994), 119.

page 118 *The opening of a big complex built by B.C. Lumber:* Baker, *Khot-La-Cha,* 130.

page 119 *Guujaaw was looking for culturally modified trees:* Years after his initial forays into the woods looking for culturally modified trees, Guujaaw filed an impact statement with the Royal Canadian Mounted Police (letter, June 10, 2004) in which he complained about culturally modified trees having been cut and removed from Kumdis, on Haida Gwaii. He made an impassioned argument for the value of CMTs, including their dollar value and the multiplier effects of carving and erecting cedar monuments. "Every tree utilized by our people tells us something of the history and movement of our people. Every tree removed, erases traces of the existence of our people."

page 121 *It* must *be saved:* Farley Mowat, in "Famous Canadians Team-Up to Save South Moresby," *South Moresby, Queen Charlotte Islands: Misty Wilderness Gem of the Canadian Pacific,* pamphlet, Western Canada Wilderness Committee, June 1985, http://www.wildernesscommittee.org/campaigns/historic/morseby/reports/VOL04NO03 (accessed February 19, 2009).

page 122 *A matter of pride for the industry:* George, *Big Trees Not Big Stumps,* 75.

page 122 *Act of aggression:* A chronology of the South Moresby dispute can be found in *Haida Laas,* Special Edition, February 1986.

SEVEN: THEY SAY

page 124 *Chilcotin War of 1864:* Alan D. McMillan, *Native Peoples and Cultures of Canada: An Anthropological Overview* (Vancouver: Douglas & McIntyre, 1988), 168.

page 125 *Convicted and hanged:* G.P.V. Akrigg and Helen B. Akrigg, *British Columbia Chronicle, 1847–1871: Gold and Colonists* (Vancouver: Discovery Press, 1977), 297–305. See also Edward Sleigh Hewlett, "Klatsassin," *Dictionary of Canadian Biography,* http://www.biographi.ca/009004-119.01-e.php?&id_nbr=4527&interval=25&&PHPSESSID=45bpogq75hb6k1gtnhgulkdkq2 (accessed February 25, 2009).

page 125 *"Hanging judge" and "Big Chief":* David Ricardo Williams, "Sir Matthew Baillie Begbie," *Dictionary of Canadian Biography,* http://www.biographi.ca/009004-119.01-e.php?&id_nbr=5958&interval=25&&PHPSESSID=kcd8115qcfdeboqrs9iavva6g7 (accessed February 25, 2009).

page 125 *Crimes of plunder or revenge:* Margaret A. Ormsby, *British Columbia: A History* (Vancouver: Macmillan of Canada, 1964), 206.

page 126 *Affecting admixture of cowboys and Indians:* Paul St. Pierre, *Breaking Smith's Quarter Horse* (Vancouver: Douglas & McIntyre, 1984). St. Pierre wrote other seminal books about the Chilcotin, including *Smith and Other Events* (Vancouver / Toronto: Douglas & McIntyre, 1971) and *Tell Me a Good Lie: Tales From the Chilcotin Country* (Vancouver / Toronto: Douglas & McIntyre, 2001).

page 126 *Logging will be the end of the Chilcotin:* Terry Glavin, "Chilcotin People Reject Logging," *Vancouver Sun,* October 26, 1985, A10.

page 127 *That matched the Haida's:* The *William* case, more properly known as *Tsilhqot'in Nation v. British Columbia,* 2007 BCSC 1700, provides a detailed history of the rights and title claim of the Chilcotin, http://www.courts.gov.bc.ca/Jdb-txt/sc/07/17/2007BCSC1700.pdf (accessed February 15, 2009).

page 127 *Fighting for rights and land as never before:* Larry Pynn, "B.C. Native Indians Fighting for Rights and Land as Never Before," *Vancouver Sun,* October 26, 1985, A10.

page 127 *Threat of a Haida protest:* Glenn Bohn, "Forest Firm Vows to Log Lyell: Haida Protest Expected," *Vancouver Sun,* October 26, 1985, A16.

pages 127–128 *Blocking the highway, breaking the law:* The passage depicting events at Athlii Gwaii relies on footage and interviews appearing in a film by Jeff Bear and Marianne Jones, *Athlii Gwaii: The Line at Lyell,* DVD (Vancouver: Ravens and Eagles Productions 2 Ltd., 2003).

page 128 *We were outgunned:* Guujaaw in Seán Hennessey, "Gwaii Haanas: How Non-violence Works," *Ideas,* Canadian Broadcasting Corporation, Radio, October 20, 1992.

page 129 *A national anthem for Haida Gwaii:* "Entrance (Lyell Island Song)," performed by Guujaaw, in Davidson et al., *Songs of Haida Gwaii,* disk 2, song 23.

pages 129–130 *Blockades are interesting:* Chamberlin, *If This Is Your Land,* 63.

page 132 *These are not criminals before you:* Miles Richardson, in Keith Baldrey, "Haidas Refuse to Knuckle under on Blockade," *Vancouver Sun,* November 29, 1985, A18.

page 132 *They have challenged the law directly:* Chief Justice Allan McEachern, in Keith Baldrey, "Judge Tells Haidas: Obey or Go to Jail," *Vancouver Sun,* November 30, 1985, A1.

page 133 *Nasty, brutish and short:* Chief Justice Allan McEachern's landmark judgement: *Delgamuukw v. British Columbia,* [1991] 3 W.W.R. 97 (B.C.S.C.). There has been much commentary about Chief Justice McEachern's use of Hobbes' phrase to characterize the lives of native people, including a commentary by James B. Waldram, Pat Berringer and Wayne Warry, "'Nasty, Brutish and Short': Anthropology and the Gitksan-Wet'suwet'en Decision," *Canadian Journal of Native Studies,* 12, no. 2 (1992), 309–316.

page 133 *The United Church rallied:* May, *Paradise Won,* 127.

page 133 *Cowardly use of the courts:* "B.C. Fed Backs Haidas, Loggers in Lyell Dispute," *Vancouver Sun,* November 28, 1985, A3.

page 134 *A poll was published:* Larry Pynn, "Talk Land Issue, Poll Tells Bennett," *Vancouver Sun,* November 30, 1985, A1.

page 134 *A showcase of evolution:* David Suzuki's narration of his second film on South Moresby and his second interview with Guujaaw are transcribed from *The Nature of Things with David Suzuki: Islands at the Edge,* videocassette, Canadian Broadcasting Corporation, Television, January 29, 1986.

page 135 *Oral cultures understand the world:* Chamberlin, *If This Is Your Land,* 19.

page 135 *The Haida account of the world begins:* John Enrico in *Skidegate Haida Myths and Histories* (Skidegate: Queen Charlotte Islands Museum Press and Council of the Haida Nation, 1995), 5. This book is a collection, translated and edited by John Enrico, of myths and histories collected by John R. Swanton from September 1900 to August 1901.

page 136 *ʔaaniis.uu tangaa ragingang ʔwan suuga:* John Sky in Enrico, *Skidegate Haida Myths and Histories,* 14–15.

page 136 *The Raven snapped up the light:* Bill Reid and Robert Bringhurst, *The Raven Steals the Light* (Vancouver: Douglas & McIntyre, 1984), 16.

page 136 *Several sub-realms of spirit beings:* Enrico, *Skidegate Haida Myths and Histories,* 7.

page 137 *Sharing equally in everything:* Edmond Bordeaux Szekely, *The Essene Gospel of Peace: Book Three* (Nelson, B.C.: International Biogenic Society, 1981), 12.

page 138 *Blood connection to the Jewish Peoples:* Nicoll Yahgulanaas, in his Buffett Award nomination letter, May 10, 2006.

pages 138–139 *Because it was told:* Guujaaw, "It Was Told," *Haida Gwaii,* xii.

page 140 *A spiritual grammar:* Chamberlin, *If This Is Your Land,* 63.

pages 139–140 *Mythological thinking has fallen into disrepute:* Karen Armstrong, *A Short History of Myth* (Toronto: Alfred A. Knopf Canada, 2005), 4–6.

page 140 *People get scared of the word 'spirituality':* Diane Brown, in Ian Lordon, "Hacking Down the Garden," *SpruceRoots,* December 2000.

page 140 *He would make a great Buddhist:* Nicoll Yahgulanaas, in his Buffett Award nomination letter, May 10, 2006.

page 142 *Trespass cabin:* George, *Big Trees Not Big Stumps,* 85.

page 142 *The Loo Taas was a newsworthy item:* Tippett, *Bill Reid,* 243.

page 143 *Trouble with Reid's assistant:* Ibid.

page 143 *The most beautiful vessel ever devised:* P.J. Reece, Thunderbirds and Thunderstorms," *Canadian Geographic,* July/August 2008, 34.

pages 143–144 *Urging visitors to see both sides of British Columbia:* Paul Pritchard, in May, *Paradise Won,* 130.

page 144 *As much of South Moresby as possible:* Tom McMillan, in May, *Paradise Won,* 136.

page 144 *An act of vandalism:* Pierre Berton, in May, *Paradise Won,* 138.

page 144 *Much to their amusement:* May, *Paradise Won,* 137–138.

page 145 *The train rolled on through the night:* May, *Paradise Won,* 140.

page 145 *Live life to the full:* May Russ, in *Haida Gwai[i]: Islands of the People,* video-cassette produced by Jeff Goodman and Mike Salisbury, BBC–Bristol in association with WNET/Thirteen [episode from the PBS series *Nature* with George H. Page], 1986.

page 146 *Renouncing their Canadian citizenship:* Ben Parfitt, "Haida Telegram Act of Frustration," *Vancouver Sun,* July 15, 1986, A8.

page 146 *No right to protect:* May, *Paradise Won,* 145.

page 146 *Fate of the Earth conference:* May, *Paradise Won,* 146–147.

page 147 *War to protect our lands:* Guujaaw, in George, *Big Trees Not Big Stumps,* 92.

page 148 *Moresby park deal reached:* Ian Gill, "Moresby Park Deal Reached: Cost and Details under Wraps," *Vancouver Sun,* July 7, 1987, A1. Daphne Bramham, "Haida Feast Celebrates Park Deal," *Vancouver Sun,* July 11, 1987, A10.

page 148 *A stopover in Hartley Bay:* May, *Paradise Won,* 292.

page 149 *The rebirth of a nation:* Thom Henley, email to the author, June 18, 2008.

EIGHT: PUSHING BACK

page 150 *Bill Reid began using repoussé:* Duffek, *Bill Reid: Beyond the Essential Form,* 15.

page 151 *The papers are shuffling in Victoria and New York:* Copy of letter from Gary Edenshaw for Islands Protection to Skidegate Band Council, November 5, 1978, University of Victoria Archives, Paul George, AR337, Acc. No. 2000-071, 2.11 First Nations.

page 151 *Whisked out of the woods: Province* staff reporter, "Indians Want Fish Put Ahead of Logging," *Province,* December 10, 1979, A4.

page 151 *A series of letters in 1979:* Guujaaw's letters, University of Victoria Archives, Canada Wilderness Committee founder Paul George, AR337, Acc. No. 2000-071, 2.11 First Nations.

pages 153–154 *Young Guujaaw told him he was on Haida land:* Jeff Lee, "Guujaaw: A Man of His People," *Vancouver Sun,* March 16, 2002, D5.

page 154 *Jailed for catching salmon:* John Cruickshank, "New Generation of Haida Talking Tough: Title to Lands Never Lost, Leader Says," *Globe and Mail,* March 24, 1987, A5.

page 154 *A festering issue:* Ernie Collison, "The Henslung Battle," *Haida Laas,* January 28, 1994, 1. The "Haida injunction" is referred to in this account. See also Terry Glavin, "Haida Force Shutdown of Resort Construction," *Vancouver Sun,* January 22, 1988, B4.

page 154 *We will not let the mine operate:* Mavis Gillie, "Gold Fever and the Haida," *Haida Laas,* July 8, 1994, 1.

page 156 *A national park shoved down our throats:* Miles Richardson, in Terry Glavin, "Haidas to Get Star Role in New Park: But South Moresby Delay Rapped," *Vancouver Sun,* January 30, 1988, A9.

page 156 *Stunned a blue-chip audience:* Terry Glavin, "Queen Charlottes Divided by Haida Band's Claims," *Vancouver Sun,* February 23, 1988, B1.

page 157 *Whose land are you standing on?:* May, *Paradise Won,* 310–311.

page 157 *Finally back on track:* May, *Paradise Won,* 311–312.

page 157 *The booklets were shredded:* May, *Paradise Won,* 312.

pages 157–158 *Permit for a mining company to drill in proposed protected area:* Les Leyne, "B.C. Gives Miners Permit to Drill in Moresby Park," *Times Colonist,* May 3, 1988, A1.

page 158 *No need for people to come up here:* Miles Richardson, in Terry Glavin, "Haida Threaten Moresby Closure," *Vancouver Sun,* July 13, 1988, B1.

page 158 *The Haida were again issuing passports:* Terry Glavin, "Haidas Declare Self-Rule," *Vancouver Sun,* January 31, 1989, A1.

page 158 *Not a place where picnic benches are the norm:* Guujaaw, quoted on the Parks Canada website at http://www.pc.gc.ca/docs/pc/rpts/heritage/prot14_e.asp (accessed February 21, 2006). This is also the page where the reference to the federally hosted potlatch was made. The link no longer functions.

page 158 *The Gwaii Haanas Agreement:* Gwaii Haanas Agreement Between: The Government of Canada, And: The Council of the Haida Nation, for and on behalf of the Haida Nation, dated January 1, 1993. The agreement was signed in Old Massett by Mary Collins, the then minister of state for the environment, and Miles Richardson, the president of the Haida Nation, http://www.pc.gc.ca/pn-np/bc/gwaiihaanas/plan/plan2a_E.asp (accessed February 15, 2009).

page 160 *A stunning reversal of previous statements:* Archipelago Management Board, "Gwaii Haanas: Haida Heritage Site and National Park Reserve," *Newsletter No. 1* (September 1993), 7.

page 160 *A Gaagixiit mask:* A Gaagixiit represents a wild man in the forest.

page 161 *Thunderbird pole:* The pole can be seen in an online gallery of Guujaaw's works at http://www.qcislands.net/guujaaw/Gallery/BgPole.html (accessed February 15, 2009).

page 161 The Spirit of Haida Gwaii: The Black Canoe: This monumental work was commissioned by architect Arthur Erickson to adorn the courtyard of the Canadian Embassy in Washington, D.C. A twin, commissioned by Vancouver's international airport authority and given a green patina, is known as *The Spirit of Haida Gwaii:*

The Jade Canoe and is on display in the international terminal building at the Vancouver airport.

pages 161–162 *To the Amazon:* David Suzuki gives a lengthy account of Paiakan's trip to Canada, and the return trip by Canadian environmentalists, in David Suzuki, "Protecting Paiakan's Forest Home," Chapter 8 in *David Suzuki: The Autobiography* (Vancouver: Greystone Books, 2006), 155–174.

page 164 *The alarmed response on the islands: The Islands Community Stability Initiative Consensus* document appears as Appendix 1 in Robin B. Clark, Inc., *Community Forest Feasibility Study for Haida Gwaii / the Queen Charlotte Islands* (Islands Community Stability Initiative, 1998), 102-121. The document can be found at: http://www.for.gov.bc.ca/hfd/library/frbc1998/frbc1998mr43.pdf.

page 164 *If we let people speak, the answers will come:* Leslie Johnson, in "The People Plan for the Forests of the People Islands," Donella Meadows, *The Global Citizen,* August 1, 1996. See http://www.pcdf.org/Meadows/people.htm.

NINE: THIS BOX OF TREASURES

page 165 *A myth is any story:* Enrico, *Skidegate Haida Myths and Histories,* 4.

page 165 *Open this box of treasures:* Guujaaw, "This Box of Treasures," in Enrico, *Skidegate Haida Myths and Histories,* vii.

pages 165–166 *And know that Haida Culture:* Guujaaw, "This Box of Treasures," in Daina Augaitis et al., *Raven Travelling: Two Centuries of Haida Art* (Vancouver: Vancouver Art Gallery and Douglas & McIntyre, 2006), 3.

page 166 *All that we say is ours is of Haida Gwaii:* Guujaaw, in Enrico, *Skidegate Haida Myths and Histories,* vii-viii.

page 166 *The Haida Nation is the rightful heir to Haida Gwaii:* Constitution of the Haida Nation, amended and adopted October 2003, House of Assembly, amended 2005, A.12.S1.a.

page 167 *Canada's own Constitution:* The *Constitution Act, 1867* (U.K.), 30 & 31 Vict., c. 3, formerly called the *British North America Act, 1867,* sets out, among other things, the terms of union of the provinces, the executive and legislative powers of the government and the division of powers between the provinces and federal government. The *Constitution Act, 1982,* being Schedule B to the *Canada Act, 1982* (U.K.), 1982, c. 11, includes Part I, Canadian Charter of Rights and Freedoms.

page 168 *The region was only mountains, forests and water:* Chittenden, *Official Report of the Exploration of the Queen Charlotte Islands,* 3.

page 169 *Needs are identified, land use zones are defined:* British Columbia, Integrated Land Management Bureau, *Integrated Land Use Planning for Public Lands in British Columbia,* http://ilmbwww.gov.bc.ca/slrp/reports/integrated_lup/index .html (accessed February 15, 2009).

page 169 *They say:* Council of the Haida Nation, *Haida Land Use Vision: Haida Gwaii Yah'guudang [Respecting Haida Gwaii],* pamphlet, April 2005. An earlier edition is available online at http://ilmbwww.gov.bc.ca/slrp/lrmp/nanaimo/qci/ docs/HLUVpublic.pdf (accessed February 15, 2009).

TEN: A RECOGNIZABLE CULTURE

page 182 *We fought with our neighbouring tribes:* Guujaaw interview with Seán Hennessey, "Gwaii Haanas: How Non-violence Works," *Ideas,* Canadian Broadcasting Corporation, Radio, October 20, 1992.

pages 182–183 *Lowered into a position:* Guujaaw, in Lordon, "Reconciling Differences and Inspiring Change," *SpruceRoots,* February 2000.

page 183 *Chief Skidegate:* Tragically, ʔAhl St'iigangaay, Chief Skidegate died in a freak boating accident early in 2008. He was to be succeeded in the chieftainship by Kingaay K̲'aajuus, Russ Jones. Pearle Pearson, "Chief Skidegate Announcement," *Queen Charlotte Islands Observer,* July 24, 2008, 13.

page 185 *An encumbrance on these forests:* Greg McDade, in "Haida Nation Moves to Stop TFL 39 Replacement," *Haida Laas,* March 9, 1995, 1.

page 186 Haida Laas: In the Haida language, Haida Laas means "good people."

page 186 *Get old mistakes out of the way:* Miles Richardson, ibid. Mr. Justice Cohen's decision dismissing the Haida petition was released on November 20, 1995.

page 187 *Make their way off their reserves:* This phrase was from "Some Comments" in Part 22 of Mr. Justice McEachern, [1991] 3 W.W.R. 97 (B.C.S.C.). The Supreme

Court of Canada's decision is reported at *Delgamuukw v. British Columbia,* [1997] 3 S.C.R. 1010, http://csc.lexum.umontreal.ca/en/1997/1997rcs3-1010/1997rcs3-1010.html (accessed February 15, 2009).

page 187 *Tide of history: Mabo v. Queensland (No. 2)* ("Mabo case"), [1992] HCA 23, para. 66.

page 187 *A legal version of checkers:* When it comes to the law regarding title and rights, New Zealand is well ahead of Canada and Australia on both counts, having apologized to Maori *iwi* (tribes) as far back as 1999, and having recognized that land is important to Maori tribes as *turangawaewae,* or "a place to stand." Two major settlements covering about half of New Zealand's land mass have been agreed.

page 187 *The prior occupation of Canada: Delgamuukw v. British Columbia,* [1997] 3 S.C.R. 1010, para. 114.

page 188 *Always a duty of consultation: Delgamuukw v. British Columbia,* [1997] 3 S.C.R. 1010, para 168.

page 188 *What's at stake here is our culture:* Guujaaw, in Ian Lordon, "Weighing in for the Title Challenge," *SpruceRoots,* September/October 2000. Terri-Lynn Williams-Davidson's comments on encumbrance appear in the same article.

page 188 *The connection of land and sea:* The Declaration of First Nations of the North Pacific Coast, also known as the Turning Point Declaration, is reprinted in *Haida Laas,* June 2006.

page 189 *On appeal, they won: Haida Nation v. British Columbia (Minister of Forests) and Weyerhauser,* 2002 BCCA 147, http://www.canlii.org/en/bc/bcca/doc/200/ 2002bcca147/2002bcca147.html (accessed February 15, 2009).

page 189 *Justice Douglas Lambert:* After subsequently retiring from the bench, and obviously taking his own opinion in the TFL 39 case to heart, Justice Lambert joined the legal team for the Haida title case.

page 190 *Williams-Davidson held the writ aloft:* An account of the filing of the writ on March 6, 2002, appears in Ian Lordon, "Negotiating Coexistence," *SpruceRoots,* April 2002, http://www.spruceroots.org/Issues%202002/Coexist.html (accessed February 15, 2009).

page 190 *A cascade of headlines rained down:* An extensive compendium of media reaction to the filing of the writ is included in a special edition of *Haida Laas* entitled "The Writ," March/April 2002. In his own analysis of the media coverage, Guujaaw said "the initial newscasts focussed on the offshore oil, probably because there is potentially billions or trillions of dollars involved. The headline 'Offshore oil is ours' is a good example of sensationalizing, especially when nobody actually said that."

page 190 *Lock, stock and barrel:* Chief Iljawass, in Suzanne Fournier, "Queen Charlottes and Offshore Oilfields Are All Ours, Haida Say," *Province,* March 6, 2002, A3, reprinted in *Haida Laas,* March 2002, 6.

page 191 *The* Washington Post: DeNeen L. Brown, "In a Canadian Court, a Native Nation Claims Offshore Rights," *Washington Post,* March 26, 2002, A10, reprinted in *Haida Laas,* March 2006, 51.

page 192 *An ageless savage:* Damian Inwood, "His mission is to save the Haida culture," *Province,* March 17, 2002, A22, reprinted in *Haida Laas,* March 2006, 50.

page 192 *The courts are doing social work:* Rafe Mair, "Editorial," CKNW Radio, March 13, 2002, transcribed and printed in *Haida Laas* March 2006, 31–33. Rafe Mair, "Interview with Guujaaw, President, Haida Nation," CKNW Radio, March 13, 2002, transcribed and printed in *Haida Laas,* March 2006, 32–35.

page 193 *I think they're sorry they asked for it:* Terri-Lynn Williams-Davidson, in Ian Lordon, "Without Equivocation," *SpruceRoots,* November 2002.

page 193 *A thousand-year plan for cedar: Haida Laas,* October 2005, 29.

page 194 *Tsuuaa 'kiing ja:* Guujaaw, *Haida Laas,* October 2005, 14.

page 195 *New-found fealty to the Haida:* Personal communication with the author, and Paul Shukovsky, "Forest Workers Sympathize with Haida; Weyerhaeuser Policy on Logging Imperils Livelihoods, They Say," *Seattle Post-Intelligencer,* June 6, 2002, B1.

page 196 *Our core action is to get rid of those tenures:* Ian Lordon, "Serving Notice: Tuning Up the Tenure Holders on Haida Gwaii," *SpruceRoots,* April 2003, http://www.spruceroots.org/April%202003/ServingNotice.html (accessed February 15, 2009).

page 196 *Amateurish attempt to gauge the public will:* Ken MacQueen, "Referendum Madness," *Maclean's,* May 13, 2002, 43.

page 196 *Particularly obstructionist:* Tony Penikett, "The Haida Don't Let Go Easily," *Globe and Mail,* September 9, 2003, A21.

page 196 *This is nothing but a* PR *game:* Lynda Lafleur, "Land claims Offer 'Designed to Be Rejected': Haida Council," *Creative Resistance,* September 4, 2003, . http://www.creativeresistance.ca (accessed March 31, 2006). This link no longer functions.

page 197 *Violation of our constitution:* Arnie Bellis, "The Haida Constitution, Business and the Environment," *SpruceRoots,* April 22, 2004, Gowgaia Institute Speakers' Series Transcript No. 5, http://www.spruceroots.org/Speakers%20Series/ ARNIE/Arnie.html (accessed February 15, 2009).

page 198 *An all island governance model:* Protocol Agreement between the Council of the Haida Nation and The Municipalities of Port Clements and Masset, signed and dated March 19, 2004. A copy of the Agreement is in *Haida Laas,* June 2006, 18–21, http://www.haidanation.ca/Pages/Agreements/PDF/Protocol_Communities.pdf (accessed February 15, 2009).

page 198 *Certainty. Certainty. Certainty.:* Jerry Lampert, "Two Perspectives on Certainty," speech to a one-day forum staged by the B.C. Treaty Commission, Venture Into a Treaty World (March 4, 2004), 16–20. In his remarks, Lampert actually used the word "certainty" eighteen times, http://www.bctreaty.net/files/ pdf_documents/Venturing%20into%20a%20treaty%20world.pdf (accessed February 15, 2009).

page 198 *A conscious effort to spoil this world:* Guujaaw, "Two Perspectives on Certainty," in *Venture Into a Treaty World* (March 4, 2004), 21–24, http://www.bctreaty .net/files/pdf_documents/Venturing%20into%20a%20treaty%20world.pdf (accessed February 15, 2009).

page 198 *The Earth is not dying—it is being killed:* U. Utah Phillips, in Naomi Klein, *No Logo* (Toronto: Vintage Canada, 2000), 325.

page 199 *The village submits they share the same concerns as the Haida:* "A Summary of Intervenor Arguments: TFL 39 Case," *SpruceRoots,* July 2004, http://www.spruce roots.org/July%202004/Arguments.html (accessed February 15, 2009).

page 199 *The old-growth forests will not survive:* Terri-Lynn Williams-Davidson, in Ian Lordon, "So Now," *SpruceRoots,* July 2004, http://www.spruceroots.org/July% 202004/SoNow.html (accessed February 15, 2009).

page 200 *A first-time beautiful moment for advocacy:* Louise Mandell, ibid.

page 201 *Fundamental legal defect:* Guujaaw letters on behalf of the Council of the Haida Nation to various individuals and government representatives.

page 203 *Canada's aboriginal peoples were never conquered: Haida Nation v. British Columbia (Minister of Forests) and Weyerhaeuser,* 2004 SCC 73, paras. 25, 74, http://scc.lexum.umontreal.ca/en/2004/2004scc73/2004scc73.html (accessed February 15, 2009).

page 204 *Slammed the brakes on governments:* Kirk Makin, "Landmark Rulings Made on Native Claims," *Globe and Mail,* November 19, 2004, A7.

page 205 *If we go out and get it:* Author notes made at the event, November 18, 2004.

ELEVEN: HOW THE WORLD GETS SAVED

page 206 *There is a field in high country:* The account of the Sacred Headwaters gathering in August 2006 is based on the author's participation in the events at that time.

page 211 *We really don't want development here:* Mark Hume, "Band Finds It's Not Alone in Fight for Wilderness," *Globe and Mail,* August 8, 2006, S2.

page 211 *They took our land and then our children:* Veronica Brodie, Ngarrindjeri elder, in Tom Trevorrow, Christine Finnimore, Steve Hemming, George Trevorrow, Matt Rigney, Veronica Brodie and Ellen Trevorrow, *They Took Our Land and Then Our Children: Ngarrindjeri Struggle for Truth and Justice,* booklet ([Camp Coorong, SA]: Ngarrindjeri Land and Progress Association, 2006).

page 212 *The souls of the dead don't rest in peace:* Vince Collison, in Penny Bailey, "There's No Place Like Home," *Wellcome Trust,* July 24, 2007, http://www.wellcome .ac.uk/News/2007/Features/WTX041039.htm (accessed February 15, 2009).

page 212 *Place of the Long Neck of Water:* Interviews with the Ngarrindjeri people of South Australia were conducted during a visit by the author in January 2008.

page 213 *Recognize Ngarrindjeri dominion:* "Ngarrindjeri Proclamation of Dominion," presented to Governor Marjorie Jackson-Nelson, December 17, 2003, in *They Took Our Land and Then Our Children.*

page 213 *For posterity:* Letter from Governor Jackson-Nelson to E.T. Trevorrow of the Ngarrindjeri Land and Progress Association, December 23, 2003, in *They Took Our Land and Then Our Children.*

page 213 *A decade going backwards:* The advent of Kevin Rudd's Labour government in 2008—whose first official act was to apologize to Australian aboriginal people—may yet signal new advances in Australia's on-again, off-again acknowledgement of aboriginal title. *Mabo* and *Yorta Yorta Aboriginal Community v. Victoria,* [2002] HCA 58.

page 217 *What our chiefs don't understand:* Herb George, "The Fire within Us," in Frank Cassidy, ed., *Aboriginal Title in British Columbia: Delgamuukw v. the Queen: Proceedings of a Conference Held September 10, 11, 1991* (Lantzville, B.C.: Oolichan Books, 1992), 55, cited in Roth, "Without Treaty, Without Conquest," 156.

page 217 *Massive Haida blockades:* Ontario Coalition Against Poverty, "Massive Haida Blockades Shut Down Weyerhaeuser" (March 23, 2005), http://ocap.ca/node/884 (accessed February 15, 2009).

pages 217–218 *The elders stood their ground:* The account of the Islands Spirit Rising blockade is compiled from a series of bulletins published on the islands during the blockade. The author also visited the blockade site near Juskatla. See the CHN website at http://www.haidanation.ca/islands/islands.html (accessed February 15, 2009).

pages 218–219 *Excellency:* A copy of the letter from Guujaaw to Her Excellency the Right Honourable Adrienne Clarkson, Governor General of Canada, March 20, 2005, is in *Haida Laas,* June 2006, 38, http://www.haidanation.ca/Pages/Haida_Laas/PDF/Journals/JL.June.06.pdf (accessed February 15, 2009).

page 219 *Standing with the Haida:* John Broadhead, "The Dollars and Sense of Haida Gwaii," April 8, 2005. Unpublished article sent to the author.

page 220 *It's a Haida Gwaii thing:* Margo Hearne, "Islands Spirits Rising," CHN website at http://www.haidanation.ca/islands/Margo.1.html (accessed February 15, 2009).

page 220 *Twenty years a'growing:* Maurice O'Sullivan, *Twenty Years A'Growing* (Nashville: J.S. Sanders and Co., 1998).

pages 220-221 *What brought the blockades down:* Understanding Arising from April 22, 2005, Discussion Between the Province [of British Columbia] and the Council of the Haida Nation, *Haida Laas,* 48–50. See CHN website at http://www.haidanation .ca/islands/Agreement.html (accessed February 15, 2009).

page 221 *Meat of the reason:* Heather Ramsay, "Optimism, No Signatures," *Queen Charlotte Islands Observer,* December 14, 2006, 44.

page 222 *Seeking appropriate compensation:* Gordon Hamilton, "Haida Deal Sparks Company Concerns: Western Forest Products Warns Victoria It Will Seek Compensation," *Vancouver Sun,* December 14, 2007, H3.

TWELVE: YES, WE CAN

page 224 *A precarious position:* Protocol Agreement, March 19, 2004. A copy of the Agreement is in *Haida Laas,* June 2006, 18–21, http://www.haidanation.ca/Pages/ Agreements/PDF/Protocol_Communities.pdf (accessed February 15, 2009).

page 226 *Where the next assault might come from:* On October 16, 2008, at a huge convention of The Nature Conservancy in Vancouver, Guujaaw gave a speech in which the audience of blue-chip, mostly American conservationists winced visibly when he invoked Iraq to make the point that he doesn't trust any government to leave the Haida alone because of their unrealized energy resources. "We all saw what they did to my cousin Saddam Hussein when they wanted *his* stuff," Guujaaw said. From author notes from the event.

page 226 *Gwaii Forest may buy* TFL: Alex Rinfret, "Gwaii Forest May Buy TFL," *Queen Charlotte Islands Observer,* October 23, 2008, 1. Randy O'Brien letter to the editor, "Elephant in the Room," *Queen Charlotte Islands Observer,* 8.

pages 226–227 *A disaster for the islands:* Heather Ramsay, "Logging Company Shuts Down Indefinitely," *Queen Charlotte Islands Observer,* January 15, 2009, 1.

page 227 *Sad news for racial equality:* "Sad News for Racial Equality on the Queen Charlotte Islands," *Canadian Constitution Foundation Newsletter* (February 2008), http://www.canadianconstitutionfoundation.ca/files/pdf/Feb%202008.pdf (accessed February 15, 2009).

page 228 *We're investing in life:* Personal communication and Erin Millar, "Trophy Lives," *BCBusiness,* September 3, 2008, 82, http://www.bcbusinessonline.ca/bcb/ top-stories/2008/09/03/trophy-lives?page=0%2C0 (accessed February 15, 2009).

page 228 *Internal Haida Nation business:* Arnie Bellis, in Alex Rinfret, "Difficult Decision Ahead over Lodge Application," *Queen Charlotte Islands Observer,* August 24, 2006, 11. The public hearing took place on Friday, August 18, 2006, two nights before Chief ʔIdansuu's potlatch.

page 229 *A massive offshore wind farm:* The wind farm threatens "significant socio-economic loss to the North Coast through loss of access or through reductions in the commercial yield of Dungeness crab," says an association representing fifty-six crab fishing vessels licensed to fish Hecate Strait. Alex Rawlings, "Crabbers Request Review of Wind Farm Project," *Queen Charlotte Islands Observer,* October 23, 2008, 4. "Naikun, Haida in New Partnership," *Queen Charlotte Islands Observer,* February 5, 2009, 4.

page 229 *Don't come flashing permits at us:* Guujaaw, speaking at the Green Economy Conference organized by PowerUp Canada, Vancouver, April 7, 2009.

page 229 *It is Haida traditional territory, full stop:* Matt Burns, speaking at the PowerUp Canada conference, April 7, 2009.

page 230 *The first woman chief in Old Massett:* While Elizabeth Moore is the first Haida woman to win election as chief in Old Massett, there was, briefly, a female president of the Council of the Haida Nation, Lavina White, elected in 1977. Her fiery but short tenure precipitated the reform of the CHN in the 1980s under the leadership of Guujaaw's uncle, Percy Williams.

page 231 *A labour market survey:* The Skeena Native Development Society labour market analysis is at http://www.snds.bc.ca (accessed February 15, 2009).

page 232 *Miles Richardson:* Miles Richardson has taken a very different political path from that of Guujaaw. He stepped down as president of the Council of the Haida Nation in order to take a position of Commissioner on the B.C. Treaty Commission, a process that Guujaaw and many Haida vehemently oppose. Two decades after declaring that he would renounce his Canadian citizenship, Buddy Richardson ran in the 2004 federal election as a Liberal (he lost). In 2008, he was inducted as a member of the Order of Canada.

page 233 *Unless we find a new way:* Williams-Davidson, "Protecting and Respecting the Earth's Soul and Aboriginal Cultural Traditions," Interfaith Summer Institute lecture, April 19, 2007.

page 233 *Tens of millions of people dedicated to change:* Paul Hawken, *Blessed Unrest: How the Largest Social Movement in History Is Restoring Grace, Justice, and Beauty to the World* (Penguin: New York, 2008), 4–5.

page 234 *The* Provider *caught barely 1,300 salmon:* Kwiaahwah Jones, "Haida Provider Expands Role," *Haida Laas,* November 2008, 9.

page 234 *Unscripted self-determination:* Naomi Klein, *The Shock Doctrine* (Toronto: Alfred. A. Knopf Canada, 2007), 221.

page 235 *One of the most exciting places in Canada:* John Ralston Saul, "Leadership and the Environment," *SpruceRoots,* Gowgaia Speakers' Series, Transcript No. 1, September 2, 2002, http://www.spruceroots.org/Speakers%20Series/JRS/JRS%20JRS .html (accessed February 15, 2009).

page 236 *We are creating magic:* Williams-Davidson, *Protecting and Respecting the Earth's Soul,* Interfaith Summer Institute lecture, April 19, 2007.

page 237 *Guujaaw is a warrior:* Spencer B. Beebe, speaking on behalf of the Final Jury Panel, 6th Annual Buffett Award for Indigenous Leadership, Ecotrust News Release, June 23, 2006, http://www.ecotrust.org/indigenousleaders/2006/2006_ Buffett_Award.pdf (accessed February 15, 2009).

page 237 *He truly has set the beat:* Michael Nicoll Yahgulanaas, while still politically active, has moved off-islands to further his career as an artist. His modernistic Haida manga has won wide acclaim, as did his Meddling in the Museum exhibit at the University of British Columbia's Museum of Anthropology in 2007. His work can be viewed at http://www.mny.ca (accessed February 25, 2009).

page 237 *Guujaaw gave the money:* Allocation of the prize money to the CHN was reported in "Buffett Award," *Haida Laas,* October 2006, 7.

page 237 *These are remarkable people:* John Ralston Saul, in Michael Valpy, "This Native Land: Our Debt to the First Nations," *Globe and Mail,* September 27, 2008, F8.

pages 238–239 *Access to ancient wisdom:* David Suzuki, Foreword, in Henley, *Rediscovery,* 14.

page 239 *Different truths exist side by side:* Bill Reid, Foreword, in Henley, *Rediscovery,* 10.

page 240 *The Haida have not ceded a single square inch:* By comparison, the Nisga'a received about $200 million in the Nisga'a Final Agreement, plus concessionary access to forestry, fisheries, wildlife harvesting, tourism and other resources. But in doing so, they settled for outright control over just 8 per cent of their traditional territory.

page 240 *An exquisitely designed economy:* Hawken, *Blessed Unrest,* 100.

page 240 *The marginal position of Indians:* Tony Penikett, *Reconciliation: First Nations Treaty Making in British Columbia* (Vancouver: Douglas & McIntyre, 2006), 249.

page 241 *Not of a lesser status than the Quebecois:* Campbell Clark and Gloria Galloway, "Kennedy to oppose 'Quebecois as nation,'" *Globe and Mail,* November 27, 2006, A1.

page 241 *Hard to retrain them:* Lordon, "Reconciling Differences," *SpruceRoots,* February 2000, http://www.spruceroots.org/February%202000/ReconDiffs.html (accessed February 15, 2009).

page 241 *The Montevideo Convention: Tony Fogarassy,* "The Haida Nation: An Independent State in International Law?" Clark Wilson, LLP brief (2006), http://www.cwilson.com/pubs/energy/haidastate.pdf (accessed February 15, 2009).

page 242 *An innately aboriginal country:* John Ralston Saul, *A Fair Country: Telling Truths about Canada* (Toronto: Viking Canada, 2008), 3–7.

page 242 *150 years to dismantle First Nations:* Penikett, *Reconciliation,* 195.

THIRTEEN: WHAT IS TO COME

page 243 *National Aboriginal Day:* National Aboriginal Day is marked in Canada on June 21 every year. The event was instituted in 1996, one of the few recommendations of the Royal Commission on Aboriginal Peoples that was acted upon.

page 243 *The soft thump thump of their fears:* Janette Turner Hospital, *The Last Magician* (Toronto, McClelland & Stewart, Inc., 1992), 79.

page 244 *Here we are at last:* Bill Reid, "The Spirit of Haida Gwaii," in Reid, *Solitary Raven,* 228.

page 246 *Probably the biggest test you can put yourself through:* Heather Ramsay, "Final Canoe Steaming Takes Place in Skidegate," *Queen Charlotte Islands Observer,* July 10, 2008, 5.

page 246 *If we don't need to, we won't do it:* Jeff King, "Land Use Agreement Signing in Vancouver: Agreement May Start to Change Relationship between Haida, Governments," *Queen Charlotte Islands Observer,* December 13, 2007, 1.

page 247 *The* William *ruling: Tsilhqot'in Nation v. British Columbia,* 2007 BCSC 1700.

page 247 *We are all here to stay: The New Relationship with Aboriginal People,* http://www.ubcic.bc.ca/files/PDF/New_Relationship.pdf (accessed February 15, 2009). For a look three years later, see Vaughn Palmer, "The 'New Relationship' Looks Good One Day, Not So Fine the Next," *Vancouver Sun,* June 13, 2008, A3.

page 247 *It's time for action:* Mark Hume, "Premier Pledges 'Historic' Legislation to Avert Protests," *Globe and Mail,* December 17, 2008, B1.

page 247 *Scuttled by the business community:* Glen Korstrom, "'Alarmist' legal views put aboriginal bill on hold," *Business in Vancouver,* April 7–13, 2009, 18.

page 248 *Giving away right to access wild lands:* Mark Hume, "Talks Must Focus on Compensation, Chief Says," *Globe and Mail,* November 6, 2008, S1.

page 248 *Highlight the gains:* Council of the Haida Nations website at http://www.haidanation.ca (accessed February 15, 2009).

page 249 *Cultural wood:* The Haida's Cultural Wood Access Program is the only co-managed process to access cultural wood in the province.

page 249 *Now more First Nations people than at the time of contact:* Ralston Saul, *A Fair Country,* 24.

page 249 *Essential to ensure there isn't a loss:* Guujaaw, [editorial], *Haida Laas,* December 2007, 12.

page 250 *It's almost like a reawakening:* Robert Davidson, in Francis Baptiste, "In the Studio with Robert Davidson," *Native Destinations,* Summer 2008, 11.

pages 250–251 *Explore new ways of getting Haida language into the community:* Heather Ramsay, "Haida Language Play Premieres This Weekend," *Queen Charlotte Islands Observer*, May 29, 2008, 1.

page 252 *We are the song:* The CD collection includes a disk featuring twenty-four songs performed by Guujaaw, including the "Entrance (Lyell Island Song)"; "Love Song," dedicated to his partner, Marcie, and "Moon Song," which "speaks to the humility that one feels upon seeing the beauty of moonlight refracting over the ocean in Haida Gwaii." These are contemporary renditions of archival songs. Also in the works is a six-disk collection of Haida songs recorded by previous generations, digitally enhanced. Guujaaw, *Songs of Haida Gwaii,* liner notes, disk 2, 2008.

page 253 *How to return the name:* Jeff King, "Haida to Give Back Name 'Queen Charlotte,'" *Queen Charlotte Islands Observer*, October 16, 2008, 1. CHN Resolution HOA 2008-06: Change of name, *Haida Laas,* November 2008, 21.

page 253 *Names are important:* Interestingly, the people of Queen Charlotte City rejected an attempt to give a Haida name, Daajing.giids Way, to their main street. After a contentious local process in which Daajing.giids Way was first chosen, then rejected, islanders opted instead for Oceanview Drive. Yet the map of British Columbia will undoubtedly get redrawn, with support coming from surprising quarters. B.C. Premier Gordon Campbell caught many observers off guard in 2008 when he supported calls to change the name of Georgia Strait, a body of water separating British Columbia's mainland and Vancouver Island, to its traditional name, the Salish Sea. See numerous stories and letters to the editor in the *Queen Charlotte Islands Observer* between September 14, 2006, and November 9, 2006.

page 253 *Good people:* Guujaaw, "Man, Myth or Magic?" in Duffek and Townsend-Gault, *Bill Reid and Beyond,* 61–63.

SELECTED BIBLIOGRAPHY

Akrigg, G.P.V., and Helen B. Akrigg. *British Columbia Chronicle, 1847–1871: Gold and Colonists.* Vancouver: Discovery Press, 1977.

Archipelago Management Board. "Gwaii Haanas: Haida Heritage Site and National Park Reserve," *Newsletter No. 1.* September 1993.

Armstrong, Karen. *A Short History of Myth.* Toronto: Alfred A. Knopf Canada, 2005.

Assembly of First Nations. *The $9 Billion Myth Exposed: Why First Nations Poverty Endures,* information sheet. Ottawa: February 24, 2007.

Athlii Gwaii: The Line at Lyell. DVD produced and directed by Jeff Bear and Marianne Jones. Vancouver: Ravens and Eagles Productions 2 Ltd, 2003.

Augaitis, Daina, et al. *Raven Travelling: Two Centuries of Haida Art.* Vancouver: Vancouver Art Gallery and Douglas & McIntyre, 2006.

B.C. Wild. *Taking It All Away: Communities on Haida Gwaii Say Enough Is Enough,* pamphlet. 1996.

Bailey, Penny. "There's No Place Like Home." *Wellcome Trust.* July 24, 2007. http://www.wellcome.ac.uk/News/2007/Features/WTX041039.htm.

Baker, Simon, and Verna J. Kirkness. *Khot-La-Cha: The Autobiography of Chief Simon Baker.* Vancouver: Douglas & McIntyre, 1994.

Baptiste, Francis. "In the Studio with Robert Davidson." *Native Destinations* (Summer 2008).

Barman, Jean. *The West Beyond the West: A History of British Columbia.* Toronto: University of Toronto Press, 1991.

Bellis, Arnie. "The Haida Constitution, Business and the Environment." *SpruceRoots.* The Gowgaia Institute Speakers' Series. Transcript No. 5, April 22, 2004. http://www.spruceroots.org/Speakers%20Series/ARNIE/Arnie.html.

Berger, Thomas R. *One Man's Justice: A Life in the Law.* Vancouver: Douglas & McIntyre, 2002.

Blackman, Margaret B. *Florence Edenshaw Davidson: During My Time, a Haida Woman,* revised edition. Seattle: University of Washington Press, 1992.

Boyd, Robert. *The Coming of the Spirit of Pestilence: Introduced Infectious Diseases and Population Decline among Northwest Coast Indians, 1774–1874.* Seattle: University of Washington Press, 1999.

Bringhurst, Robert. *A Story as Sharp as a Knife: The Classical Haida Mythtellers and Their World.* Vancouver: Douglas & McIntyre, 1999.

British Columbia. Integrated Land Management Bureau. *Integrated Land Use Planning for Public Lands in British Columbia.* http://ilmbwww.gov.bc.ca/slrp/reports/integrated_lup/index.html.

British Columbia. Royal Commission on Indian Affairs. *Report.* Vol. 3 (1916).

———. *The New Relationship with Aboriginal People.* http://www.gov.bc.ca/themes/new_relationship.html.

Broadhead, John, ed. *Islands at the Edge: Preserving the Queen Charlotte Islands Heritage.* Skidegate: Island Protections Society; Vancouver / Toronto: Douglas & McIntyre, 1984.

Calder v. British Columbia (Attorney General), [1973] S.C.R. 313.

Canada. *An Act to Further Amend the Indian Act, 1880.* S.C. 1884, 47 Vict., c. 27, s. 3.

———. *Constitution Act, 1867* (U.K.), 30 & 31 Vict., c. 3, formerly called the *British North America Act, 1867.*

———. *Constitution Act, 1982,* being Schedule B to the *Canada Act, 1982* (U.K.), 1982, c. 11.

———. House of Commons. *Debates,* April 22, 1983, 24771.

———. *Indian Act,* R.S.C. 1985, c. I-5.

Canadian Broadcasting Corporation, Radio. "How Non-violence Works." *Ideas.* Transcript of documentary by Seán Hennessey. October 20, 1992.

Canadian Broadcasting Corporation, Television. "Islands at the Edge." *The Nature of Things with David Suzuki.* Videocassette. January 29, 1986.

———. "Windy Bay." *The Nature of Things with David Suzuki.* Videocassette. January 27, 1982.

Cardinal, Harold. *The Unjust Society: The Tragedy of Canada's Indians.* Edmonton: Hurtig, 1969.

Chamberlin, J. Edward. *If This Is Your Land, Where Are Your Stories? Finding Common Ground.* Toronto: Alfred. A. Knopf Canada, 2003.

Chittenden, Newton H. *Official Report of the Exploration of the Queen Charlotte Islands for the Government of British Columbia.* Victoria: Queen's Printer, 1884.

Clark, Robin B. *Community Forest Feasibility Study for Haida Gwaii / the Queen Charlotte Islands.* Islands Community Stability Initiative, 1998. http://www.for.gov.bc.ca/hfd/library/frbc1998/frbc1998mr43.pdf.

Cole, Douglas, and Bradley Lockner. *To the Charlottes: George Dawson's 1878 Survey of the Queen Charlotte Islands*. Vancouver: University of British Columbia Press, 1993.

Council of the Haida Nation. *Haida Land Use Vision: Haida Gwaii Yah'guudang [Respecting Haida Gwaii]*, pamphlet, April 2005. An earlier edition is available online at http://ilmbwww.gov.bc.ca/slrp/lrmp/nanaimo/qci/docs/HLUVpublic.pdf (accessed February 15, 2009).

Dalzell, Kathleen E. *The Queen Charlotte Islands, 1774–1966*. Madeira Park, B.C.: Harbour Publishing, 1968.

Davidson, Reg, Robert Davidson, Guujaaw, Marianne Jones and Terri-Lynn Williams-Davidson. *Songs of Haida Gwaii: Haida Gwaii Singers Anthology*. Four-CD set with companion booklet. Surrey: Haida Gwaii Singers Society and Haida Nation, 2008.

Davis, Wade (text), and Graham Osborne (photos). *Rainforest: Ancient Realm of the Pacific Northwest*. Vancouver / Toronto: Greystone Books, 1998.

Dawson, George M. *Report on the Queen Charlotte Islands 1878*. Ottawa: Geological Survey of Canada, 1880.

Delgamuukw v. British Columbia, [1991] 3 W.W.R. 97 (B.C.S.C.).

Delgamuukw v. British Columbia, [1997] 3 S.C.R. 1010, appeal and cross-appeal from (1993), 104 D.L.R. (4th) 470, [1993] 5 W.W.R. 97 (B.C.C.A.), varying an order of McEachern C.J. (1991), 79 D.L.R. (4th) 185, [1991] 3 W.W.R. 97 (B.C.S.C.), and dismissing British Columbia's cross-appeal as abandoned. Appeal allowed in part; cross-appeal dismissed. http://csc.lexum.umontreal.ca/en/1997/1997rcs3-1010/1997rcs3-1010.html.

Dr. Seuss. *The Lorax*. New York: Random House, 1971.

Duffek, Karen. *Bill Reid: Beyond the Essential Form*. Museum Note No. 19. Vancouver: University of British Columbia Press in association with the UBC Museum of Anthropology, 1993.

Duffek, Karen, and Charlotte Townsend-Gault (eds). *Bill Reid and Beyond: Expanding on Modern Native Art*. Vancouver: Douglas & McIntyre, 2004.

EAGLE (Legal Counsel for the Council of the Haida Nation). "A Summary of Intervenor Arguments: TFL 39 Case." *SpruceRoots*, July 2004. http://www.spruceroots.org/July%202004/Arguments.html.

Enrico, John (ed. and trans.). *Skidegate Haida Myths and Histories*. With a foreword by Guujaaw ("This Box of Treasures"). Skidegate: Queen Charlotte Islands Museum Press and Council of the Haida Nation, 1995.

Fisher, Robin. *Contact and Conflict: Indian-European Relations in British Columbia, 1774–1890*. Vancouver: University of British Columbia Press, 1977.

Fogarassy, Tony. "The Haida Nation: An Independent State in International Law?" Clark Wilson, LLP brief (2006), http://www.cwilson.com/pubs/energy/haidastate.pdf (accessed February 15, 2009).

George, Herb. "The Fire within Us." In *Aboriginal Title in British Columbia: Delgamuukw v. the Queen: Proceedings of a Conference Held September 10, 11, 1991*, edited by Frank Cassidy. Lantzville, B.C.: Oolichan Books, 1992.

George, Paul. *Big Trees Not Big Stumps: 25 Years of Campaigning to Save Wilderness with the Wilderness Committee*. Vancouver: Paul George and Western Canada Wilderness Committee, 2006.

Gowgaia Institute. *Forest Economy Trends and Economic Conditions on Haida Gwaii*. 2007. http://www.spruceroots.org/Booklets/ForTrends.pdf.

Guujaaw. "Entrance (Lyell Island) Song." Disk 2 of Reg Davidson, Robert Davidson, Guujaaw, Marianne Jones and Terri-Lynn Williams-Davidson. *Songs of Haida Gwaii: Haida Gwaii Singers Anthology*. CD. Surrey: Haida Gwaii Singers Society and Haida Nation, 2008.

———. "It Was Told." Foreword to *Haida Gwaii: Human History and Environment from the Time of Loon to the Time of the Iron People*, edited by Daryl W. Fedje and Rolf W. Mathewes. Vancouver: University of British Columbia Press, 2005: xii–xiii.

———. "Man, Myth or Magic?" In *Bill Reid and Beyond: Expanding on Modern Native Art*, edited by Karen Duffek and Charlotte Townsend-Gault. Vancouver: Museum of Anthropology at the University of British Columbia and Douglas & McIntyre, 2004: 61–63.

———. "Two Perspectives on Certainty." Speech to a one-day forum by the B.C. Treaty Commission. *Venture into a Treaty World*, March 4, 2004, 21–24. http://www.bctreaty.net/files/pdf_documents/Venturing%20into%20a%20 · treaty%20world.pdf.

Gwaganad (Diane Brown). "A Non-Haida Upbringing: Conflicts and Resolutions." In *Bill Reid and Beyond: Expanding on Modern Native Art*, edited by Karen Duffek and Charlotte Townsend-Gault, 64–70. Vancouver: Douglas & McIntyre, 2004.

Haida Gwai[i]: Islands of the People. Videocassette. Produced by Jeff Goodman and Mike Salisbury. A production of BBC–Bristol in association with [New York] WNET / Thirteen [episode from the PBS series *Nature* with George H. Page], 1986.

Haida Nation v. British Columbia (Minister of Forests) and Weyerhaeuser, 2004 SCC 73, appeals from a judgment of the British Columbia Court of Appeal, 2002 BCCA 147, with supplementary reasons, 2002 BCCA 462, reversing a decision of the British Columbia Supreme, 2000 BCSC 1280. Appeal by the Crown dismissed. Appeal by Weyerhaeuser Co. allowed. http://scc.lexum.umontreal.ca/en/2004/2004scc73/2004scc73.html.

Harris, Christie. *Raven's Cry*. Vancouver: Douglas & McIntyre, 1966.

Harris, Douglas C. *Landing Native Fisheries: Indian Reserves and Fishing Rights in British Columbia, 1849–1925*. Vancouver: University of British Columbia Press, 2008.

Hawken, Paul. *Blessed Unrest: How the Largest Social Movement in History Is Restoring Grace, Justice, and Beauty to the World.* Penguin: New York, 2008.

Henley, Thom. *Rediscovery: Ancient Pathways, New Directions.* Foreword by Bill Reid. Foreword by David Suzuki. Edmonton: Lone Pine Publishing, 1996.

Hennessey, Seán. "Gwaii Haanas: How Non-violence Works." Transcript from a documentary aired on *Ideas.* Canadian Broadcasting Corporation, Radio, October 20, 1992.

Hewlett, Edward Sleigh. "Klatsassin." *Dictionary of Canadian Biography,* http://www.biographi.ca/009004-119.01-e.php?&id_nbr=4527&interval=25&&PHPSE ssID=45bpogq75hb6k1gtnhgulkdkq2.

Islands Protection Committee (Masset). *About Time for an Island* (Winter 1975).

————. *All Alone Stone* [2] (1975).

————. *All Alone Stone* 3 (1976).

Islands Protection Society. *All Alone Stone* 4 (Spring 1980).

Kii?iljuus (Barbara J. Wilson) and Heather Harris. "Tllsda X̲aaydas K̲'aaygang. nga: Long, Long Ago Haida Ancient Stories." Chapter 7 in *Haida Gwaii: Human History and Environment from the Time of Loon to the Time of the Iron People,* edited by Daryl W. Fedje and Rolf W. Mathewes. Vancouver: University of British Columbia Press, 2005.

Klein, Naomi. *No Logo.* Toronto: Vintage Canada, 2000.

————. *The Shock Doctrine.* Toronto: Alfred. A. Knopf Canada, 2007.

Lampert, Jerry. "Two Perspectives on Certainty." Speech to a one-day forum by the B.C. Treaty Commission. *Venturing into a Treaty World,* March 4, 2004: 16–20. http://www.llbc.leg.bc.ca/public/PubDocs/bcdocs/368336/venture_ into_a_treaty.pdf.

Lordon, Ian. "Hacking Down the Garden." *SpruceRoots,* December 2000. http://www.spruceroots.org/December00/Hacking.html.

————. "Negotiating Coexistence." *SpruceRoots,* April 2002. http://www.spruceroots.org/Issues%202002/Coexist.html.

————. "Reconciling Differences and Inspiring Change." *SpruceRoots,* February 2000. http://www.spruceroots.org/February%202000/ReconDiffs.html.

————. "Serving Notice: Tuning up the Tenure Holders on Haida Gwaii." *SpruceRoots,* April 2003. http://www.spruceroots.org/April%202003/ServingNotice.html.

————. "So Now." *SpruceRoots,* July 2004. http://www.spruceroots.org/July%20 2004/SoNow.html.

————. "Weighing In for the Title Challenge." *SpruceRoots,* September/October 2000. http://www.spruceroots.org/SeptOct.00/Title.html.

————. "What Do You Do with Old Rednecks?" *SpruceRoots,* July 1998. http://www.spruceroots.org/July98/RL.html.

————. "Without Equivocation." *SpruceRoots,* November 2002. http://www
.spruceroots.org/Nov%202002/Without.html.

Mabo v. Queensland (No. 2), [1992] HCA 23.

MacDonald, George F. *Haida Art.* Vancouver: Douglas & McIntyre: 1996.

MacDonald, George F., Bill Reid and Richard J. Huyda. *Haida Monumental Art:
Villages of the Queen Charlotte Islands.* Vancouver: University of British
Columbia Press, 1994.

McKinnon, Bruce. "Aboriginal Title: After Marshall and Bernard, Part II."
Advocate, 65, Part 5 (September 2007), 611–632.

McMillan, Alan D. *Native Peoples and Cultures of Canada: An Anthropological
Overview.* Vancouver: Douglas & McIntyre, 1988.

MacQueen, Ken. "Referendum Madness." *Maclean's,* May 13, 2002. Microfiche.

————. "West Coast Renaissance." *Maclean's,* October 20, 2003. Microfiche.

Mann, Charles C. *1491: New Revelations of the Americas before Columbus.* New
York: Alfred A. Knopf, 2005.

Marchak, M. Patricia, Scott L. Aycock and Deborah M. Herbert. *Falldown:
Forest Policy in British Columbia.* Vancouver: David Suzuki Foundation
and Ecotrust Canada, 1999.

May, Elizabeth. *Paradise Won: The Struggle for South Moresby.* Toronto:
McClelland & Stewart, 1990.

Millennium Ecosystem Assessment. *Ecosystem and Human Well-Being: Synthesis.*
Washington, D.C.: Island Press, 2005.

O'Sullivan, Maurice. *Twenty Years A'Growing.* Nashville: J.S. Sanders and
Co., 1998.

Ontario Coalition Against Poverty, "Massive Haida Blockades Shut Down
Weyerhaeuser," March 23, 2005, http://ocap.ca/node/884 (accessed February
15, 2009).

Ormsby, Margaret A. *British Columbia: A History.* Toronto: Macmillan of
Canada, 1964.

Penikett, Tony. *Reconciliation: First Nations Treaty Making in British Columbia.*
Vancouver: Douglas & McIntyre, 2006.

Pinkerton, Evelyn. "Taking the Minister to Court: Changes in Public Opinion
About Forest Management and Their Expression in Haida Land Claims."
B.C. Studies, no. 57 (1983): 68–85.

Ralston Saul, John. *A Fair Country: Telling Truths about Canada.* Toronto:
Viking Canada, 2008.

————. "Leadership and the Environment." *SpruceRoots.* Gowgaia Speakers'
Series, Transcript No. 1, September 2, 2002. http://www.spruceroots.org/
Speakers%20Series/JRS/JRS%20JRS.html.

Rammell, George. "Goldsmith/Culturesmith." In *Bill Reid and Beyond:
Expanding on Modern Native Art,* edited by Karen Duffek and Charlotte

Townsend-Gault. Vancouver: Museum of Anthropology at the University of British Columbia and Douglas & McIntyre, 2004, 44–58.

Reece, P.J. "Thunderbirds and Thunderstorms." *Canadian Geographic*, July/August 2008.

Reid, Bill. *Solitary Raven: Selected Writings of Bill Reid*. Introduction by Robert Bringhurst. Vancouver: Douglas & McIntyre, 2000.

Reid, Bill, and Robert Bringhurst. *The Raven Steals the Light*. Vancouver: Douglas & McIntyre, 1984.

Roth, Christopher Fritz. "Without Treaty, Without Conquest: Indigenous Sovereignty in Post-*Delgamuukw* British Columbia." *Wicazo Sa Review* 17, no. 2 (Fall 2002): 143–165.

Royal Commission on Indian Affairs for the Province of British Columbia (McKenna-McBride Commission), *Report*, vol. 3 (1916), 726.

Smyly, John, and Carolyn Smyly. *Those Born at Koona*. Saanichton, B.C.: Hancock House, 1973.

St. Pierre, Paul. *Breaking Smith's Quarter Horse*. Vancouver: Douglas & McIntyre, 1984.

Statement of Claim re: Haida Nation v. British Columbia (Attorney General) (6 June 2003), Vancouver L020662 (B.C.S.C.).

Statement of Defence of the Defendant Her Majesty the Queen in Right of the Province of British Columbia re: Haida Nation v. British Columbia (Attorney General) (6 June 2003), Vancouver L020662 (B.C.S.C.).

Statement of Defence of the Attorney General of Canada re: Haida Nation v. British Columbia (Attorney General) (6 June 2003), Vancouver L020662 (B.C.S.C.).

Stearns, Mary Lee. *Haida Culture in Custody: The Masset Band*. Seattle: University of Washington Press, 1981.

Steltzer, Ulli, and Robert Davidson. *Eagle Transforming: The Art of Robert Davidson*. Vancouver: Douglas & McIntyre, 1994.

Stewart, Hilary. *Cedar: Tree of Life to the Northwest Indians*. Vancouver: Douglas & McIntyre, 1984.

Suzuki, David. "Ecological Millennium: Setting the Bottom Line." Presented to the Canadian Conference on International Health, November 14–17, 1999. http://www.idrc.ca/uploads/user-S/10271047150suzuki.pdf.

———. *David Suzuki: The Autobiography*. Vancouver: Greystone Books, 2006.

Szekely, Edmond Bordeaux. *The Essene Gospel of Peace: Book Three*. Nelson, B.C.: International Biogenic Society, 1981.

Tennant, Paul. *Aboriginal Peoples and Politics: The Indian Land Question in British Columbia, 1849–1989*. Vancouver: University of British Columbia Press, 1990.

Tippett, Maria. *Bill Reid: The Making of an Indian*. Toronto: Vintage Canada, 2004.

Titley, E. Brian. *A Narrow Vision: Duncan Campbell Scott and the Administration of Indian Affairs in Canada*. Vancouver: University of British Columbia Press, 1986.

Trevorrow, Tom, Christine Finnimore, Steve Hemming, George Trevorrow, Matt Rigney, Veronica Brodie and Ellen Trevorrow. *They Took Our Land and Then Our Children: Ngarrindjeri Struggle for Truth and Justice,* booklet. [Camp Coorong, SA]: Ngarrindjeri Land and Progress Association, 2006.

Tsilhqot'in Nation v. British Columbia 2007 BCSC 1700. http://www.courts.gov.bc.ca/ Jdb-txt/SC/07/17/2007BCSC1700.pdf.

Turner, Nancy J. *Plants of Haida Gwaii.* Winlaw, B.C.: Sono Nis Press, 2004.

Turner Hospital, Janette. *The Last Magician.* Toronto: McClelland & Stewart, 1992.

University of Victoria Archives. Canada Wilderness Committee founder Paul George. AR337, Acc. No. 2000-071, 2.11 First Nations. Includes Guujaaw's letters.

Vaillant, John. *The Golden Spruce: A True Story of Myth, Madness and Greed.* Toronto: Alfred A. Knopf Canada, 2005.

Waldram, James B., Pat Berringer and Wayne Warry. " 'Nasty, Brutish and Short,' Anthropology and the Gitksan-Wet'suwet'en Decision." *Canadian Journal of Native Studies* 12, no. 2 (1992): 309–316.

Williams, David Ricardo. "Sir Matthew Baillie Begbie." *Dictionary of Canadian Biography.* http://www.biographi.ca/009004-119.01-e.php?&id_ nbr=5958&interval=25&&PHPSESSID=kcd8115qcfdeboqrs9iavva6g7.

Williams-Davidson, Terri-Lynn. "Protecting and Respecting the Earth's Soul and Aboriginal Cultural Traditions." Lecture presented at the Interfaith Summer Institute for Justice, Peace and Social Movements, Vancouver, April 19, 2007.

Wright, Robin K. *Northern Haida Master Carvers.* Seattle and Vancouver: University of Washington Press and Douglas & McIntyre, 2001.

Wright, Ronald. *An Illustrated Short History of Progress.* Toronto: Anansi, 2006.

York, Geoffrey, and Loreen Pindera. *People of the Pines: The Warriors and the Legacy of Oka.* Toronto: McArthur & Company, 1991.

Yorta Yorta Aboriginal Community v. Victoria, [2002] HCA 58.

ACKNOWLEDGEMENTS

Content: This book would not exist without the tremendous contributions of many people, on Haida Gwaii and off it. First, my thanks to Guujaaw, a mostly reluctant subject who nonetheless gave me sufficient room with which to work. Part of Guujaaw's reticence about the writing of this book stems from a concern that he might be seen to be taking undue or excessive credit for events that have involved many other people. To be clear, Guujaaw did not seek for this book to be written, nor has he been asked to endorse it; but to the extent that he agreed to be interviewed on various occasions, encouraged others to do the same and allowed access to some of the files of the Council of the Haida Nation, I am indebted to him. I think it is also important to acknowledge that Guujaaw has expressed dissatisfaction with this book, which I regret.

A number of people were interviewed for the book, or in other ways provided access to vital material. Among them are: Chief ?Idansuu (Jim Hart), the late Chief Skidegate (Dempsey Collinson), Chief Iljawass (Reynold Russ), Elizabeth Moore, Raven, Ron Russ, David Phillips, Arnie Bellis, Jenny Nelson, Michael Nicoll Yahgulanaas, Nika Collison, Miles Richardson, Gwaai Edenshaw, Jaalen Edenshaw, Rosemary Hart, Lucille Bell, Diane Brown, Art Lew, April Davis (Churchill), Wanagan (Captain Gold), Reverend Ian MacKenzie,

George F. MacDonald, Dave Porter, Tony Pearse, David Suzuki, Thom Henley, the late Jim Fulton, Adrienne Clarkson, Doug Gould, Robert Davidson, Terri-Lynn Williams-Davidson, George Rammell, Geoff Plant, Doug Caul, Kelly Brown, Lynn Pinkerton and Wade Davis.

Others helped me to find material or refine what I did with it, including Lenore Lawrence at Premier Creek Lodging, two anonymous readers on the islands, forestry analyst Ben Parfitt, mapmaker Eliana MacDonald, filmmaker Michael Bourquin and linguist Robert Bringhurst.

In Australia, Neil Ward, Matt Rigney, John Butcher and Peter Seidl helped me, to paraphrase T.S. Eliot, arrive where I had started and know the place for the first time.

Inspiration: Scott McIntyre had the courage to instigate the project and has been stalwart and faithful in the struggle to complete it; Scott Steedman was a keen-eyed ally; Ric Young introduced me to William Blake and so much more besides, and is a constant friend; Louise Dennys added critical insights and encouragement; Spencer Beebe rescued me from mere reporting and opened my mind to so much more; Liz Woody gave me the courage to tell this story my way.

Logistics: May Russ and her husband, Stan Hansen, got me safely to and from Daalung Stl'ang; Chris Ashurst and Meredith Adams helped my family and me live well at North Beach; Wendy Riley at the Moon Over Naikoon café almost adopted the kids and kept them warm and fed while we ignored them; Susan Musgrave was a pal. And again, David Phillips was just brilliant in every way. Meanwhile, I will always be indebted to Mike and Manon Hobbis and their talented crew for expert navigation of Haida Gwaii in the sv *Duen*.

Off the islands, but no less critical to the creation of time and space to think and to write, George Patterson and Josie Osborne put me up, and put up with me, at the Tofino Botanical Gardens; and Peter Buckland, Neil Weizel and Katrina Kadoski were generous with their hospitality at Cougar Annie's Garden.

Coherence: Barbara Pulling edited this book with diligence and determination. Her advocacy was boundless, and I am indebted to her for her calm, careful and persistent interventions.

Family: Books are always hard on families. To my children, Jasper, Fergus and Lucy, I hope that my many absences, even when I've been present, have not been unduly difficult to bear, and that our six-week adventure in the cabin on North Beach will be remembered for more than just the rain and the mice. As for Jennifer, who has been a tireless researcher, critic, editor, organizer, champion and provider of sober second thought, much of what this book has become owes directly to her. Come to think of it, much of me does, too.

Grateful acknowledgement is made for permission to quote from the following sources:

One Man's Justice, by Thomas Berger, published in 2002 by Douglas & McIntyre Ltd. (now D&M Publishers Inc.) Reprinted with permission of the publisher. / *Rainforest*, by Wade Davis with photos by Graham Osborne, published in 1998 by Greystone Books, an imprint of D&M Publishers Inc. Reprinted with permission of the publisher. / "This Box of Treasures," by Guujaaw, found in *Raven Travelling*, published in 2006 by Douglas & McIntyre Ltd. (now D&M Publishers Inc.) and the Vancouver Art Gallery. Reprinted with permission of the publisher. / "Man, Myth or Magic?" by Guujaaw, found in *Bill Reid and Beyond*, edited by Karen Duffek and Charlotte Townsend-Gault, published in 2004 by Douglas & McIntyre Ltd. (now D&M Publishers Inc.) Reprinted with permission of the publisher. / *If This Is Your Land, Where Are Your Stories?* by J. Edward Chamberlin. Copyright © 2003 J. Edward Chamberlin Consulting Inc. Reprinted by permission of Knopf Canada. / Excerpts from *Paradise Won: The Struggle for South Moresby* by Elizabeth May © 1990. Published by McClelland & Stewart Ltd. Used with permission of the publisher. / *Bill Reid: The Making of an Indian* by Maria Tippett. Copyright © 2003

The page-number suffix "n" indicates an endnote; suffix "c" indicates chronology.